# INTER-FAITH ORGANIZATIONS, 1893–1979: AN HISTORICAL DIRECTORY

## OTHER BOOKS BY MARCUS BRAYBROOKE

*Faiths in Fellowship* (London, 1976).

*Inter-Faith Worship: A Report of a Working Party*
(Galliard, 1974).

*Together to the Truth: A Review of Changing Attitudes
in Hinduism and Christianity Since 1800*
(Madras, 1971).

*The Undiscovered Christ: A Review of Recent Develop-
ments in the Christian Approach to the Hindu*
(Madras, 1973).

# INTER-FAITH ORGANIZATIONS, 1893–1979: AN HISTORICAL DIRECTORY

BY
MARCUS BRAYBROOKE

THE EDWIN MELLEN PRESS
NEW YORK AND TORONTO

*Copyright* © *1980*

The Edwin Mellen Press
New York and Toronto


Library of Congress Cataloging Number 79-91620

ISBN 0-88946-971-7

*Texts and Studies in Religion, ISBN 0-889-46-976-8*


Printed in the United States of America

# CONTENTS

# INTRODUCTION

Religious pluralism is not new. At many times and
in many countries, members of different religions have
lived in proximity. It is only in the last eighty years,
however, that there has been an increasing desire that
such co-existence should be based on mutual respect and a
growing hope that religious variety may be enriching,
rather than divisive. With isolated exceptions, such as
Aśoka and Akbar, the concept of religious tolerance is
very new. The rival orthodox schools of Hindu philosophy
disputed vigorously with each other[1] and in Western Europe,
Christians of different persuasions fought each other. In
England, it was not until this century that all the dis-
abilities from which non-Anglicans suffered were removed.
Still, in many parts of the world, religious freedom and
tolerance are lacking and people are discriminated against
because of their beliefs.

In Christianity first, and increasingly in other religions, there have been ecumenical movements, drawing together those who belong to the same religion, even if to
different traditions and denominations. Parallel to these,
but a weaker and more struggling infant, has been a "wider
ecumenical" or "inter-faith" movement, seeking co-operation, fellowship and unity between members of different religions. The growth of this infant to, perhaps, adoles-
cence is the subject of this study.

It may first be worth recalling, by way of contrast,
other ways in which, in a plural situation, members of different religions have related to each other. One religion
may be dominant, being also the religion of the ruling

power, and another religion exist with varying degrees of freedom. The situation of Jews in Europe through the centuries illustrates this. At times almost completely proscribed, at other times Jews were allowed to exist within strict limits. The position of Hindus in India under the Moghul Emperors is another example. Again, there may be direct military opposition, as between Christians and Muslims in Mediaeval Spain or during the Crusades, or as in the eighteenth century between Sikhs and Muslims in India. At other times, religions may be rivals, competing for adherents, as was the case between Buddhists and Hindus in ancient India, and is the case between Muslims and Christians in parts of Africa today. Another pattern is that of the legalized co-existence of separate communities as in the *millet* system in Israel, where each religious group, Jews, Muslims, Christians of different denomination and Druze are treated as, in measure, self-governing communities. They occupy the same land space, but there is no human meeting. In the Far East, by contrast, people may belong to more than one religion. Some contemporary states, such as India, have adopted a secular model, in which no religion has a preferential position. This is different to the Communist states, which in theory are anti-religious, and in which, to varying degrees, there is discrimination against all religions.

Those who are the subject of this study share a concern that the relationship of religions to each other should be co-operative and creative. The influence of one religion on another is not new. What is new is the conscious and deliberate search for mutual knowledge and influence. Through the centuries, religions have influenced each other. The doctrines of the Upanishads, that the Atma is Brahman, may have been developed in response to Buddhist teaching. Śankara's writings were partly intended to combat Buddhism. From the Bible, it can be seen that the faith of Israel was influenced by the Baal, nature worship of the Canaanites and, during the exile in Babylon, by Zoroastrian ideas about angels and immortality. It was through the writings of the Muslim Averroes that Aquinas learned of Aristotle's thought.

Such influences were unacknowledged. The deliberate attempt to study religious traditions other than one's own, not to refute them, but in the hope that thereby one's own religious life may be enriched, is quite new. There are various factors that have contributed to the contemporary meeting of religions. The imperial expansion of Europe coincided with the industrial, scientific and technological revolutions. This has meant the spread across the world of a common technological culture, with instant communication in "the global village". The European expansion was not just political and technological. Nineteenth century imperialism was accompanied by religious and cultural expansion. The educational pattern of Europe was exported with its belief in liberal values and political democracy. The nineteenth century was also the great era of Christian missions from Western Europe and the United States of America. The Gospel was taken to almost every country, and many missionaries shared in educational work. This century has seen the reassertion of traditional Asian and African values, but these have been reasserted in reaction to European cultural and religious expansion.

In this century there has been the "counter-attack" from the East. An awareness of African and Asian cultures and religions has influenced European culture. The influence of African art on European art in this century of Oriental music on European music  are examples of this. The pioneers of this development were often Europeans such as Schopenhauer, Margaret Noble or Annie Besant, who became enamoured of Eastern values, but now, Africans and Asians confidently commend the traditional values of their societies and many Westerners look to Africa and the East for values that seem to be lacking in their own society.

The work of scholars has made the teachings and texts of religions other than Christianity widely available. Man Westerners have travelled to or lived in Asia, and recently, largely through immigration, Western Europe is becomin a religiously plural society. Recent figures for France show that Muslims are the second largest religious communi ty after Roman Catholics. There are about two million Mus lims, as against an estimated fourteen million practising Roman Catholics and one and one-quarter million Protestant Jews in France number about 900,000 and Buddhists about 80,000. In Britain, Muslims are second to Christians and there are sizeable Hindu and Sikh minorities.[2]

The great religions are encountering each other in a new way. Do they meet as rivals and opponents or as frien and fellow pilgrims? Those who have hoped that the meetin will be one of friendship and co-operation are the subject of this study.

My own involvement has been primarily with the World Congress of Faiths. Because of this personal knowledge, a Honorary Secretary for ten years and now as Editor of the journal, *World Faiths,* and Chairman, the Congress will fea ture prominently in this study. I know many of the person alities and have had easy access to the records. The atte to assess the contemporary role of the Congress has involv looking back to its origins and indeed to the beginnings of organized inter-faith co-operation. The Congress is only one amongst various inter-religious bodies, and a study of other organizations shows, by comparison, the suc cesses and failures and the differing purposes of inter-

faith meetings. Broadly speaking, inter-faith organizations are either primarily concerned with a deepening understanding of truth or with working for peace. The World
Congress of Faiths, the Temple of Understanding, and The
Fellowship of the Friends of Truth are typical of the
first concern; The World Conference on Religion and Peace,
of the second. Recently, the churches have set up agencies
for relations with other religions. The word "dialogue"
is often used, but the official approaches of the churches
are necessarily different from the work of bodies which
are inter-religious in aim and composition. A study of
the work of the Vatican Secretariat for Non-Christians and
of the World Council of Churches Sub Unit on Dialogue between Men of Living Faiths and Ideologies shows the tension for official bodies between "open" dialogue and compromise of their basic belief. To some extent,individual
believers who participate in inter-faith bodies experience
in themselves a similar tension, for example whether they
can with integrity take part in "inter-faith" services.

"Multi-lateral" dialogue, or "multilogue", in which
members of several religions meet together, has a different character to "bilateral" dialogue in which discussions
are between members of only two religions. Mention will
be made of Christian-Muslim and Christian-Hindu meetings,
but the special characteristics of "bilateral" dialogue
will be mainly exemplified by Jewish-Christian encounter.
In Israel this has the added complication of being subject
to political tensions.

The view taken of the relation of religions to each
other influences the way in which religion or religions
are taught. In general the academic study of religions
has sought to be disinterested and has remained aloof from
inter-faith organizations. At the school level, especially in Britain, many of those who have taken an interest

in the teaching of world religions, have done so because
of their desire to encourage harmony between members of
different religious and ethnic communities.

Beyond the histories of particular organizations,
there are more general questions about the relation of
religions. Are the differences essentially unimportant?
This is the implication of the Theosophical Movement.
Significant as this movement has been, it is not discussed
in detail, because it is not an "inter-religious" movement in the usual sense, and some limits to the field of
study have to be determined. Must an acceptance of the
validity of other religions lead to a modification of a
religion's own traditional teachings and beliefs? Such a
question is implied for Christianity in the discussion
following the publication of *The Myth of God Incarnate*.[3]
Is the meeting of religions the threshold of a new development in man's religious consciousness? Such is the view
of those who think California today is the "wave of the
future".[4] These and similar questions are beyond the
scope of this study, but suggest the profound significance
that may lie in the contemporary meeting of religions.

The aim here is more modest; to look at the efforts
and ideals of some of those who have worked to encourage
inter-faith understanding. I am grateful to many people
for their help and co-operation.

I have been privileged to attend the Geneva and Harvard
Conferences of the Temple of Understanding, and the Second Assembly
of the World Conference on Religion and Peace at Louvain, the Guru
Nanak Seminar at Patiala, the Second Annual Conference
Towards A Global Congress of World Religions, and to spend at Bost
three months studying at the Ecumenical Institute for Advanced Theological Study in Jerusalem.

The officers of the organizations discussed have been
generous in giving me time and information. Dr. Homer

Jack of the World Conference on Religion and Peace, Mrs.
Judith Hollister of the Temple of Understanding, Dr.
Stanley Samartha of the World Council of Churches, Dr.
Coos Schoneveld of the Ecumenical Theological Research
Fraternity in Israel, Dr. Bernard Resnikoff, of the Ameri-
can Jewish Committee in Israel, Sister Mary Kelly of Jews,
Christians and Muslims, Rev. W. W. Simpson of the Council
of Christians and Jews, the Rt. Rev. George Appleton, the
Rev. Jack Austin and Mrs. Heather McConnell of the World
Congress of Faiths, and Professor E. G. Parrinder of London University, have, at some stage, read the material
relevant to their organizations. Opinions and errors remain my responsibility, but without their help, there
would have been a number of mistakes. Often information
and records are incomplete and a knowledge of what happened depends on the memory of those involved. I am
grateful to Dr. Warren Lewis for his help and to Mrs. E.
I. Charlton and Mrs. Una Crist for their meticulous typing.
I thank those who have given me financial help to assist
me with my studies and with the cost of travelling. My
thanks to Mary, Rachel and Jeremy for their patience,
interest and support; and to the parishoners of Swainswick,
Woolley and Langridge for their forbearance.

I hope that this study may be some permanent record
of the dedication of those who have worked for fellowship
and harmony amongst believers and may inspire others to
continue their work.

Marcus Braybrooke

August 1979

# CHAPTER ONE

# THE WORLD PARLIAMENT OF RELIGIONS

The greatest achievement of the first major inter-religious gathering, the World Parliament of Religions, held in Chicago in 1893, was that it met.  It had been decided that Chicago should mark the four-hundredth anniversary of the discovery of America by Christopher Columbus, by holding a World Fair.  To accompany this, a series of Congresses  on the chief areas of knowledge were to be arranged.  Should there be such a Congress on religion? Would it not perhaps create discord and division?

In 1891, Charles C. Bonney, who was head of the World's Congress Auxiliary, appointed a General Committee on Religious Congresses to discuss the matter.  The Committee was varied in its composition.  It included the Roman Catholic Archbishop, the Protestant Episcopal Bishop of Chicago, members of the larger Protestant Churches, a Unitarian, a Quaker, a Universalist, and a member of the New (Swedenborgian) Church as well as Dr. E. G. Hirsch, who was Minister of Sinai Temple and Professor of Rabbinic Literature.  The Rev. J. H. Barrows, pastor of the First Presbyterian Church of Chicago, was chosen as chairman.

Although so predominantly Christian, the Committee soon decided that the Congress should try to represent the many religions of the world, not just one or two.  This novel idea[1] itself became a major subject of discussion, both during the preparations and at the Parliament itself.  On what basis was it possible for members of different religions to meet together and what did such a meeting imply as to the relationship of religions to each other?

In June 1891, the General Committee sent out a parliamentary address, explaining the proposed purpose of the Congress.  Calling attention to the importance of religion as a factor in human development, it expressed the hope that all great historic faiths would co-operate.  The committee believed that the time was ripe for a new manifestation of human fraternity, and noted that the sacred scriptures were increasingly studied in a spirit of candour and brotherhood.  There was no desire to create a

1

mood of indifferentism. Rather the hope was that a
friendly conference of eminent men, strong in their personal conviction, would show what are the supreme truths
and the light that religion could throw on the great
problems of the time.[2]

More than three thousand copies of the Preliminary Address
were sent to religious leaders across the world. There
was a considerable welcome for the suggestions. Those,
like Max Müller, who were working in the field of comparative studies of religion, hoped the conference would increase interest in their subject. Others hoped it would
provide an opportunity to show the superiority and suf-
ficiency of their particular form of Christianity. Other
who felt that their religion had been misunderstood saw
this as a chance to correct these misconceptions. Some
hoped that the conference would draw Christians closer to
each other, whilst the more progressive and broad-minded
"championed the Parliament from the feeling that they, as
Christians, might wisely and rightly show a more brotherl
spirit towards representatives of other faiths".[3]

There was also some opposition. Gladstone, whilst wishin
the Parliament well, wrote, "I am one of those who look
more to improved tempers and conceptions in the individua
than to the adoption of formulated plans for the promotio
of religious unity".[4] The Sultan of Turkey also opposed
the idea, but it was the opposition of the Presbyterian
Church in the USA and of the Archbishop of Canterbury whi
caused most disappointment.

In 1892, the General Assembly of the Presbyterian Church
in the USA, at Portland, passed a resolution expressing
strong disapproval. The resolution was passed hurriedly
at the end of a session, without debate, but it was a
blow to the Chairman and prime-mover Henry Barrows, who
was himself a Presbyterian. It seems to have made some
of his statements about the aims of the Parliament move
defensive. In fact, Presbyterian opinion was divided.
Several Presbyterian journals gave support and several
Presbyterians accepted appointments on the Advisory Council. The church's Board of Foreign Missions also gave
general approval.

The Archbishop of Canterbury, E. W. Benson, said that his
difficulties rested "on the fact that the Christian religion is the one religion. I do not understand how that
religion can be regarded as a member of a Parliament of
Religions, without assuming the equality of other intended members and the parity of their position and claims".

He then objected to the assumption that the Church of
Rome was the Catholic Church and the implication that the
Church of England was outside the Catholic Church. He
also raised the question of how those outside a tradition
could come to appreciate its inner life of devotion.
"While I quite understand how the Christian religion
might produce its evidences before any assembly, a 'pre-
sentation' of that religion must go far beyond the question of evidences, and must subject to public discussion
that faith and devotion which are its characteristics,
and which belong to a region too sacred for such treatment".[5]

An answer, on behalf of the Committee, was sent to the
*Review of the Churches* by the Rev. F. Herbert Stead. He
said that the treatment of Christianity would be fraternal, devotional and courteous. Calling churches by the
name which they themselves chose was a matter of courtesy.
No one, he continued, would "be expected to regard all
other faiths as equal to his own".[6] The Archbishop's opposition, however, continued. Some members of the Church
of England did, nevertheless, agree to serve on the Advisory Council, whilst the Bishops of the Protestant
Episcopal Church were, on the whole, in favour of the Parliament.

When the conference opened on September 11th, 1893, more
than four thousand people crowded the Hall of Columbus.
At ten o'clock, representatives of a dozen faiths marched
down the aisle, arm in arm. On the platform the central
position was taken by Cardinal Gibbon, who, after the
singing of Watts' paraphrase of the hundredth Psalm, led
everyone in saying the Lord's Prayer. An opening address
was given by President Bonney, Chairman of the World's
Congress Auxiliary, who voiced the high ideal that "when
the religious Faiths of the World recognize each other as
brothers, children of one Father, whom all profess to love
and serve, then, and not till then, will the nations of
the earth yield to the Spirit of concord and learn war no
more". He insisted that although delegates met in a spirit of mutual respect, no one was asked to compromise his
individual convictions.[7]

The General Programme of the Parliament lasted for seventeen days and took place in the Hall of Columbus. There
were addresses on a wide range of subjects from a great
variety of speakers. In the nearby Hall of Washington,
representatives of the various faiths gave expositions of
their beliefs. Simultaneously a number of different denominations of the great faiths held independent congresses

to expound their views.  A number of kindred organizations also held congresses.  The size of the Congress
needs to be appreciated.  The Hall of Columbus was usually crowded and on the fourth day, the attendance was so
large that the Hall of Washington had to be used for an
overflow meeting.  Although some people attended most sessions, the size meant that most people came as an audience to listen rather than as participants.  The fact, too,
that several different lectures and meetings might be
taking place at the same time made the gathering diffuse.
Yet there was some real meeting by the delegates and
speakers with each other.  A number of receptions and
social gatherings were held and many of the visitors from
abroad were given hospitality in local homes.

For the final session, more than seven thousand people
crowded the Halls of Washington and Columbus.  (There was
a black market for tickets).  After the singing of "Lift
Up Your Heads, O Ye Gates", the assembly stood in silence
and asked for God's blessing.  Then they sang the hymn
"Lead Kindly Light", and this was followed by numerous expressions of thanks and impressions.  The Chairman, John
Henry Barrows, and the President, Charles C. Bonny, made
their concluding addresses, Bonney ending with the words,
"Henceforth the religions of the world will make war, not
on each other, but on the giant evils that afflict mankind".  Finally, led by Dr. Hirsch, a Rabbi from Chicago,
all together said the Lord's Prayer.[8]

Throughout the Parliament the relation of religions to
each other was a dominant issue.  Some were quite clear
that their religion was destined to triumph.  Count Bern-
storff, a German Evangelical Protestant, said "We meet
together, each one wishing to gain the others to his own
creed".[9]  Mohammed Alexander Russell Webb, an American
convert to Islam, whose paper was one of the very few to
arouse vocal opposition, began by saying, "There is not
a Mussulman on earth who does not believe that ultimately
Islam will be the universal faith".[10]  The Rev. G. F.
Pentecost of London argued that the ultimate triumph of
Christianity was assured by its essential superiority to
all other religions, whilst the Rev. J. S. Dennis of New
York asserted, "Christianity is uncompromising and it is
uncompromising because it is true".[11]

The view most commonly voiced by Christians was that other faiths contained some reflections of the light which
was fully revealed in Christianity.  "In all religions",
said the Roman Catholic Archbishop Redwood of New Zea-
land, "there is a vast element of truth".[12]  The Rev.

Henry M. Field, a Presbyterian journalist, said that in
his travels across the world he had everywhere "seen
evidence of God's presence": "I have found that 'God has
not left himself without witness' in any of the dark
climes or in any of the dark religions of this world".[13]
This was also the position taken by the Chairman, Henry
Barrows. T. E. Slater, a missionary in India, argued
that Christianity fulfilled the aspirations of other religions—a view later made well-known in Farquhar's book,
*The Crown of Hinduism*. A comparison of the Bible with
other scriptures, said Slater, "establishes Christianity's
*satisfying* character in distinction from the *seeking*
spirit of other faiths. The Bible shows God in quest of
man rather than man in quest of God. It meets the questions raised in the philosophies of the East and supplies
their only true solution".[14]

Some Christians made a distinction between Christ and
Christianity. "It is not Christianity" said Rev. Lyman
Abbott, "that we want to tell our brethren across the
sea about; it is the Christ".[15] Interestingly, in view
of later ideas of a Cosmic Christ, Dr. William R. Alger
of Boston said, "I don't think it is heresy to say that
we must not confine the idea of Christ to the mere historic individual, Jesus of Nazareth; but we must consider
that Christ is not merely the individual. He is the com-
pleted genus incarnate".[16] Some Christian speakers also
suggested that there might be something to learn from
other religions. Rev. F. W. M. Hugenholtz of the Liberal
Church of Holland, suggested that if people saw something
in another religion that was lacking in their own, they
should try to enrich their own religion with "spiritual
treasures found elsewhere".[17] Henry Barrows in his opening address asked, "Why should not Christians be glad to
learn what God has wrought through Buddha and Zoroaster—
through the Sages of China, and the prophets of India
and the prophet of Islam".[18] George Candlin, at the
closing session, also suggested that God was at work in
other religions. "So surely as God is our common Father
our hearts alike have yearned for him, and our souls in
devoutest moods have caught whispers of grace dropped
from his throne".[19]

The Roman Catholic Archbishop Feeham suggested that the
ground of meeting was not religion but common humanity—
a theme that has recurred in inter-faith gatherings. "No
matter", he said, "how we may differ in faith or in religion, there is one thing that is common to us all, and
that is a common humanity".[20]

A few speakers moved towards a universalist position, although the organizers were always careful to disavow such
a position.[21]   Dr. Momerie, Dean of Westminister and a
Professor of King's College London, who died before the
Parliament began, had prepared a paper for it in which
he wrote: "It cannot be that the New Commandment was inspired when uttered by Christ and was not inspired when
uttered, as it was uttered, by Confucius and by Hillel.
*The fact is all religions are fundamentally more or less
true and all religions are superficially more or less
false.*   And I suspect that the Creed of the universal
religion, the religion of the future, will be summed up
pretty much in the words of Tennyson:

                 The whole world is everywhere
                 Bound by gold chains about the feet of God".[22]

Colonel T. W. Higginson took a similar position: "For
most of us in America the door out of superstition and
sin may be called Christianity; that is our historical
name for it; it is the accident of a birthplace.   But
other nations find other outlets, they must pass through
their own doors, not through ours; and all will come at
last upon the broad ground of God's providing, which bear
no name".[23]   T. Estlin Carpenter of Manchester New Colleg
Oxford, spoke also on the need for a wider conception of
revelation.   The Bible of humanity required a view of
revelation not confined to any particular revelation. The
history of religions is the history of God's continual
revelation.   "However much we mar and frustrate it, in
this revelation each one of us may have part.   Its forms
may change from age to age; its institutions may rise and
fall; its rites and usages may grow and decline.   These a
the temporary, the local, the accidental; they are not
the essence which abides.   To realize the sympathy of religions is the first step towards grasping this great
thought.   May this Congress hasten the day of mutual unde
standing, when God, by whatever name we hallow him, shal
be all in all".[24]

A similar vision of the essential unity of religions was
voiced by Vivekananda.   Swami Vivekananda, the disciple
of Sri Ramakrishna, was one of the outstanding personali-
ties of the Parliament.   Indeed, the *New York Times* said
he was "undoubtedly the greatest figure in the Parliamen
of Religions".[25]   In his address at the opening session,
he delighted the audience by beginning, "Sisters and
Brothers of America".   He went on to say, "I am proud to
belong to a religion that has taught the world both toler
ance and universal acceptance.   We believe not only in

universal toleration, but we accept all religions to be true".[26]  Speaking on the final day, he rejected the attempt of religions to win converts from each other.  "The Christian is not to become a Hindu or a Buddhist, nor a Hindu or a Buddhist to become a Christian.  But each must assimilate the others and yet preserve its individuality, and grow according to its own Law of growth".  The editor notes that there was not much general approval of this speech.[27]

Because the question of the relation of religions to each other and especially of Christianity to other faiths has remained to the fore throughout this century, it is natural to concentrate on this and to note that the wide range of positions that have been adopted in the subsequent debate are nearly all foreshadowed at the Parliament. Certain other aspects of the Congress should also be remembered.

In view of later discussions about the propriety of interfaith prayers and worship, it is noteworthy that sessions always began with silence and the Lord's Prayer.  The opening and closing session included some hymns, such as "Lead Kindly Light". A committee of the Parliament suggested that the following hymns were suitable: "Nearer My God to Thee", "Come Thou Almighty King", "All People That on Earth", "God is Love, His Mercy Brightens", "O Life That Makes All Things New".  Several devotional meetings were held in the early hours under the leadership of Theodore F. Seward, who was the Founder of the Brotherhood of Christian Unity.

The papers, especially of the Scientific Section, contain a mass of interesting information about the religions represented.  There was, in addition, some attempt to relate the Parliament to the concerns of the world.  It was hoped that greater knowledge of one another and of one another's beliefs would strengthen peace and human understanding.  Certain specific issues were talked about, including drunkenness and prostitution, the erring and criminal classes, the women of India, religion and labour, religion and wealth, and crime and its remedy.  On the thirteenth evening the Archbishop of Zante read a protest against popular views that Jews used the blood of Christian children in their religious rites.  He was afraid, lest this falsehood would occasion attacks on Jews.  It is interesting that efforts were made to involve women in the proceedings and a women's committee was formed. Another committee was set up to suggest accurate books on various bodies.

It may be doubted whether discussions on specific topics
had much practical result.  The influence of the Parliament lay more in making those who attended, mainly Americans, aware of the existence as living forces of religions other than Christianity.  The presence of speakers from the great faiths challenged Christians to re-
think some of their assumptions.  Criticisms of missionary work were voiced, but the organizers felt this was
outweighed by the favourable impression of Christianity
given to those of other faiths who attended.  The participation of Roman Catholics and Greek Orthodox may have
encouraged the search for Christian unity.

The disappointment perhaps was that no plans were made
for a continuing structure or for future gatherings.  As
a conference, the Parliament seems to have been successful and harmonious, thanks in particular to the careful
preparation and hard work of the Chairman.  No doubt it
was an educational experience for those who participated
and some kept in touch with those whom they met there.
The publication of the records extended its influence.
Yet, whilst the Parliament seems to have been something
of a seventeen-day wonder, and only possible because it
was held under the auspices of an international exposition, it remains a remarkable pioneer event, and no subsequent inter-faith gathering has come near to it in
size or complexity.

# CHAPTER TWO

## IS ACADEMIC STUDY DISINTERESTED?

When *Le Premier Congrés International d'Historie des Religions* was convened in Paris in 1901, in connection with *L'Exposition Universelle,* it was devoted exclusively to the scientific study of religions. The circular advertising the conference said that "the proposed Congress is of an exclusively historical nature."[1] In the event, the papers justified this claim.

The Paris Congress was to be the first of a series. At each congress an international continuation committee was appointed, with responsibility for arranging the next congress. These were held at Basel (1904), Oxford (1908), Leiden (1912), Paris (1923), Lund (1929) and Brussels (1935). No permanent organization, however, was established until after the second world war. Soon after the war, Professor Gerardus van der Leeuw helped to found a Dutch Society for the history of religions. From this body a request went to the surviving members of the continuation committee appointed at Brussels for permission to organize a congress in Amsterdam in 1950. Preparations were also made to form a permanent body consisting of national societies. The desire for a permanent body was partly so that the work could be related to UNESCO.[2]

At the Amsterdam Congress, an international organization was set up with a permanent secretariat. At first the organization was called *The International Association for the Study of the History of Religions* (IASHR): but the name was later shortened to *The International Association for the History of Religions* (IAHR). The first statute states the purpose of IAHR to be "a worldwide organization which has as its object the promotion of the academic study of the history of religions through the international collaboration of all scholars whose research has a bearing on the subject".[3] The intention of Van der Leeuw and the other founders was that the history of religions should not be isolated from other related studies, such as the psychology and

sociology of religion:[4] but their overriding concern
was for the academic or "scientific" study of religions.

The post-war period has seen much discussion of methodology in the study of religions.  This is well described
by Professor Eric Sharpe in his *Comparative Religion*.[5]
In this context, the important question is whether the
academic study of religions is an end in itself or
should serve the cause of inter-faith and international
understanding.  This came to a head after the ninth
International Congress which was held in 1958 in Tokyo.
This was the first time a Congress had been held outside
Europe.  Despite initial fears, the registration of
scholars from outside Japan was satisfactory.  One hundred and thirty came from twenty-six foreign countries,
including a large number from the USA and about thirty
scholars from Afro-Asian countries.[6]  Even so, with the
presence of many Japanese scholars, the Congress became
aware that the Oriental approach to the study of religions was different to the dominant academic tradition
in Europe.  "The West", writes Professor Sharpe, "had
generally tended to look upon religion for scholarly
purposes as something static, a collection of data, or
alternatively as an organism to be dissected.  Typically
the West had long been accustomed to spending most of
its labours on the ancient religious traditions.  Perhaps by the 1950s its approach was no longer purely
genetic: But well-established conventions die hard.  The
East, on the other hand, could as a rule conceive of no
purpose for the study of religion other than to deepen
one's apprehension and understanding of reality: certainly it could never look upon religion merely as a
passive object stretched out on the scholar's operating
table.  Religion is there to be lived, and if study does
not help the student to live better or more fully, then
there can be little or no part in it".[7]

The "Eastern" view had some "Western" sympathizers, such
as Friedrich Heiler, who delivered an address at the
opening session.[8]  The issue was also raised by the fact
that the Congress was immediately followed by a symposium, arranged as part of a UNESCO East-West project, on
"Religion and Thought in Orient and Occident: A Century
of Cultural Exchange".

Heiler, a pupil and friend of Rudolf Otto, had in 1956
revived Otto's *Religious League of Mankind,* which was
affliated to the World Congress of Faiths.[9]  He began
his opening address with the quotation, "Have we not all one
father?  Has not one God created us?"  He welcomed Arnold Toynbee

book, *An Historian's Approach to Religion,* and its criticism of the exclusive attitude of so many Christians. The modern science of religion, Heiler argued, refuted the narrow Christian view which denied every other revelation and claimed there was no unity of Gospel and religions. Quoting Schleiermacher's words, "The deeper you progress in religion, the more the whole religious world appears as an indivisible whole", Heiler outlined "seven principle areas of unity which the high religions of the earth manifest".[10] The reality of the transcendent, he said, is immanent in human hearts, is man's highest good, and is ultimate love. The way to God is a way of sacrifice. Equally all religions teach love for one's neighbour as well as saying that love is a superior way to God. "Thus there is an ultimate and most profound unity of all high religions".[11] One of the most important tasks of the science of religion", he continued, "is to bring to light this unity of all religions. It thereby pursues only one purpose, that of pure knowledge of the truth. But unintentionally there sprouts forth from the root of scientific inquiry into truth not only a tree with wondrous blossoms but also with glorious fruit—Its inquiry into truth bears important consequences for the practical relationship of one religion to another".[12] "A new era", he concluded, "will dawn upon mankind when the religions will rise to true tolerance and co-operation on behalf of mankind. To assist in preparing the way for this era is one of the finest hopes of the scientific study of religion".[13]

Such questions had normally been avoided by scholars as "unscientific". Their unease was increased by the fact that the next Congress was to be held in Marburg, which was Heiler's own university. In an article in the *Hibbert Journal,* Professor Zwi Werblowsky of Jerusalem voiced his dissent, although he did not mention Heiler by name. He argued that whilst individuals who studied religion might advocate mutual understanding and co-operation, they could not do so as students of religion. "Students of religion cannot by definition preach mutual understanding—if they speak of mutual understanding, then they do so as protagonists of a certain ideology (i.e., of tolerance, charity, liberalism, etc.) but not as students of religion—there is, as I can see it, neither room nor justification for an 'Applied Comparative Religion'".[14]

Matters came to a head at Marburg. The Secretary, Professor C. J. Bleeker, presented a paper to the General Assembly of the I.A.H.R. on "The Future Task of the

History of Religion". He mentioned the new dimension,
introduced by the presence of Oriental scholars at the
Tokyo Congress. He then dealt with criticisms of the
UNESCO symposium on "Religion and Thought in East and
West, a Century of Cultural Exchange". The intention
was that the problems should be discussed in a historical context, although some participants may have trans-
gressed the borders of purely scientific research. He
admitted that the theme could not be discussed in complete disinterestedness, because it touched directly on
the burning issues of the day. Claiming that Oriental
scholars were equally capable of strictly scientific
research, he pointed out that there were Western thinkers who believed that the history of religions should
contribute to the reconstruction of cultural and religious life. Many students were motivated solely by
pure love for the work and performed their studies according to the strict rules of science "without asking
whether the outcome of their investigation can serve
the cultural or religious wellbeing of mankind".[15] Others, however, felt that, not as a scholar, but as a man
of science and as a citizen, it was right for them to
share in the struggle for the preservation of the moral
and religious values of humanity. Bleeker, whilst
adopting a mediating approach and stressing the scientific nature of the study of religions, concluded: "I
think we can hardly withdraw from taking into account
the express wish that the study of the history of religions should give its contribution to the clarificatic
of present religious questions".[16] He then mentioned
four questions: "What is true religion?"; the need for a
survey of different types of religion; the value of religion for the present and the future, and the idea of
sympathy and tolerance.

In the ensuing discussion, Professor Zwi Werblowsky
submitted a short paper containing "the basic minimum
conditions for the study of the history of religions".
A variety of scholars had signified their general agreement with the statement. The first point rejected the
distinction between Occidental and Oriental. "There are
*Religionswissenschaftler* in the East as there are 'in-
tuitionists' in the West".[17] Secondly, *Religionswissen-
shaft* is seen as a branch of the Humanities. "It is an
anthropological discipline, studying religious phenome-
na  as a creation, feature and aspect of human culture—
the discussion of the absolute value of religion is ex-
cluded by definition, although it may have its legitimate place in other completely independent disciplines

such as,e.g., theology and philosophy of religion."[18]
Thirdly, the statement that "the value of religious phe-
nomena can be understood only if we keep in mind that
religion is ultimately a realization of a transcendent
truth" is rejected. Fourthly, it is said: "The study of
religions need not seek for justification outside itself
so long as it remains embedded in a culture pattern that
allows for every quest of historical truth as its own
*raison d'être*. Whatever the subsequent use made by the
individual scholar of his special knowledge, and whatever the analyzable sociological functions of scientific
activity in any specific cultural and historical situation, the *ethos* of our studies is in themselves".[19] Finally, it is stated, "There may or may not be room for
organizations in which students of religion join with
others in order to contribute their share towards the
promotion of certain ideals—national, international,
political, social, spiritual and otherwise. But this is
a matter of individual ideology and commitment, and must
under no circumstance be allowed to influence or colour
the character of IAHR."[20]

Although the discussion revealed differences of emphasis,
the general thrust of Professor Werblowsky's paper was
accepted. Summarizing the discussion, Professor Bleeker
ended by saying, "We should made a clear distinction between our scientific work and the Ecumenical movement or
the World Congress of Faiths—we are only a congress for
scientific study of the history of religions. It is our
duty to spread our light to people who do not know pro-
perly what religion is. But our task is not conversion
to faith whatsoever, but simply enlightening".[21]

Discussion of methodology in the study of religions continues: but the debates within IAHR from Tokyo to Marburg
make clear the distinction between the academic study of
religions and both theology on the one hand and the promotion of inter-faith understanding on the other. In his
scientific work, the student of religions must hold his
personal beliefs in suspension and not confuse his study,
which is an end in itself, with other causes,however
worthy. Those concerned with inter-faith organizations
have often not fully appreciated the nature of the academic discipline. This had led to misunderstanding and
suspicion. Many scholars have kept aloof from inter-
faith bodies for fear that they would be placed in a
false position or that their scholarly reputation would
be jeopardized. This has seriously weakened inter-faith
organizations, which have also lacked the support of religious leaders, afraid that their orthodoxy might be

compromised. As a result inter-faith gatherings have
often lacked the depth and scholarship that would have
been beneficial. Recently however, there has been a
broadening of religious studies, with some scholars
taking more interest in believers' self-understanding
of their faiths, and, as inter-faith dialogue becomes
more widespread, a greater appreciation of the contribution that the academic study of religions can make to
this.

Whilst the academic study of religions does not itself
carry implications about the relation of religions to
each other, the great increase of knowledge for which
it has been responsible has done much to    foster awareness of and interest in other religions. Spreading information has also been an aspect of the work of inter-
faith bodies. The *Religions of The Empire* Conference
held in London in 1924, may be taken as an example of
this, as its purpose was only informative.

The conference was arranged to coincide with the British
Empire exhibition. Sir Denison Ross, an expert on Oriental languages and joint author of *The Heart of Asia*, in
agreeing to become chairman of the organizing committee,
insisted "that the Congress should not take a controversial form".[22] To ensure this, all speakers from the
platform were accorded an equal status. They were not
allowed to introduce matters which were either religiously or politically controversial. In any case, their
papers had to be submitted in advance to the committee.
No discussion was allowed. The intention of the conference was strictly informative, not comparative.[23] This
also was the reason why no papers were given on Christianity or Judaism. This was a deliberate decision of
the organizers as "they considered that their function
was chiefly to familiarize those attending the lectures
with the religions of the Empire relatively little known"
in Britain.[24]

The other condition Sir Denison Ross laid down was "that
the spokesman of each religion should be one who pro-
fessed such religion".[25] The papers were given by scholarly adherents of the particular religion and the choice
of speakers was well made. Here is an interesting point
of principle which is still discussed. Can someone who
is not a member of a faith speak adequately of it, or
must an outsider inevitably miss the "feel" of a religion? This is an issue that has come to the fore in the
teaching of world religions in British Schools. It is
often said that the aim is not just to provide informa-

tion about a religion, but to help pupils understand
the world-view of adherents of a particular religious
tradition.  Certainly it is easier for a member of a religion to convey what it feels like to belong to it:
but the number of adherents of Indian religions in Britain who have been readily able to communicate their
faith has been very limited.  Sympathetic teachers,
making use of the wide range of audio-visual aids which
are now available, have shown that they can convey to
their pupils considerable insight into faiths other than
their own.

The universities, however, had first to be opened to the
study of "comparative religion".  Through his benefi-
cence, H. N. Spalding, who believed that a study of world
religions was vital for mankind's future, exercised an
important influence.  He and his wife gave Oxford a
Chair of Eastern Religion and Ethics, Lectureships in
Chinese Philosophy and Religion and in Eastern Orthodox
Culture, an Advisorship in Eastern Art, and four temporary Senior Research Fellowships in Indian History and
Religion, as well as a  wildlife and plant sanctuary on
the Cherwell.  He also founded and nurtured the School
of Eastern Religious Studies at Durham and gave books
to libraries across the world.  With Dr. Radhakrishnan
and a group of men eminent in church and state and
learning all over the world, in 1951 he helped to found
at Oxford a Union for the Study of the Great Religions.

H. N. Spalding had various objectives in promoting the
study of religions.  He believed that knowledge and understanding would encourage tolerance.  Secondly, he
believed that every great civilization had been inspired
by the possession of a spiritual content shared by all
its members.  Europeans, even if ignorant of the Bible
and the classics, were subconsciously moulded by the
legacy of Hellenized Rome and Christianized Judaism.
Recent specialization was destroying this shared heritage, whilst the technological unity of the world required a broader base for any new shared spiritual culture.  The belief of the founders of the union for the
Study of the Great Religions was that "just as European
civilization achieved unity in diversity on a basis of
Christianity and Hellenism, so a world culture could be
built up and a world renaissance made possible if educational institutions throughout the world were inspired
by a common study of the spirit of man as reflected in
his approach to God.  The great cultures and religions
of East and West—of the Far East, India, Islam, ancient
Greece and Palestine, Slav, Latin and Nordic Europe, and

North and Latin America—should be impartially studied
and compared in their independence, integrity and fruitful diversity".[26]

Spalding's third objective was the "restoration of faith
in humanity and of happiness in living",[27] which require
the exercise of self-control.

Through his trusts, much, in a quiet way, has been
achieved. The first two holders of the Spalding Chair
at Oxford, Dr. Radhakrishnan and Dr. Zaehner, exercised
wide influence through their writings. The Spalding
trust has subsidized books, libraries, lectureships,
and individual scholars. It has encouraged various new
projects such as the Shap Working Party. The Union for
the Study of Great Religions, although it seldom meets
as a body, has had distinguished members.[28] It circu-
lates a periodic report on current developments and a
half yearly compilation of notes on a wide range of
books—the work of Archimandrite Lev Gillet. Through its
then chairman, Sir Richard Livingstone, it played a part
in the setting up of the School of World Religion at
Harvard. The union was also responsible for the conception and implementation of the periodical *Religious
Studies*.

What the Spalding trust and the Union for the Study of
Great Religions have tried to do for scholars and universities, the Shap Working Party has sought to do for
teachers and schools in Britain. Its task has been to provide
adequate material for teachers of world religions. At
a conference held at Shap, in the Lake District, in 1969
a working party was set up with the intention:

"(1)   To identify the practical problems at various
        educational levels involved in teaching about
        world religions.

 (2)   To study and provide relevant syllabus mater-
        ial.

 (3)   To generate new ideas, and to explore the pos-
        sibilities of future conferences and in-
        service training courses for teachers.

 (4)   To act as a clearing house for information on
        visual aids, books, conferences or working
        parties on related topics."[29]

Since its formation, the Shap Working Party has done
much to fulfill its aims.[30] It is interesting that,

although many of its leaders commend the wider significance of the study of world religions for its bearing on
good community relations and the search for religious
truth, nothing to this effect is included in the aims of
the Working Party.

The agreed terms of reference of the Standing Conference
on Inter-Faith Dialogue in Education are also non-commit-
tal,[31] although dialogue has been seen as not just com-
municating information but also a growing in truth.  The
Selly Oak Conference in 1974 agreed that "essential in-
gredients for meaningful dialogue are honesty and integrity and a 'wanting to know', so that it becomes not
merely a question of communication, though of course it
is that, but something that involves discovering truths
about ourselves, and that involves an openness that puts
those of us who participate at risk.  It does this because we are asked to face up to, amongst other things,
the question of truth and the recognition of incompati-
bles—dialogue can provide us with deeper insights into
our own faiths—it has a social value and implications
both for the world community and for world peace".[32]
Here the significance of dialogue for international and
inter-faith understanding is recognized as well as its
importance in the quest for religious truth.  In other
bodies, such as the Council of Christians and Jews, the
value of education has been seen in removing ignorance
and the causes of prejudice, thereby helping "to check
and combat all forms of religious and racial intolerance".[33]  The Inter-Religions Organization of Singapore
has also hoped that providing accurate information about
the religions practiced there has helped "to create a
climate in which religious disturbances are less likely".[34]

An ambitious project is The World Order for Cultural Exchange.  It is intended to enrol  as many children at
birth as possible on a twin international registration
basis, from different countries and conditions, keeping
them informed as to what their twin is doing for a period
of twenty years.  It is further intended to enrol  a
guardian from a third country, who will also be kept informed of the two children's welfare.  It is also planned
to set up Peace Libraries.  These suggestions came from
Fr. Alfred Woodard, whose grandfather Nathaniel Woodard,
founded the Woodard Schools.  The Provost is Father
Michael Woodard, the son of Alfred Woodard.  It is hoped
to win the support of the eleven "ideologies" or religions.  At present, books on each of them are being prepared.  It is also hoped to purchase a centre for inter-

faith study and meditation.

Clearly the motives for studying world religions are
varied.  At one extreme is disinterested scientific
study—"Truth for truth's sake"—at the other such study
is encouraged in the belief that it will foster human
unity and the search for truth.  Implicit in the views
of those who have this latter hope is the belief that
world religions have much in common.  In between are
those who see the value of knowing what others believe,
as this can help mutual understanding between religious
communities, but who do not wish to compromise the truth
claims of their own faith.  The attitude to the study of
religions therefore reflects a person's or organization's
view of the relation of religions.  Confusion is sometimes caused because these underlying premises are not
examined.

Whatever the motivation, this century has seen an enor-
mous increase in information about world religions.  In
many countries, such information is readily available
and people can quite easily acquire a basic knowledge of
the beliefs of other religious traditions.  Ignorance,
which may be a cause of prejudice, is, even so, still
widespread.  Inter-faith bodies therefore have a continuing task of providing accurate information and helping
members of one religious community to meet and get to
know those of other communities.  Yet increasingly, this
work is being done by the religions themselves, or by
the growing academic study of the subject.  This means
that inter-faith bodies can concentrate on their particular and specific tasks, which are different to those
of the academic study of the subject.

# CHAPTER THREE

## A MYSTICAL UNITY OF RELIGIONS?

Amongst those most active in seeking inter-faith fellowship have been those who stress the mystical unity of
religions. This approach has been particularly associated with the World Congress of Faiths and, more recently, the Temple of Understanding.

The claim was made by the nineteenth-century Hindu leader, Sri Ramakrishna, that he had discovered that the
mystical experience at the heart of every religious discipline was essentially the same. On this claim, Swami
Vivekananda based his call for tolerance at the World
Parliament of Religions. For, if the essential experience is similar, the differences said to be caused by
theological and cultural conditioning become inessential.
Instead of competing, religions should therefore co-operate. This, it has also been felt, was timely, at a
moment in history when modern communications were making
the world one.

These views have been eloquently expounded by Dr. S.
Radhakrishnan, who spoke at early gatherings of the World
Congress of Faiths and later became its Patron, and who
also became a supporter of the *Temple of Understanding*.
In the Preface to *Eastern Religions and Western Thought*,
he reveals his universal interest. He sees a new humanism on the horizon, embracing the whole of mankind, because there is a growing world consciousness. The supreme task of our generation is to give a world soul to
this growing world consciousness. "Should we not", he
asks, "give a spiritual basis to the world which is now
being mechanically made to feel its oneness by modern
scientific inventions?"[1] In his opinion, a world community, of which the various nations are the units, and universal religion, of which the various historical religions are the branches, should arise as the social and
spiritual counterparts of the scientific progress of this
century. International contacts through improved means
of communications and the growth of commerce are only the
body of the new world. A feeling of brotherhood among

all nations, a spirit of co-operation in the pursuit of
common peaceful aims, international fellowship and universal toleration——these should form the soul of that
world. In his Kamala Lectures, he argued that through
the influence of science and trade a world culture is
shaping itself and that as religions adapt to this new
world and express themselves in a new idiom so they are
"approximating to one another". The universal elements
in them will be emphasized and the "gradual assimilation
of religions will function as a world faith".[2] "The
time has come", he wrote in his book *Religion in a Chang
ing World,* "for us to join in unity of spirit".[3] His
view rests on two premises. First, that the underlying
mystical experience of the great religious leaders is
closely related. "The seers describe their experiences
with an impressive unanimity. They are near to one another on mountains farthest apart".[4] The second premise
is that each individual must discover the truth for himself and that it will differ as each individual's development differs. This allows for the acceptance of variety and of different views of truth.


THE WORLD CONGRESS OF FAITHS


Francis Younghusband

It was his own mystical experience that led Francis
Younghusband to work for inter-faith fellowship.

Francis' father was Major-General J. W. Younghusband and
his mother was Clara Jane Shaw, who was the sister of
Robert Shaw, an explorer of Central Asia. Francis,
their second son, was born at a hill station on the
North-West Frontier on May 31, 1863. He was taken home
at seven months by his mother with the rest of the family to her mother who lived in Bath. After grandmother'
death, the family returned to India, but Francis was sen
back when five or six to England for his schooling.
In 1876, he started at Clifton College, Bristol and was
expected to conform to the rather conventional public
school version of Christianity. Yet already at his confirmation he was thinking for himself. He had some
doubts about the virgin birth and the physical resurrec-
tion and ascension of Jesus. During this time, he paid
a visit to the Alps, which he said, "did far more for me
than all the sermons I had ever heard".[5]

In 1881 he entered Sandhurst and the following year set

sail for India. His choice of reading for the journey
showed that already he had considerable interest in religion. Amongst many biographies, lives of Christ were
prominent. He had time to think and determined that in
the future he would take nothing on authority. Ritual
and dogma were unimportant. He came to think of Jesus
Christ as a real man, with all the frailties of men,
who became great because of indomitable courage. Already his basic convictions were largely fixed. They
were to develop in two main ways: in greater experience
of the mystery of the universe and in broadening sympathy with, and understanding of, other faiths.

The highlights of the next few years of military service
were his journeys of exploration to Manchuria and across
the Gobi Desert. In 1888 he was granted a short leave,
so that he could lecture about his travels to the Royal
Geographical Society. He tried, unsuccessfully, to communicate to his parents his new sense of spiritual values. He had met and spoken with Christians of many denominations and with both educated and simple adherents
of other faiths. He did not think one alone could be
true and the other false. In the Gobi Desert, he had
studied Darwin's work. He had found confirmation for
his views on the gospels in Renan's *Life of Jesus* and
Seeley's *Ecce Homo*. The book that had impressed him
most was Tolstoy's *The Kingdom of God is Within You*.
For him, at the time, the essence of Christianity was
that the divine Spirit, which in Christ was a living
flame, was latent in all men. All therefore were children of the same Father and should seek to develop the
divine Spirit. Thus by 1889, he had made his own religion for himself.[6]

On his return to India, after a time of "arid and mean-
ingless" soldiery, he was asked to explore all the Himalayan passes from the north. He was in his element as
an explorer, but even so,during his leave in England in
1891, he again discussed with his father his project to
leave the service and devote his life to the conduct of
a spiritual campaign. This would not have been as an
official of any church, but in some undefined way.
Events on the frontier, however, demanded his immediate
return to duty. In 1903, he was asked by Lord Curzon,
the Viceroy, to lead a mission to Tibet. This was a
difficult and dangerous undertaking. At Lhasa, he successfully signed a treaty, but his work was repudiated
by the politicians. It was as he was leaving Lhasa that
he had a decisive spiritual experience which largely

determined his future life.  He described it in his book
*Vital Religion:*

> The day after leaving Lhasa I went off alone
> to the mountainside, and there gave myself
> up to all the emotions of this eventful
> time.  Every anxiety was over——I was full
> of good-will as my former foes were convert-
> ed into stalwart friends.  But now there
> grew up in me something infinitely greater
> than mere elation and good-will.  Elation
> grew to exultation, exultation to an exal-
> tation which thrilled through me with over-
> powering intensity.  I was beside myself
> with untellable joy.  The whole world was
> ablaze with the same ineffable bliss that
> was burning within me.  I felt in touch with
> the flaming heart of the world.  What was
> glowing in all creation and in every single
> human being was a joy far beyond mere good-
> ness as the glory of the sun is beyond the
> glow of a candle.  A mighty joy-giving Power
> was at work in the world——at work in all
> about me and at work in every living thing.
> So it was revealed.

> Never again could I think evil.  Never again
> could I bear enmity.  Joy had begotten love.[7]

Already for some fifteen years, religion had been Francis Younghusband's primary interest.  He was aware of
the Higher-Critical study of the scriptures and of
scientific advance.  As a result he was dissatisfied
with the conventional religion in which he had been
brought up.  "I had visions of a far greater religion
yet to be, and of a God as much greater than our English
God as a Himalayan giant is greater than an English
hill".[8]

Already he wished to communicate this "greater religion",
but he knew that first he had to clarify the intellectual
framework of his conception of the universe.  Convinced
that the universe was governed by its own laws and not
by external interference, he continued his study of
science and came, for a while, under the influence of
Herbert Spencer.  Yet, a variety of experience and his
reading of nature-mystics, such as Blake and Wordsworth,
made him dissatisfied with Spencer's "petty-minded hatred
of religion".[9]  A study of McTaggart's *Some Dogmas of
Religion* and *Studies in Hegelian Cosmology* led him to

seek the acquaintance of the author, which issued in a
close friendship.

Having tested his faith against intellectual criticism,
he set to work to give it shape and definition in a
book to be called *The Inherent Impulse*. As the work was
nearing completion, he met with an accident in Belgium,
which was followed by prolonged illness. This experience led him to revise his book, which, eventually, was
published in the autumn of 1912, with the title *Within*.
This was the first of several books in which he described
his religious views.[10]

His basic conviction was that joy was the ground and
crown of all religion.[11] Joy, he claimed, was at the
heart of Christ's message. Hindu, Buddhist and Muslim
saints had also declared the same; and the Psalms were
full of its expression. Although love was usually regarded as more fundamental, he held that joy was both
deeper and higher.[12] This emphasis did not mean that
he disregarded evil and suffering. He believed, however,
that the joy of life not merely counterbalanced the suffering and wickedness but could transform it into good.[13]

It is important to recognize that his conception of a
fellowship of faiths sprang from a mystical sense of the
unity of all people. The "brotherhood of man" was for
Sir Francis  not a religious slogan  but a truth realized
in religious experience. In such an experience, a person
is "lifted right out of himself and wafted up to unbe-
lievable heights. He seems to expand to infinite distance and embrace the whole world".[14]

In working for the Congress, Sir Francis made it clear
that there was no intention of formulating another eclectic religion. It was rather to help members of all
faiths become aware of the universal experience which had
been his. The Congress, he hoped, "would awaken a wider
consciousness and afford men a vision of a happier world-
order in which the roots of fellowship would strike down
deep to the Central Source of all spiritual loveliness
till what had begun as human would flower as divine".[15]
The human fellowship that he  sought to promote was in-
extricably linked to communion with the divine. The
Congress, therefore, was an attempt to give practical
expression to the mystic's vision of unity.

## The World Congress of Faiths 1936

Sir Francis Younghusband played an active part in the

Religions of Empire Conference in 1924. Although the
intention of the conference was that it should only present information, Sir Francis, in his opening address,
made clear that he saw in it an expression of the fundamental unity of religion. He asserted that religion was
the ultimate basis on which the Empire must stand, and
that the conference was against exclusive views. "We
may each of us hold that our own religion is more completely perfect than any other. But even then we may
recognize that God reveals himself in many ways, and
that to the followers of other religions than our own
may have been revealed much that may be of value to us.
And we may hope to seize from each some of that Divine
Spirit which inspires every religion in diverse ways".[16]

Besides recognizing that God reveals himself through the
various religions, Sir Francis was also suggesting that
members of one faith might learn from the revelation
given in other faiths. Recognizing the significance of
the difference between religions, Younghusband went on
to say, "We need never lose our faith that all the time
there may be an underlying and overarching harmony which
may reconcile them all, if only we could reach it".[17]

There was no direct follow-up to this conference, but
some of those responsible for it helped to establish the
Society for the Study of Religions. The Society (which
arranged and published lectures), after the second World
War, merged with the World Congress of Faiths. Sir
Francis became chairman of the Society's committee. Sir
Francis also supported the Inter-Religious Fellowship
which was organized by Reverend Leslie Belton, who was
at that time the editor of *The Inquirer*.[18] In 1933, Sir
Francis attended the World Fellowship of Faiths conference held in Chicago in "conscious imitation" of the
1893 World Parliament of Religions. He also took part
in similar gatherings held in New York and other American
cities in 1934. He was in touch, too, with the attempts to
arrange an Inter-Religious Peace conference.[19] The organizers of these efforts urged him to inaugurate an
Inter-Faith Congress in London, and by the time he returned to England in 1934, he felt that the moment was
ripe for such an initiative.

He therefore invited a number of people to a meeting on
November 12, 1934, at which it was agreed to establish
a British National Council of the World Fellowship of
Faiths. H. H. Maharaja Gaekwar of Baroda became president and Sir Francis was elected chairman and organizer
of the British National Council. Soon afterwards, Sir

Francis published his chairman's proposals for the Congress, stressing that the aim was not to formulate a new synthetic faith, but to provide a meeting ground for followers of different religions.

The Congress itself was held at University College, London, from July 3rd to 18th, 1936. Sir Francis succeeded in getting outstanding members of the main traditions to speak. He was an aristocrat at heart and was keen to ask those whom, in his diaries, he called "the best people". Participants included Yusuf Ali, known for his carefully annotated translation of the Qur'an, the Russian Nicolas Berdiaeff, Dr. Surendranath Dasgupta, author of a massive History of Indian Philosophy, C. E. M. Joad, Dr. G. P. Malalasekara from Ceylon, Dr. Joseph Needham, Dr. Radhakrishnan, Sir Herbert Samuel and Dr. Suzuki.

A wide range of views was represented. Besides the main traditions, there were speakers from the Church of the Latter Day Saints, from Caodia or Renovated Buddhism, "a new faith" which claimed one million adherents, from Jainism and from the Baha'i faith. An Abyssinian priest and a humanist also spoke.

The Congress was not residential and this restricted the social intercourse between participants. Yet for the first time at an inter-religious gathering, discussion was allowed and was carried on in good humour. The chairmen and leaders of debate were carefully chosen.

Many of the published papers are of a high quality. Perhaps most interesting is the different attitudes they display towards the relationship of religions. On the one hand, the Reverend P. T. R. Kirk claimed that Christianity must be accepted by the whole of mankind and Mr. Moulvri A. R. Dard made a similar claim for the Ahmadiyya community. By contrast, the paper by Professor Haldane, who died shortly before the conference, included this passage: "Many Christians entertain the ideal of converting non-Christian peoples to Christianity. I think that a much higher ideal is to understand and enter into sympathy with the religions which exist in other countries and use the understanding and sympathy as a basis for higher religion".[20] Several speakers, such as the Chief Rabbi and Canon Barry, stressed the difference between religions, whereas Ranjee G. Shani said the differences were trivial. "Jesus and Buddha, Shakespeare and Ramakrishna—are in essence 'members one of another'".[21]

In general it was agreed that the aim of the Congress
was not to create one new synthetic religion, but to
generate understanding and a sense of unity between the
religions of the world.  Rabbi Dr. Israel Mattuck,
Chairman of the Executive of the World Union for Progressive Judaism, put it like this:  "I am not pleading
for one religion to include all men.  I like diversity.
I should no more want a world with one religion than I
should want only one coloured rose in my garden.  But we
can have diversity without enmity and when we do this,
I believe, the world will be more ready to receive our
message about human unity and human peace".[22]

Several speakers hoped that the world religions could
together work for peace and spiritual uplift.  Professor
Marcault, a French Professor of Psychology, highlighted
the important question of what in practice religions can
actually do together.  It is not easy to find areas of
practical co-operation in which to give concrete expression to the desire to work together.  "Peace and fellowship", he said, "can only be constructive if they are
incarnated in some positive religious aim in whose realization all faiths can agree to co-operate, and whose
universality maintains them united".[23]

In his foreword to the published papers, *Faiths and Fellowship,* Sir Francis Younghusband stressed again that
the one aim of the Congress was to promote the spirit of
fellowship.  He ruled out certain misunderstandings.
There was no intention of formulating another eclectic
religion, nor of seeking the lowest common denominator,
nor of appraising the value of existing religions and
discussing respective merits and defects.  It was not
maintained that all religions are  the same, nor equally
true, nor as good as one another.  The hope was to "in-
tensify that sense of community which is latent in all
men" and to awaken a livelier world-consciousness.  Sir
Francis mentioned that through discussion and reflection,
the conception of God grew greater and that by coming
closer to each other, members of different religions
deepened their own spiritual comunion.[24]

In estimating the value of the Congress, the question
that has to be asked, as it has to be of the subsequent
life of the World Congress of Faiths, is, whether, however worthy, the aims are sufficiently precise.  The
question of the relation to each other of the world religions is still much debated.  The position of the Congress rules out the view that any one religion has a
monopoly of truth.  It assumes that, despite differences,

the world religions have an affinity, and share a recognition of spiritual reality and of ethical values. Many
adherents of missionary religions have, therefore, opposed the Congress, because they claim that their religion is the truth and because they are reluctant to
grant even limited validity to other religions. On the
other hand, the Congress rules out the attempt to create a new synthetic religion. It insists that differences are important and must be respected. It is therefore criticized by those who advocate a new unified religion and by those who hold that differences are only
external and irrelevant.

Is, then, the promotion of a spirit of fellowship and
world loyalty a sufficient aim to engender enthusiasm?
Clearly it is for some, but the number of those people,
even religious leaders, with a world consciousness and
interest is small. Their number in Britain has declined
as the Empire has disappeared, although immigration has
recently helped to create a new interest in inter-faith
dialogue.

How fellowship is understood may vary considerably. It
may imply learning to appreciate others whose values and
ways of life are different. In a world of prejudice,
this is important, but somewhat negative. Fellowship
may be concerned with the discovery of areas of ethical
agreement and perhaps with taking common action on certain moral issues.

At its deepest level, the search for fellowship becomes
a search for truth and flows from communion with the
divine. Here it is assumed that the truth is greater
than the understanding of any individual or of any one
religion and that by sharing together with members of
other faiths, each individual will be deepened in his
knowledge of truth and usually in his appreciation of
his own religious tradition. It seems that Sir Francis
Younghusband saw the development of all these aspects of
fellowship as part of the work of the Congress, although
he was aware of the difficulty of conveying exactly what
he meant by fellowship. He perhaps came nearest to
expressing his understanding in a talk given soon after
the outbreak of war. "When I speak of fellowship", he
said, "I have found subtler and deeper meanings emerge
as I study the idea more closely. It is not exactly
either friendship, or companionship, or neighbourliness,
or co-operation, though these may develop from it. And
the sentiment from which it springs is something more
than compassion, for compassion concerns itself with

unhappiness alone rather than with both happiness and
unhappiness.  Even sympathy is associated rather with
suffering than with enjoyment.  At its intensest and
highest, fellowship seems to be a communion of spirit
greater, deeper, higher, wider, more universal, more
fundamental than any of these—than even love."[25]  Whatever brought people together, he continued, so long as
it increased their enjoyment, led to fellowship.  The
highest enjoyment and therefore fellowship came from the
meeting together of people who were profoundly interested
in religion.  The aim of the Congress was to develop both
the meeting of people with each other and their communion
with the Divine so that the unity of mankind might become
more obvious and complete.[26]

The History of the Congress

On the morning after the Congress ended, a meeting was
held at which it was unanimously agreed to set up a continuation committee, of which Sir Francis was elected
chairman.  It was agreed that activities would continue
under the auspices of the World Congress of Faiths (Continuation Movement) and that individual membership would
be invited.  This was an important decision, as it gave
the Congress its own independent life.  The Executive
Committee is answerable to the members, and whilst this
may mean that there is an imbalance of the religions represented, it allows the Congress freedom of activity. To
have sought official representation from religious groups
—even had it been forthcoming—might have gained wider
support for the Congress, but would have restricted its
freedom.

The committee soon arranged another congress, which was
held at Oxford in 1937 and was residential.  In the next
year, one was held at Cambridge, and in 1939, in Paris.
The latter conference helped to sow the seeds of a French
group, "L'Union des Croyants".

The outbreak of war severely restricted the work of the
congress.  Communications with friends abroad became
difficult and international congresses impossible.  Sir
Francis, like many others, thought the war would not
last long and was concerned that the world religions
should be ready to share in the post-war task of reconstruction.  Inviting members to a meeting, he wrote: "A
new world order is now the dream of men, but for this a
new spirit will be needed.  This is the special concern
of men of religion, in this case men of all religions—

non-Christians as well as Christians—all combined to
create a world loyalty, and a sense of world fellowship
and to provide the spiritual impetus, the dynamic and
the direction to the statesmen and economists, whose
business is to give it bodily expression".[27] Again when
the Atlantic Charter was proclaimed, he at once arranged
a series of meetings on an inter-religious foundation
for the Atlantic Charter, saying that "of all the forces
which are to be marshalled behind the Charter, the force
which may be engendered by all the religions working together in unison will be incontestably the most potent".[28]

To maintain communications with the scattered membership,
a "Chairman's Circular Letter" was started. By 1941 this
had developed from a typewritten sheet to a four-page
printed pamphlet. In one, Sir Francis urged members to
meet together locally and at Bournemouth, Lady Lees took
the initiative in forming a local group.

In 1942, despite many difficulties a congress was held
in Birmingham. At it, Sir Francis was taken ill and he
died soon afterwards at the home of Madeleine, Lady Lees
in Dorset. A memorial service was held in St. Martin-in-
the-Fields on the 10th of August, 1942; appropriately
the service included short lessons from the sacred scriptures of the world.

The death of Sir Francis was a heavy blow to the Congress,
because it depended so much on his inspiration and effort
and because no plans had prepared for this possibility. Many, too, had taken part out of personal regard for
Sir Francis. Lord Samuel temporarily became chairman,
but Baron Erik Palmstierna soon took his place.

Baron Erik Palmstierna was for a short while Foreign Minister of Sweden and from 1920 to 1937 he was Swedish Ambassador in London. After his retirement he settled in
England. His two books, *Horizons of Immortality* and
*Widening Horizons,* show his concern for spiritualism. He
found Sir Francis a kindred spirit, and took a leading
part in the 1939 Paris conference. Like Sir Francis he,
too, believed in an essential mystical unity of religions.
In his book, *The World: Crisis and Faith,* he wrote that
"a striking congruity of views and aims occurs among
Saints and Mystics belonging to races which were alien
to each other".[29] Of the Congress, he said, "We are not
looking for any super-world religion which ought to replace existing historical institutions and dogmas—but
we search for organic elements of religious experience."[30]
The Baron's five-year chairmanship was marked by important

international contacts and he gave much attention to
*The Three-Faith Declaration on World Peace.* In a speech
in the House of Lords, Dr. Bell, the Bishop of Chichester, suggested that an international authority, backed by
the monotheistic faiths, might secure the rule of law in
international affairs. The Baron contacted the Bishop,
and a small committee met to explore the suggestion.
It was decided initially to see what support existed
for the *Three-Faith Declaration on World Peace* that had
been issued in America in October,1943.[31] There was an
encouraging response from all,except the Christian
churches. Without their support,the idea came to nothing, but it is evidence of a hope, often repeated in the
history of the Congress, that religions together might
be able to exert an influence for peace and world order.

The Baron was succeeded by Sir John Stewart Wallace, who
had been Chief Land Registrar for England and Wales. He
was particularly keen to encourage "seekers"—those without a definite religious commitment but who were interested in spiritual matters—to join the Congress. This
move met with some opposition, but Sir Francis in choos-
ing the title Congress of Faiths rather than Congress of
Religions had hoped that such seekers might join the
movement. Sir John also tried to introduce a deeper
spirit of devotion into the Congress  by encouraging
All Faiths Services and also meditation meetings, which
were led by Rev. R. G. Coulson, Bhikkhu Thittila, and
Swami Avyaktananda. Conferences again began to be held,
but on a smaller scale than before the war.

After Sir John Stewart Wallace's resignation, Baroness
Ravensdale took the chair  and the day-to-day running
of the Society was in the hands of Rev. Arthur Peacock,
who became Hon. Secretary. In  1937 Arthur Peacock became a minister of the Universalist Church, but with the
decline of Universalism, he decided in 1951 to become a
Unitarian minister. His motto was a verse of Elizabeth
Barrett-Browning's:

> Universalism - universe religion - the unity
> of all things,
> Why it's the greatest word in our language.

An energetic secretary, he helped to develop the work of
the Congress. The predominance, however, of universalist unitarian and neo-Hindu views tended to discourage
those with more orthodox religious views, especially
Christians, from participating in the Congress, and it
was regarded in some quarters as "syncretistic", although

the Congress repudiated this charge. Syncretism, a term
originally used by Plutarch (*De Fraterno Amore* 19) of the
fusion of religious cults which occurred in the Graeco-
Roman world, is usually used in a pejorative sense of an
artificial mixing of religions. Christians, many of whom
at the period were deeply influenced by the theology of
Barth and Kraemer who stressed that the Gospel was dis-
continuous from world religions, were suspicious of any
such mixing of religions.

In 1959 the Rev. Reginald Sorensen, M.P., who in 1964
was created a baron, became chairman and retained the office until his death in 1970. A tireless worker for
numerous causes, he and his wife Muriel brought to the
Congress their gift of friendship and concern for individuals of all races and conditions. His interest was
especially in seeking the common moral values contained
in the teachings of the world religions. The emphasis
shifted, therefore, away from the mystical.

Conscious of the obscurantist and reactionary character
of so much religion, he had a love-hate relationship
with organized religion. In his *I Believe in Man*, he
criticized religion's opposition to new knowledge, to
scientific advance and social progress. He disliked all
intolerance and found orthodox Christianity too rigid
and dogmatic. Yet he never doubted that the human spirit
could commune with the divine and sought to commend a
"modern faith".[32] "I affirm that we should not be se-
duced into thinking that the only reality is the tangi-
ble and the sensuous, but that reality is vaster and more
permeative of our material environment than we can neatly
tie up with intellectual string".[33]

With his belief in a divine spirit went a deep and opti-
mistic belief in the human spirit and in man's ability
eventually to overcome evil and suffering in the world.
He held that this belief was enshrined in all the great
religious traditions and hoped that the Congress could
help the religions emphasize the ethical values which
they held in common. Impatient with doctrinal debate or
theological dialogue—despite his questioning mind—in
his addresses, again and again he came back to matters
of ethical and moral concern.

He was well aware of the endless variations of moral patterns or "mores", but held that in the world religions
could be found an essential moral content beyond trans-
ient communal codes.[34] "It is necessary", he said at a
conference service, "to distinguish between paramount

moral values and what I term 'moral patterns'".[35] "Moral patterns vary considerably, but penetrating, yet
transcending those variables are moral values, that,
with degrees of priority and emphasis, exist within all
faiths and religions. Among these are justice, mercy,
compassion, integrity, courage, sacrifice, fidelity and
fraternity. Here is where all can meet on common
grounds".[36] He believed that despite differences of
metaphysics and custom, all religions could agree on
these moral values and that such agreement was vital
for the world. "I would claim that only a measure of
inter-religious, international and inter-racial agreement on essential moral values can enable mankind to
dwell on this earth in co-operation, amity and peace".[37]

Whilst the Congress has continued to seek for common
moral values and to work for international peace and
the development of a world community, in recent years
there has been a deepening of inter-faith dialogue within the Congress. Committed members of world religions
have taken a more active part and both the President,
the Very Rev. Edward Carpenter, who is Dean of Westminster, and the recent chairman, the Rt. Rev. George Appleton, who was Anglican Archbishop of Jerusalem, are
distinguished church leaders, and the vice-chairman,
Rabbi Hugo Gryn, is the Rabbi of an important Reform
Synagogue in London. At the same time, the mood in Britain has changed. The presence in Britain, through immigration of sizeable Muslim, Hindu and Sikh communities,
has given new importance to inter-faith relations. The
attitude of Christians has become more open and inter-
faith dialogue is widely encouraged. The teaching of
world religions has also been a major development in
religious education and there is an interest in world
religions amongst a wider public.

Yet whilst inter-faith dialogue is now more common, there
remains a particular emphasis to the work of the World
Congress of Faiths. Much dialogue is at the level of
seeking to understand what others believe and practise,
in the hope that this will promote tolerance and goodwill. The Congress goes beyond this and sees dialogue
as a "truth-seeking" exercise. The assumption is often
voiced that there is a truth which transcends any one
world religion, and that the coming together of religions
is mutually enriching. In a lecture at the Fortieth Anniversary Conference of the Congress in Canterbury in
1976, Bishop George Appleton distinguished certain stages
in the meeting of religions. "There is first of all the
stage of self-affirmation, in which adherents of any

particular faith feel the need to proclaim and propagate
their own faith".[38]   Then comes a period of self-criti-
cism.   "Finally there should be a stage of renewal and
a deepened sense of vocation and mission.   I believe
that each religion may have a mission, which in theistic
terms might be spoken of as God's mission to the world
through Hinduism, Buddhism, Judaism and Islam, while our
Baha'i brethren may with some justice claim that they
were an early ecumenical movement among the world religions.

So each religion has a mission, a gospel, a central affirmation.   Each of us needs to enlarge on the gospel
which he has received, without wanting to demolish the
gospel of others.

In this deeper fellowship of spirit we can understand
the way of salvation perceived and sometimes enjoyed  by
others—the "moksha" or liberation of the Hindu, the en-
lightenment or "satori" of the Buddhist, the rule of God
as accepted by the Jew or the Muslim, the reconciliation
of sinful man through the Cross.

Inevitably when we learn about the discoveries and insights of other Faiths, we relate them to our own and assess them by our own basic convictions.   So we can enlarge and deepen our initial and basic faith by the experience and insights of people from other religions and
cultures, without disloyalty to our own commitment".[39]

Edward Carpenter has suggested that the recovery of belief
requires  the coming together of the insights of many
faith traditions.[40]

Yehudi Menuhin, in a message to the 1976 conference said,
"Until you transform your various weaknesses into a single strength, into an evolved conception of life and
eternity, into a unified force, you will carry no weight
with the behaviour of man".[41]

The emphasis is therefore on the mutual enrichment that
may come from the meeting of people of various faiths.
Whilst in part this is an intellectual task, as in the
approach adopted by Professor John Hiek in his book
*Death and Eternal Life*,[42] it is also an attempt to enter
into one another's spirituality, as practised and reported by Swami Abhishiktananda, Dom Bede Griffiths or
Fr. Murray Rogers.   The Congress itself has arranged a
number of small meditation weekends with leaders belong-

ing to different faiths to explore each other's spiritual disciplines.

This current emphasis, whilst it re-echoes the sense of
the mystical unity of religions which is to be found in
the writings of Sir Francis Younghusband, is rather
richer and deeper than the "universalism" of the nineteen-fifties. Instead of stressing only what is common,
it sees the great religions as complementary—each with
particular insights and treasures to share with others.
Such an approach does justice to the variety and actuality of the world religions and at the same time suggests
that their coming together may be mutually beneficial.

## Activities

The work of the Congress has been primarily educational.
It has helped to remove the prejudice and ignorance that
has often existed between members of different religions
and encouraged them as they become friends together to
seek for deeper truth.  The annual conferences have been
important in drawing members together.  A wide range of
topics have been discussed, with speakers drawn from
many religions.  Regular lectures have been held
in  London,    provincial centres and, on the Continent,
arranged by the overseas groups.

The journal *World Faiths* has appeared regularly since
1949,[43] and goes to many parts of the world.  Whilst not
an "academic" journal, it keeps members in touch with
each other and gives news of inter-faith activities and
has a wide range of articles.

The World Congress of Faiths has been a pioneer of inter-
faith worship.  Sir Francis wished that the Religions
of Empire Conference (1924) had included times of devotion, but this was not possible, although the Reverend
Tyssul Davies arranged an inter-faith gathering at the
Theistic Church.  At the 1936 conference, there were some
readings from the sacred scriptures and members of the
conference attended Anglican services at St. Paul's and
Canterbury Cathedral.  It is, however, only since the
second World War that attempts have been made to develop
inter-faith worship.  This goes beyond the attendance of
members of one faith at the worship of another to the
attempt to arrange a joint service in which members of
several faiths can share.

One of the first services in which people of several

faiths took part was the memorial service for Sir Francis Younghusband at St. Martin-in-the-Fields in 1942. In 1946 an "All Faiths" service was arranged during the Annual Conference at the Institut Français. In 1949, the Reverend Will Hayes, who for some years had been experimenting with universalist worship, compiled and conducted a service for the World Congress of Faiths, called "Every Nation Kneeling".[44] On the occasion of the Coronation of Queen Elizabeth II, inspired by her request that people of all religions should pray for her, the Congress organized a special service, at the Memorial Hall, Farringdon Street, London. About six hundred people attended and this success led the Executive Committee to decide on an annual service. At the first of these, held at the King's Weigh House, Oxford Street, the preacher was the Reverend Edward Carpenter. Subsequent services have been held at churches of several denominations, including Roman Catholic, Anglican, Baptist and Unitarian. They have also been held at Reform and Liberal synagogues. Until recently, other faiths have not possessed large enough buildings in central London for the Annual Service.

Amongst the most memorable services was that held at the West London Synagogue in 1973, when the speaker was His Holiness the Dalai Lama, who said he was deeply moved by the collection of prayer readings from different religious groups. The following year saw the introduction of a religious dance-mime at the conclusion of the service, which vividly expressed the search for unity. A problem of inter-faith services is to ensure real participation without asking those present to compromise their particular beliefs. Hymns have therefore to be chosen with great care and it is only recently that there has been sufficient trust to join together in prayer and affirmation.

A number of Christians have expressed their disapproval of inter-faith services. Archdeacon Carpenter, as President, therefore gathered together a small group of Christians, of several denominations, to consider the theological rationale for such services. The report of the group[45] suggests that those taking part believed that members of all faiths worshipped the same God, the Creator of all, and that such services witnessed to the ethical values upheld in every faith. The group rejected the view that attendance at such services implied disloyalty to Jesus Christ. Although the discussion centers on matters of Christian theology, the report contains comments from members of many religions.

In recent years the number of inter-faith services has
been increasing.  In 1966 a Multi-Faith Act of Witness
was held on Commonwealth Day for the first time and
similar ceremonies have been held in subsequent years.[46]
The Week of Prayer for World Peace has been marked by
inter-faith services.  Several local groups of the United
Nations Association and some councils for community relations have held similar services.  It seems clear that in
the religiously plural situation in Great Britain, the
need for inter-faith worship will continue to grow.  Indeed the psychologist, Professor Thouless, told the 1952
conference that such services might well be the best way
of forwarding the aims of the Congress.

At the Annual Conferences, members of different faiths
are asked to lead times of devotion.  Another area of
growth is in the desire to learn from each other about
prayer and meditation.  This was evident during the
festival "Ways of the Spirit", held in London in 1975,
and with which the Congress co-operated.  This desire
has also prompted plans for some small devotional conferences.

As yet, little thought has been given to more personal
situations, such as a wedding where bride and groom belong to different faiths but wish for a religious ceremony.  Quite a lot of thought, however, has been given
to school assemblies and the possibility of children of
different faiths worshipping together.  This whole area
is still very new.  Yet, as the thrust of the inter-
faith movement is increasingly towards co-operation and
common action, the desire to worship together can be expected to increase.

A growing concern of the Congress has been religious
education.  It was one of the first bodies to advocate
the teaching of world religions and to express concern
about provision for the religious education of children
of minority faiths.  An article in *World Faiths*, March,
1961, said there was a need for an "Advisory Council for
Inter-Faith Understanding in Education", "on which would
be representatives of the teachers' bodies, local education authorities, teachers' training colleges, the
churches and such organizations as the W.C.F. and the
Council of Christians and Jews".[47]  On more than one occasion, Lord Sorensen raised the matter in Parliament.[48]
In 1965 Bernard Cousins, a member of the Congress, published a booklet giving examples of his own efforts to
introduce world religions into the classroom.  "The

study of one faith in isolation", he wrote, "with
scarcely any reference to the greatness of others can
produce a narrowness of outlook, an arrogance and ex-
clusiveness which give rise to suspicion, contempt and
dislike for the unfamiliar".[49]   In the same year, Rev.
John Rowland compiled an All Faiths Order of Service
for World Childrens' Day.[50]

In 1969, the Congress convened an Education Advisory
Committee.  At that time it was thought that a new Education Act was being prepared, so the Committee's first
task was to draw up a statement, issued in July,1970,
about the provision of Religious Education in local
authority schools "with particular reference to the
teaching of world religions and the needs of all children in a plural society".[51]   The Committee, on which
all major religions were represented, argued that religious education should have a place in schools, primarily on educational grounds.  "We believe that religious
education should have a continuing place in our schools.
The primary reason for this is educational.  A knowledge
of man's religious history is essential to an understanding of our culture and our fellow beings.  The spiritual
dimension is a part of human experience and pupils
should be given the opportunity to understand and assess
religious claims.  As people of faith we believe that
individuals and society need a spiritual basis.  Moral
values, too, although they may be independent, are often
closely related to religious faith".[52]   In calling for
the teaching of other religions, besides Christianity,
the group said that what was needed was "the imaginative
sympathy that enables a child to appreciate what living
by another faith means to its followers".[53]   The committee suggested that assemblies might sometimes be inter-
faith in character.  Subsequently the committee has discussed assemblies in greater detail[54] and the misunderstandings that religious communities have about each
other.

The resources available to the Congress have been very
limited and the leadership in this field has increasingly been taken by the SHAP Working Party and the Standing
Conference on Inter-Faith Dialogue in Education.[55]   The Religious Education Council,although its scope is wider,has
also been concerned about the teaching of world religions.[56]

The provision of information on a wide variety of religious subjects has been another important task of the
Congress.  This work has been especially developed in Holland.

The Dutch branch, *Wereldgesprek der Godsdietsten*, was
founded in 1947 and is now called *Interreligio Netherlands*.[57]

The last twenty years have seen a considerable change
in the population of the Netherlands, which is now a
plural society. The center attracts many who are not
in contact with the main religious bodies but who are
concerned for spiritual values and religious experience.
It deals with inquiries about specific practices of the
world religions, requests for educational material, for
speakers, and for information on new religious developments. It maintains contact with similar centres abroad
especially through the newsletter *Lifesign*, which goes t
about five hundred people or institutions overseas. The
center has provided help for teachers of world religions
and arranged exhibitions. It has started meetings for
those working for the media, to encourage more responsible reporting of religious matters. Recently the society took the initiative in establishing a Council on
Religions, on which the main religious groups in Holland
are represented.[58]


## Achievements

It is hard to estimate what has been achieved by the
World Congress of Faiths. Indeed it is always difficult
to assess the results of bodies concerned to change attitudes by the long-term education of the public. Certainly the relationship of religions to each other in
Britain is now more open than it was forty years ago.
Yet there are many reasons for this. The number of adherents of religions other than Christianity has increased significantly. Christianity's position in society has declined and is less dominant. The theologica
mood is more open and sympathetic to dialogue. The existence of the Congress, however, although numerically
and financially a very weak organization, has, at times
when the climate of British opinion was less sympathetic
to religions other than Christianity, served to witness
to the possibility of another view. Some of its members
have been influential in public life and others have
been strengthened to find they were not alone in their
views.

Now, as inter-faith dialogue becomes more popular and is
given a fresh urgency by the desire for good community
relations, the Congress can contribute by its experience and by concentrating on the "truth-seeking" dialogu

which is its *métier*.[59]  Whilst such "truth-seeking"
dialogue may be discursive or theological, it should
also deepen into the interior dialogue which is the common exploration of spirituality and needs to express
itself in a common concern for world community.  If the
Congress concentrates on "truth-seeking" dialogue, in
its various aspects, it can make others aware how easily,
now that dialogue is fashionable, it can be perverted
for political, polemical or proselytizing purposes.

## THE TEMPLE OF UNDERSTANDING

The story begins in the sunporch of a house on Maher
Avenue, Greenwich, Connecticut.  One afternoon in 1959,
Mrs. Judith Hollister was talking to a friend.  Discussing the world situation, the friend had the idea of
gathering together in one building the great religions
of the world.  "We spend hours at the conference table—
but no time at all in trying to understand what is going
on in the other man's mind".[60]  In the excitement of the
moment, Mrs. Hollister contacted the Ford Foundation and
spoke to William Nims.  He suggested that she contact
other inter-faith foundations and bring her committee
to see him.  In fact, she had no committee and her
friends were skeptical of the idea.

Yet Mrs. Hollister persisted.  Since the age of eighteen
she had been fascinated by the study of the world's religions.  As a layperson, she had taken courses at the
Union Theological Seminary and at Columbia University.
She had had the chance to meet a number of Eastern religious leaders.  Her husband, Dickerman Hollister, a
lawyer, who was conservative in thought and action, became convinced that the plan was more than a passing
enthusiasm.  He suggested that she should discuss the
project with Mrs. Roosevelt.

She hesitated to approach her, but it so happened that
six days after her husband had made his suggestion, she
found herself at a dinner party sitting next to a cousin
of Eleanor Roosevelt.  Mrs. Hollister mentioned her ad-
miration for Mrs. Roosevelt, and the cousin suggested
she join him in going to tea with her the next day.
This was an opportunity, but she had nothing to show
Mrs. Roosevelt.  She contacted her architect friend,
Lathrop Douglass, and by tea time the next day, he had
sketched a plan of the proposed building.

When Mrs. Hollister arrived at the tea party she was
taken aback to find "the whole room was filled with
beards and turbans".  She wondered if she would have
any chance to share her dream with Mrs. Roosevelt; but
Mrs. Roosevelt leaned across the table and asked "My
dear Mrs. Hollister, is there anything in particular
that you wish to discuss with me?"  Soon the plans of
the building were unrolled and Mrs. Roosevelt expressed
her interest and offered to help.[61]

At Mrs. Roosevelt's suggestion and with letters of introduction from her, six weeks later Mrs. Hollister set
out to meet international religious leaders to discover
if there was were support for the scheme.

On this initial tour in 1960, accompanied by her eleven-
year-old redheaded son, she went first to Rome, where
she saw Pope John, but did not receive any official
blessing.  She also met Mr. Nehru, the Prime Minister of
India, and Mr. Anwar El Sadat, who was then Secretary
General of the Islamic Congress in Cairo, both of whom
were helpful.  Mrs. Hollister spent a week in 1963 in
Lambarene with Albert Schweitzer and gained his sympathy
In 1968, after the Calcutta Summit Conference, she visited the Dalai Lama.  On her initial tour, she received
little encouragement from Christian leaders, but on her
return to the states she gained the backing of some
Christian leaders in New England.  Gradually with an
international list of sponsors, a board of directors
was set up and the Temple of Understanding was registere
in 1960 as a non-profit, tax-deductible educational corporation.  The name was the suggestion of Mrs. Ellsworth
Bunker, who was the wife of the American Ambassador at
the time Mrs. Hollister visited New Delhi during her
initial world tour.  In 1965, the Executive Office was
moved from Mrs. Hollister's home to Washington, with Mr.
Finley Peter Dunne as Executive Director.[62]

In 1966 twenty acres of forest land on the Potomac River
were purchased and dedicated, and appeals were launched
for money.  In 1967, Mrs. Hollister was received by Pope
Paul VI in a special audience at the Vatican, and he
promised to pray for "il Tempio della Comprensione".
In the same year, an International Committee was formed
under the Chairmanship of Mrs. Basant Kumar Birla, of
Calcutta, India.

Spiritual Summit Conferences

Gradually the emphasis moved away from a building to
creating an international fellowship. In 1968 two important Conferences were held: the First Washington Conference on Inter-Religious Understanding, in January and
the First Spiritual Summit Conference, in Calcutta in
October. The Washington Conference was a one-day meeting. A panel of speakers each talked on "The Validity
Which Each of the Religions Accords to Other Religions".[63]
What emerged most distinctly from the day was a ringing
affirmation, phrased in as many kinds of theological
terminology as there are religions, that the great faiths
of man do possess the capacity and the will to join hands
for the common good, and that none of them considers that
this would call for any compromise of their essential
doctrines or rituals.[64]

Already preparations were in hand for the First Spiritual
Summit Conference, which was held in Calcutta from 22nd
to 26th October, 1968. The conference brought together
some thirty leaders of ten world religions, together
with about forty members of the Board of Directors and
Friends of the Temple, a few scholars, and a few representatives of youth. The public was invited to some
sessions. On Friday 25th, the entire conference crossed
the Ganges River by steamboat to the Calcutta Botanical
Gardens to join in prayer for peace and the salvation
of mankind.[65]

The Second Spiritual Summit Conference was held in Geneva, Switzerland, from March 31st to April 4th, 1970, on
the theme "Practical Measures for World Peace". Several
aspects of present-day life were discussed, such as "The
Human Factors in World Peace", "The Population Problem",
"The Role of World Business", and "The Role of Women in
Peace". The opening address was given by Dr. Eugene
Carson Blake, the General Secretary of the World Council
of Churches, on "The Ambiguous Role of Religions in Relation to World Peace". He reminded his audience that
religion often does not make for peace. He warned
against trying to create any sort of super-authority and
any tendency towards syncretism.

In an effort to carry forward the spirit of the conference it was decided to create the "Continuing Conference
on World Religions", "To promote understanding and en-
during appreciation of the different faiths, and to
bring to bear all the resources at our disposal towards
the solution of human problems, both personal and

social".[66]  A distinguished executive was chosen, but
it seems that this body has never become active.

The conference concluded with a significant ceremony
in the thirteenth-century Cathedral of St. Pierre.  In
the church where John Calvin had preached, representatives of the religions present prayed in their own sacred languages.  Pastor Henry Babel of the Cathedral,
who had faced some opposition in agreeing to the ceremony, read from the Bible and the writings of Calvin,
and the sermon was preached by Dr. Lowell Ditzen.  At
the conclusion, all delegates said the Lord's Prayer.

Some forty four leaders and sixty others took part in
the conference.  Christians were in the majority (twenty
seven) with seven Buddhists and Muslims, but only a
couple of Hindus, although nearly all religions had
some representative.  There was a Jain, a Sikh, a Zoroastrian, but no member of the Baha'i faith.  A number
of special advisors added their expertise to the discussions, which in general were well informed and of a
high quality, bringing together religious leaders and
experts on the matters discussed.  The conference was
certainly a valuable educational experience for those
who took part.  It is difficult to assess what outside
impact it had, other than through its effect on participants.  Considerable effort was made to attract coverage by the media, but whilst the novelty of the occasion
might merit a story, it is unlikely that this had much
lasting effect, other than in adding, in a cumulative
way, to a change of mood.

The next spiritual summit was held at Harvard Divinity
School in October, 1971, and began the useful pattern of
arranging such conferences in conjunction with an educational institution.  It was intended to demonstrate in
America "that the religions of the world do know how to
collaborate, and that understanding, as we mean it in
the Temple of Understanding, can become a great source
of hope for mankind in this doubting and pragmatic century".[67]  The subject was "Religion in the Seventies".
The challenge of science and technology to religion was
considered and the questioning of traditional religions
by young people—this discussion was enlivened by the
presence of a good number of local students and some
"hippies" from California, who demonstrated an alternative life-style.  There was some feeling that religions
need to free themselves from inherited cultic and cultural patterns.  The Harvard conference was followed by
gatherings at Princeton University, Sarah Lawrence

College, Manhattanville College, and Wainwright House
in Rye, New York.

The next year a weekend symposium was held at Cornell
University, Ithaca, and in 1973, a weekend colloquium
was arranged at Yale. This was on "meditation" and con-
sisted of meditation sessions as well as talk about it.
In May, 1974, another, larger gathering was held again at
Cornell, on the theme "Toward World Community". The
Conference explored various means, such as publications
and education, through which a sense of world community
could be fostered, and coincided with the opening of a
Centre for World Community at Cornell. Amongst those taking
part were Ven. Maha Thera Piyananda, of the Washington
Buddhist Vihara; Swami Adiswarananda, of the Ramakrishna
Vendanta Center, in New York; Rabbis Samuel Silver and
Herbert Weiner; Fr. Masson from the Vatican; Archbishop
George Appleton, Chairman of the World Congress of
Faiths; Sir Zafrulla Khan and Master Chitrabhanu.

In February, 1975, a spiritual symposium was held at
Sarah Lawrence College, New York, on "Mysticism and
Meditation", led by Pir Vilayat Inayat Khan, Shimano
Eido Roshi, Rabbi Herbert Weiner and Rev. Robley E.
Whitson.

The most recent major gathering of the Temple of Understanding was the Fifth Spiritual Summit Conference held
at the Cathedral Church of St. John the Divine, in October, 1975, on "One is the Human Spirit". The imaginative programme opened with a colourful ceremony at the
Cathedral, at which the Dean, the Very Rev. James P.
Morton, the Rev. Toshio Miyake, of Konko-Kyo Church,
Osaka, and Dr. Jean Houston, conference chairperson and
president of the Foundation for Mind Research, spoke
briefly, before Dr. Margaret Mead, the distinguished
anthropologist, gave the keynote address. She suggested
there was "new hope" for the human race, because it
shared a common problem—threats in the atmosphere.
"Whereas people fought each other in the name of trivial
boundaries they now, together, face the challenge of pol-
lutants and airborne warfare".[68]  "At the heart of each
religion", she said, "we find the same overriding concern for our common humanity".[69]

A large part of the conference was spent in panel discussions, one on each morning from Monday to Thursday.
The first was on "Unity with Diversity", suggesting
that the world faiths were complementary rather than
rivals.  "Many flowers make the garden beautiful", said

the Jain Munishri Chitrabhanu, "and the world will be
sustained and beautified by different approaches to
life".[70]   On Tuesday, "Ecology and the Spiritual Environ
ment" was discussed.  Two main viewpoints emerged.  The
first was that man's technological growth is unbalancing
the ecology and tending to destroy it.  The second was
that man and technology are part of a much larger evolutionary process.  Dr. Mitchell, the former astronaut,
expressed the second approach: "Technology is neither
good nor bad, it just is.  It is our problem to adapt to
what is, not to revert to what was.  We must develop
better ways to use our tools".[71]

An interesting aspect of the discussion was the participation of a Sioux and a Hopi medicine man.  On Wednes-
day the theme was "Creating the Future Community".  Different degrees of emphasis were placed on the need for
unity and diversity.  Rabbi Weiner stressed the need
for diverse religious traditions, saying, with William
James, that the Divine is much too large for any one
faith to express it.  Pir Vilayat Khan, however, looked
to the younger generation as  pioneers of a new syncret:
community which will encompass all religious traditions.
Dr. Homer Jack, of the World Conference on Religion and
Peace, stressed the need to solve urgent, immediate problems before speculating on the future community.  Religious groups needed to develop experts for advisory
positions in practical matters of state and on political
decisions.  The fourth morning was devoted to "Women,
Religion and World Community".  This panel discussed the
role of women and asserted their equality.

In the afternoons, seminars were held to discuss further
the issues raised in the mornings and to help prepare
the Joint Statement, which was read at the United Nations on Friday, October 24, the thirtieth anniversary
of the United Nations.  This was a historic occasion,
as, although Pope Paul VI had addressed the U.N. in 196!
this was the first time that representatives of the
world religions had gathered at the U.N.  Even so, the
objection of some countries to a religious presence
meant that the gathering had to be held in the Dag
Hammarskjöld Auditorium rather than the General Assembly
The programme began with a meditation by Sri Chinmoy,
Director of the U.N. Meditation Group; followed by an
introduction by Charles Mills, President of the Temple
of Understanding; and remarks by Edna McCallion, President of the Religious Non-Governmental Organizations at
U.N.  Then Secretary-General Kurt Waldheim gave a brief
address, assessing the present and future role of the

U.N. Dr. Cousins introduced the religious leaders who
were to speak: Srimata Gayatri Devi, founder of two
Vedanta Ashrams in America; Lord Abbot Kosho Ohtani,
Chief Abbott of the Nishi Honganj Temple in Kyoto; Rabbi
Robert Gordis, former president of the Synagogue Council
of America; Mother Teresa, foundress of Missionaires of
Charity in India; and Dr. Seyyed Hossein Nasr, Director
of the Iranian Academy of Philosophy, Teheran. The
speakers stressed the responsibility of the U.N. and
the need for it to take note of mankind's spiritual aspirations. Lord Abbot Kosho Ohtani said that "religion
must assume an important role" in helping to solve the
world's problems.[72] Mother Teresa directed attention
to the poor: "Let us today, when we have gathered to
prove to the whole world that we are one, let us be one
in this love to the poorest of the poor in the world".[73]

After the religious leaders had spoken, Dr. Jean Houston
read the Joint Statement, and Brother David Steindl-Rast,
O.S.B., Chairman of the Centre for Spiritual Studies,
ended the session with a prayer, for which all were
asked to stand: "Let our standing be a mindful gesture;
mindful of the ground on which we are standing, the one
little plot of land on this earth not belonging to *one*
nation, but to all nations united. It is a very small
piece of land, indeed it is a symbol of human concord,
a symbol of the truth that this poor, mistreated earth
belongs to all of us together. As we stand, then, like
plants standing on a good plot of ground, let us sink our
roots deep into our hidden unity. (Allow yourself to
feel what it means to stand and to extend your inner
roots). Rooted in the soil of the heart, let us expose
ourselves to the wind of the Spirit, the one Spirit who
moves all who let themselves be moved. Let us breathe
deeply the breath of the One Spirit. Let our standing
bear witness that we take a stand on common ground. Let
our standing be an expression of reverence for all those
who before us have taken a stand for human unity".[74]

The Joint Statement said that the technological unity of
mankind had yet to be matched by social and moral unity
and this required the utilization of religions' spiritual resources. Religion itself had often been divisive:
but there had been a move towards unity within and between world religions. "The great religions and spiritual movements of our time stand ready to unite around
their common spiritual and moral vision and to contribute
to the development of a morality and ethics which is
mindful of and actively concerned with basic human rights
and freedoms, the natural world and our shared environ-

ment, and the vital need for world peace".[75]   The statement praised the U.N. for its achievements, but said
that immense tasks remained and that there had been in-
sufficient progress on disarmament, economic development and human rights.  There was reference to the need
for world-wide religious freedom, and the conference
recommended that the U.N. should consider the "creation
of an agency which will bring the much-needed resources
and inspirations of the spiritual traditions to the solution of world problems".[76]

The statement is well written, although general in its
terms.  Its main significance seems to lie in asserting
the united concern of religions about the future of mankind and in urging the U.N. to recognize and make use of
the spiritual resources of the world religions.  Prob-
ably, as so often, the lasting impact of the conference
is on and through those who took part.

Unlike most inter-religious conferences, this was not
just a matter of words.  Each day at 8:30 am and at
noon, meditative rituals from the various religions
were held.  On Monday evening, a new symphony, "One is
the Spirit of Man", especially written for the occasion
by Maia Aphrahamian, was performed by the Symphony for
United Nations.  Performances were also given by Hamza
El Din, Donald Swann, the Levitown Madrigal Singers, the
Newark Boys Choir, the First Musicians, and other groups.
The Sufi Order presented five times a Cosmic Mass, which
had a cast of three hundred people.  Written and nar-
rated by Pir Vilayat Khan, an elaborate pageant depicted
the evolutionary stages of the world religions and suggested how they might eventually meet on a transcendent-
al plane of universal understanding.  An art exhibition
was also arranged to coincide with the conference.

The opportunity to appreciate art and music and also to
meditate, enriched the gathering, as it allowed delegates to share experiences together as well as discussing
concepts.  Indeed, several people have suggested that
shared experiences are more likely to develop a sense
of oneness than are speeches and debates.


Changing Patterns

Besides international conferences, the Temple of Understanding has arranged for religious leaders to speak at
a variety of schools.  It has organized youth camps  and
a tour to India.

In 1974, the Temple of Understanding acquired a new
piece of land, consisting of 83 acres of forest land
surrounding the ten acre Lac des Anges (Lake of the
Angels), to be used as the site for a meditation and religious study centre. The land is about an hour's
drive south of Washington, near St. Mary's City, Maryland. It was at St. Mary's City in 1649 that the first
Act of Religious Tolerance was written, enacted and en-
forced. In June, a simple ceremony was held to conse-
crate the land. During the summer of 1975, youth groups
stayed on the land and started to clean up the forest.

There have been changes in the organization. At the
Board meeting in December, 1970, Charles J. Mills of
Byram, Connecticut, was elected President, and Mrs. Hollister became Chairman of the Board, which relieved her of
day-to-day details of the work. Charles Mills, a graduate of Yale, had been an executive of the F.M.C. Corporation before retiring to devote himself full time to
the Temple of Understanding. Dr. Ditzen, as vice-presi-
dent, continued to be chairman of the Committee on Plans
and Programmes. In 1972, Finley P. Dunne, who had been
Executive Director since 1964, retired and was succeeded
by John Gillooly. Gillooly, who had taught European and
Russian history at the University of Massachusetts, came
to the Temple of Understanding from the Laymen's Movement at Wainwright House in Rye, New York, of which he
was Executive Director. In 1975, Mrs. Hollister retired as chairperson. She was invited to remain as
honorary chairperson, but was succeeded by Finley Peter
Dunne as chairperson. Recently inflation and financial
pressures have hampered the Temple of Understanding. As
a result, the offices have been moved from Washington and
are now based at Wainwright House, Rye, New York. In
1976 the first issue appeared of a new journal of world
religions, called *Insight,* published by Finley Peter
Dunne and edited by Professor K. L. Seshagiri Rao, of
the University of Virginia, supported by a strong advisory editorial board.

In nearly twenty years, the Temple of Understanding has
grown from small beginnings to involve important religious leaders of all traditions. The initial emphasis
on a building has somewhat faded, but the emphasis on
meditation and religious study remains. The conferences
have been primarily directed to increasing understanding
and communication between religious communities. Although matters of topical concern have been discussed,
no organization has developed to try and see that recommendations are implemented. Rather, in its conference

and its educational work,the Temple of Understanding
has helped people to learn more about faiths other than
their own and to break down exclusive attitudes to
others, which are still strong in the predominantly
Christian USA. Like other bodies in this field, whilst
supported by important individuals, it has failed to
get official backing and financial support from religious groups,which is necessary if the work is to be
maintained at the level required. Yet if much remains
to be done, it has created in many minds the dream of
religious fellowship and co-operation.

## Towards a Global Congress of the World's Religions

A new attempt to fulfill this dream is the projected Glc
Congress of the World's Religions. The sixth annual Int
national Conference on the Unity of the Sciences,
sponsored by the International Cultural Foundation, foun
by the Rev. Sun Myung Moon, was held in San Francisco in
1977. Afterwards some participants stayed on to discuss
proposal prepared by the faculty of the Unification Theological
Seminary, Barrytown, New York.

This begins by saying that the world family has entered
an international era and that the future of the religious faiths is necessarily an interdependent one. "We
are moving towards active participation in one another's
lives and faiths. Towards this inevitable goal, we pro-
pose the formation of a Global Congress of World Religions".[77] There then follow certain affirmations.
First, each religion has its own profound truths and
absolute value. Secondly, one purpose of religion is
to make a better world, but no religion can do this in
isolation and by itself. "Practical co-operation of
the world's faiths in solving specific human problems
is required as a means both of releasing new energies
against these problems and of acting out spiritual
values common to the religions themselves".[78] The world
religions can provide leadership for the new age and
bring the human family together in healthy wholeness.
"If the world's religions do not offer the required
leadership, the inevitably resulting void is liable to
be filled by militarists or reductionists or material-
ists".[79] Religions should provide an alternative to the
threats of totalitarian communism and reactionary fasc-
ism.

The statement proposes a "global forum in which the reli
gions can take the public initiative which humanity may
rightfully expect of them—we support the work of unifi-

cation of the world's religions. 'Unification' is
a non-sectarian word which means for us neither union nor
uniformity, neither creedal alignment nor imposed or implicit agreement on theological issues. We hold, rather,
that there is already a sufficient basis in common, human,
spiritual insights which would allow for a problem-sol-
ving orientation according to which we could work together even though we disagree doctrinally. We acknowledge that the religious situation is and shall continue
to be a pluralistic one: we, too, are comfortable with
the mutual tolerance and independence which pluralism implies. At the same time, we are convinced that communication, co-operation and confederation of the world's religions is desirable as an expression of the essential unity
of human hearts and necessary as a means of solving basic
problems".[80]

It has been worth quoting this initial document quite
fully, as subsequent discussion has refined the idea,
but not seriously modified it. At San Francisco, a con-
sensus was reached that "it is a good idea to hold a
Global Congress of World Religions as soon as feasible,
to provide a universal forum in which representative religious hearts and minds may clarify the common issues of
life and the reality of global humanity. There was a constant affirmation of the value and healthiness of religious pluralism and, at the same time, a sense of common
religious community—no one spoke in favour of organizational or doctrinal unity".[81] The tentative plan suggests holding a global congress perhaps in 1981 and then
possibly every three years.

The initiative was left with the Unification Theological
Seminary and especially with Dr. Warren Lewis, who is a
free churchman from Texas, professionally employed to
teach at the Seminary. Since 1978, Lewis has carried the
project forward on two fronts. Conferences on contemporary African religion have been held at Barrytown and
Bristol, and progress reports were made at the Second and
Third Annual Conferences Towards a Global Congress of the
World's Religions at Boston (1978) and Los Angeles (1979).
An African Institute for the Study of Humanistic Values,
under the direction of Dr. Francis Botchway, assisted by
Dr. Kwarne Gyekye and Dr. A. J. Ohin, has been established at the University of Berrin, Lome, Togo. An international, inter-faith board of advisors has been as-
sembled by Botchway to oversee the work of the Institute,
which is dedicated to the study of human value within the
context of the tripartite religious framework of African
experience—Christian, Muslim, and African autochthonous
religions.

At the Boston and Los Angeles Conferences, Lewis chaired
further discussions of the original idea and will be developing plans. At Boston, Dr. K. L. Seshagiri Rao,
Editor of *Insight,* the journal of the Temple of Understanding, and I, as editor of *World Faiths,* both spoke
in an individual capacity. At Los Angeles, Finley Peter
Dunne, board member of the Temple of Understanding, and
Isma'il R. al-Faruqi, Professor of Islamics at Temple
University in Philadelphia, Pennsylvania, continued the
discussion, each of us exploring the concept in terms of
respective areas of expertise. Ninian Smart, Professor
of Comparative Religions at Lancaster and at Santa Barbara, announced the formation of an international, inter
faith Committee for the Global Congress. This Committee
functioning as an independent body comprising individual
dedicated to the founding of the Global Congress and kno
for their inter-religious concerns, shall have the responsibilities of refining the idea, setting the agenda,
and calling the Global Congress of the World's Religions
into its first session.

A difficulty of finding institutional co-sponsors has re
lated to the initial sponsorship by the Unification Theo
logical Seminary, which is a graduate theological instit
tion founded by the Rev. Sun Myung Moon. The prime purpose of the Seminary is to offer a Master's programme in
religious education to the leadership of the Unification
Movement, although other students are welcome. The faculty is intentionally pluralistic and international,
with Christians of various denominations, a Jew from Ro-
mania, a Korean Confucianist, and two members of the Uni
fication Church.

The Rev. Sun Myung Moon and the Unification Church have
been the subjects of much hostile publicity. Partly thi
relates to the source and use of the Rev. Moon's money,
partly to his political sympathies, partly to the proliferation of organizations using different names, and
mainly to methods by which his followers are recruited
and trained. The USA Congress mounted an inquiry.[82]
Methods of fund-raising and over-enthusiastic recruitmen
have been criticized by the leadership of the Unificatio
Church itself. Some of the external criticisms may have
been evoked by jealousy of the movement's growth, and
many are still suspicious of the Unificationist activity

A full study of the Unification Church is impossible her
and would require a discussion of "new religions" in gen
eral. The fact that some of the Rev. Moon's teachings
differs from traditional Christian views or that some of

his followers regard him as the new Messiah is not relevant here. Any global congress should have maximum freedom for all to share their particular beliefs. The difficulty for other organizations is to know whether to appear to associate with the Unification Church. Support for the global congress would not imply support for the Unification Church, but the implications of the Seminary's sponsorship need to be clarified. Other bodies have to be satisfied that the global congress would be genuinely independent and not part of plans for the growth of the Unification Church. There is always a fear that financial dependence may limit freedom. To meet these hesitations, initiative for the Global Congress is now being taken by the small, independent Committee for the Global Congress. They act as individuals, rather than as official representatives of their respective organizations. The Unification Seminary continues to give financial backing, but the responsibility for the Congress now belongs solely to the steering committee. It remains to be seen whether such a committee can enlist the wide support necessary for the Congress to become a truly representative and global body.

## "We are Already One"

The question raised by the World Congress of Faiths and the Temple of Understanding is whether there is a common core of mystical unity which transcends the differences of the world religions. Both bodies expressly repudiate syncretism and take a positive view of differences—that they contribute to a richer whole. In his Preface to *The World Religions Speak*, Finley P. Dunne writes of the Temple of Understanding that its purpose is not syncretic. "There is no intention of trying to combine any religion with any other, no thought of changing the elements of creed and faith, ritual and scripture, ethics and cultural content that give each religion of mankind its distinctive character. Rather, each religion is honoured...for its own unique traditions. The differences...are to be cherished, both for themselves and the sanctities and beauties they reveal, and for the insight they give us into the true nature of each of them".[83] The World Congress of Faiths, on its membership leaflet, repudiates any syncretistic aim. The approach is, rather, as Bishop Appleton said at the Canterbury Conference, to listen to and to share the central affirmations of each world religion, that thereby all may be enriched.[84] Yet the assumption that world religions are complementary—an assumption that many would question—suggests there is a unity of religions, even if that unity is still undiscovered.

To all who seek the mystical unity of religions, the wor
of Thomas Merton, spoken at the First Spiritual Summit
Conference, remain as a promise and a challenge.  "My
dear brothers, we are already one, but we imagine that w
are not.  What we have to recover is our original unity.
What we have to be is what we already are".[85]

# CHAPTER FOUR

## PEACE THROUGH RELIGION

By a sad irony, it was on the very day that the First
World War began that one of the earliest inter-faith
conferences for peace held its first meeting. This
tragic coincidence highlights the continuing question
that such efforts have had to face. "Can religions,
even if they act together, exert any effective influence on political decisions and events?"

Here the interest is with those inter-faith bodies, and
in particular the World Conference on Religion and Peace,
for which the search for peace has been the dominant
concern. The World Congress of Faiths and the Temple
of Understanding have both hoped that their work would
contribute to peace and world order, but as a long-term
result of a revival of spiritual values. The World Conference on Religion and Peace has, by contrast, tried to
enable world religions to have effective political influence, and has eschewed the discussion of theological
differences. Certainly it has helped to create a new
climate of friendship and trust between members of different religions. It has educated some religious leaders in an awareness of contemporary problems. Through
it, representatives of world religions have called on
humanity to live at peace. It is, however, by no means
clear to what extent the people of the world have lis-
tened or responded to this call.

The most influential inter-faith body working for peace
is the World Conference on Religion and Peace. Attention will centre on its work. As it is in part the cul-
mination of earlier efforts, especially in the USA and
Japan, dating back to early in this century, it will be
helpful first to consider these. They show how those
involved primarily in peace-work have become aware of
the inter-religious dimension of their endeavours. Their
initial motivation is therefore different from those who
were prompted to search for unity amidst the diversity
of mankind's religious beliefs and practices. These
earlier efforts also highlight some of the problems involved in this work.

1914 to 1963

Three phases in the peace movement in the USA in the
nineteenth century can be distinguished.  From about
1815 to 1867, the movement was primarily ethical and essentially religious, but not ecclesiastical.  From about
1867 to 1890, there was increasing emphasis on the political aspects of the search for peace with advocacy of
proposals for arbitration.  From 1890 until the outbreak
of the first World War, peace propaganda seemed to become more effective and the government explored some
suggestions.[1]

In February, 1914, the industrial magnate, Andrew Car-
negie, invited Protestant, Roman Catholic and Jewish
representatives to his house and asked them to become
trustees of money which he wished to give for the aboli-
tion of war.  From this came into being the Church Peace
Union, in which twelve religious bodies—Roman Catholic,
Protestant, and Jewish—co-operated. This at the time
was very unusual.  The day after the gathering at Car-
negie's house, Edwin Mead said to Charles Macfarland,
"May not the time come when all religions will unite for
peace?"

In August of that year members of the Church Peace Union
shared with members of the World Alliance for International Friendship in a conference at Constance, Switzerland.  Sadly, they met there in August, 1914, on the very
day that war broke out, so they quickly dispersed and
some had difficulty in reaching their homes.

A decade was to pass before the hope of holding an inter-
faith conference for peace was again suggested.   On December 11, 1924, Dr. Henry Atkinson, who was General
Secretary, presented to the Church Peace Union "a plan
to hold a World Religions Congress on behalf of International Friendship and Goodwill".  The outline suggested
forming an international committee of a thousand members,
drawn from all religions.  They would be invited to serve
as individuals, rather than as representatives of a religion.  This principle, because of the lack of hier-
archical or representative structures within most religions, has been found necessary at almost all inter-
faith gatherings.  The conference, Atkinson suggested,
should be autonomous and the committee, when set up,
should decide its venue.  He tentatively suggested 1930
as a date for the conference.  The Church Peace Union
accepted the proposal and agreed to shoulder responsibility for setting up and calling the Congress.[2]

The earliest announcement of the plan is interesting as
it shows what its originators had in mind.  The representatives, it said, "will not meet to discuss or compare religions, nor to form a league of faiths, least
of all to find a least common denominator of their beliefs.  They will assemble in order, if possible, to
harness to the cause of international goodwill and peace
the spiritual force of all their religious faiths".  The
results that were hoped for were that:

1.  It might create a clearer knowledge of the
    record, ideals, and attitude of each religion
    in its relation to world peace.

2.  Each religion would be challenged and stimulated
    to set itself in the best light and to emphasize
    its noblest ideals and principles.

3.  Leaders would be drawn together in a better
    mutual understanding.

4.  A realization of common objectives would help
    promote unity of spirit and action.

5.  There might emerge the possibility of a co-oper-
    ation, through a loose form of organization,
    whereby all the religions of the world might
    exert a united pressure at critical times.[3]

Another document voiced the hope that agreement might be
expressed on:

1.  Human brotherhood as essential to all religions.

2.  The fact that world peace could only be estab-
    lished by the recognition of universal brother-
    hood.

3.  The possibility of world religions co-operating
    by each working in their own sphere for the
    attainment of these ideals.

Atkinson was asked to seek support for the proposal,
especially amongst the religions of the East.  Advice
was sought from many quarters, including Sir Eric Drum-
mond, Secretary General of the League of Nations, and
Mr. Franklin D. Roosevelt.  Sponsors in America included
Jews, Protestants, Roman Catholics, and some not identified with any religious body.  There was considerable
support, although there was also opposition from some

Christians who feared that Christian claims would be
compromised, and from others who thought the idea chi-
merical or utopian.

By 1928,Atkinson had got together a preliminary committee which included religious leaders from India, China,
Japan, Ceylon, England, Sweden, Germany, France, Holland,
and the USA. Amongst the religions represented were
*Christian, Jew, Hindu, Confucian, Muslim, Baha'i, Shinto,
Buddhist, and Theosophist.* One hundred and ninety delegates—one hundred and twenty five of them Christians—
attended a Preliminary Committee meeting at Geneva in
September,1928. At this it was decided to call a conference in "1930 if possible". Dean Shailer Mathews was
elected chairman of the conference. At the committee
meeting various speakers, including Dr. Joseph O. Hertz,
Chief Rabbi of the British Empire, and the missionary,
C. F. Andrews, outlined the fundamentals of their religions. There were some devotional exercises, based on a
book of worship, which included passages from the sacred
scriptures, prepared by Professor Robert E. Hume. The
Preliminary Committee adopted a statement of purpose,
saying that the conference's sole intention "will be to
rouse and to direct the religious impulses of humanity
against war in a constructive world-wide effort to
achieve peace...The Universal Conference designs neither to
set up a formal league of religions, nor to compare the
relative values of faith, nor to espouse any political,
ecclesiastical, or theological or social system". The
specific objects would be to state the highest teaching
of each religion on peace and the cause of war, to record the efforts of religious bodies to further peace,
to seek out ways in which people of all religions can
work together for peace, and to look for opportunities
for concerted action.[4]

The Preliminary Committee elected a central committee of
seventy people, which next met at Frankfurt in August,
1929. In the meantime, Atkinson had visited India,
China, Japan, and several other countries. He had met
Gandhi and Tagore, and had managed to set up committees
in India, Burma, Ceylon and Japan, and had discovered at
least a dozen groups which were trying to secure similar
co-operation. In Japan especially, the Japan Religious
Association had also envisaged a World Conference. On
hearing of the American plan, they postponed their own
scheme and decided to co-operate with the Church Peace
Union. They did,however, in 1928 hold a National Religious Conference, attended by about 1,500 people.[5] In
the interval also, an administrative committee, appointed

by the Central Committee at Geneva, had met at Paris in
December, 1928.  At this it was agreed that the Church
Peace Union should remain the administrative agency,
with Shailer Mathews as Chairman and Atkinson as Secretary.  The Paris meeting also set up a small committee
which reported to the Frankfurt meeting of the Central
Committee on the preparations required for the conference.  Because of the conference's importance, it suggested that the topic "What can religions contribute to
the establishment of Universal Peace" be divided into
three issues to be explored separately by three commissions.  The three questions were:

1.  What are the influences in the world that
    make for war?

2.  What are the spiritual resources of mankind
    with which these influences can be met?

3.  How can these resources be set in motion and
    directed to bear upon the causes of war?

A fourth commission should look at the practical question
of how these resources could be activated.  The group
also recommended that the number of addresses should be
strictly limited, and that outstanding religious leaders
should be invited to preach, where possible in an appropriate church or synagogue.  The Central Committee at
Frankfurt decided to change the name to *World Conference
for International Peace through Religion*.  The proposed
date of the conference was advanced to 1931.

At the next Central Committee meeting at Berne in August,
1930, the date was again advanced, now to 1932, and the
venue chosen was Washington.  It was now felt that preparations pointed to a "world-wide movement rather than
to the holding of a single meeting", and other assemblies
in Geneva and Tokyo were envisaged.  Visitors to the
Berne Committee meeting included Rabindranath Tagore and
Professor Salvadore de Madariaga of the League of Nations.
At the next Central Committee meeting, held at Geneva in
August, 1931, plans were again both enlarged and deferred.

The Commission reports show a strong desire to submit to
the will of God and not to use religion as a "means".
Considerable attention was given to the relation of religion and education, and also to the attitude of religions to peace and justice and the question of the practical contribution which they can make.  It was now
thought that effective inter-faith committees for peace

were needed in local areas.  In effect, the work for
which the conference was originally envisaged was now
seen as a necessary preliminary to holding such a conference.  Answers to questions about the contribution
of religions to peace and the establishment of local
committees were now desired before an international conference should be held.  Inevitably, as the scope and
objectives had become so enlarged, the conference was
deferred.

Meanwhile in Japan, a National Religious Conference for
International Peace was held in May, 1931, with 345 delegates.  Addresses were given by the Prime Minister of
Japan and religious leaders.  On the third day, at a
general meeting, twelve resolutions were adopted unanimously.  Part of the main resolution, as it comes from
one of the earliest conferences, is worth quoting:

> If all religionists in the world co-operate and do
> their utmost, then our ideal of a warless world
> will not only exist in our religious faith  but
> also it will become a matter of practical interna-
> tional affairs.  Therefore, we appeal to public
> opinion at home and abroad, proclaiming our belief
> and decision:
>
> 1.  The Conference declares that we religionists
>     should assume responsibility for the frequent
>     occurrence of war.
>
> 2.  The Conference declares that all religions can
>     and ought to co-operate to bring about interna-
>     tional peace, admitting the unique characteris-
>     tics of each religion.
>
> 3.  It is our conviction that the moral law should
>     govern international relations as well as per-
>     sonal relations.
>
> 7.  The Conference hopes for the total removal of
>     all racial and religious discrimination.
>
> 8.  The Conference declares that religionists should
>     take the leadership of the League of Nations and
>     the Treaty for Renunciation of War.

The Conference also urged the establishment of an institute for studying the means and ways of promoting international peace through the co-operation of all religions.
It suggested the creation of a permanent religious peace

movement to make a world league of religions, and
pledged Japan's leadership in such a movement.  These
high hopes were to be bitterly disappointed by events
leading up to and during the second World War.  Yet, a
few of those involved in the 1931 conference were again
to become active in post-war inter-faith work for peace,
and Japan has indeed become one of the leaders in the
World Conference on Religion and Peace, of which the
first conference was held in Japan at Kyoto.[6]

It seems that the next meeting of the Central Committee
of the World Conference for International Peach through
Religion was not held until September,1937, again at
Geneva.  In the meantime, the international situation
had deteriorated and the "economic debacle on the part
of the nations" had made the original plans for the conference impossible.  Shailer Mathews had again visited
India and the Near East.  The agenda centred  on the
question "How can religion function in the field of international affairs?"  It was agreed that the conference
should be held at an early date, if possible in 1939.
Meanwhile regional conferences might begin at once and
an approach should be made to the World Alliance for
International Friendship to include the findings of the
committee in its programme for 1938.  In a message—
which proved to be the committee's final message—it
was affirmed that only religion could create the spirit
of goodwill necessary to effect the changes required to
create lasting peace.  Events had overtaken the committee.  Before a conference was held, the world was
plunged into war.

Even so, Charles Macfarland claimed a reserve of strength
was gathered by the movement.  "First, new connections
and associations have been made between men of goodwill
among the religions of East and West, including Britain
and India.  Secondly, the Executive (or Central) Committee has gathered a fund of experience and information,
the want of which, in earlier years, retarded its efforts.  There is now a new basis of understanding.
Thirdly, the organization of forces will be ready when
the moment comes".[7]

With hindsight, it seems that the efforts were too ambitious.  For a conference on the scale and of the scope
envisaged, the preliminary preparations were perhaps
ideally necessary, but circumstances are never ideal,
and if one waits for perfection, one waits forever. Even
so, the smaller committee meetings and preparatory commissions created many fruitful and on-going contacts

and produced some useful material—as much perhaps as
would have come from a single large isolated conference.
Indeed, the failure in fact to convene such a conference
may reflect hidden doubts about its value. The question
is whether it is best to start from the top with an inter
national conference and hope that from this, local initia
tives will follow, or whether to be fruitful, local group
are needed first. It seems that the Central Committee in
creasingly came to recognize the prior need of local
groups. The committee also wrestled with the question,
which remains the central problem of inter-faith efforts
for peace: how in practise can religions effectively promote international peace and justice? In the harsh world
of power politics, moral exhortation and public opinion
are often ignored. Certainly they were not strong enough
to stem the fateful tide of violence which was rising in
the thirties. Economic depression also worked against
the committee, whilst the Christian theological mood had
changed. A comparison of the International Missionary
Council's meeting at Jerusalem, in 1928, with the next
meeting at Tambaram, Madras, in 1938, shows this change.
Instead of, as at Jerusalem, seeing signs of God's activity in other religions, at Tambaram, led by Kraemer,
Christians emphasized the Gospel's discontinuity from
world religions.

War did not, however, completely extinguish the hope of
inter-religious co-operation for peace. In 1943, a
statement entitled *Pattern for Peace* was signed in the
USA by various religious bodies, including the National
Catholic Welfare Conference, the Synagogue Council of
America, the Federal Council of the Churches of Christ
in America, and some orthodox groups. The statement asserted that the Moral Law must govern World Order and
that the rights of individuals, of the oppressed,and of
minorities should be respected. It called for an International Institution to maintain peace with justice and
for international economic co-operation.

At the San Francisco conference, which laid the foundations for the United Nations, non-governmental organizations concerned for peace were invited. After the war,
the Church Peace Union concentrated on building up support for the United Nations and in going beyond the World
Council of Churches in creating links with Roman Catholics and Jews. A committee report, from the late forties
showed that the desire for wider contacts had survived.
"Our leadership must not be exclusively Catholic, or
Protestant, or Jewish, but must be inspired by a sincere
effort to achieve inter-faith solidarity in action for
world peace".[8]   Yet it was not until the nineteen-

sixties that significant developments occurred.

It is true that many religious people, in the period
after the second World War, were deeply concerned for
peace, and there was much discussion about the morality
of nuclear weapons.  This concern, however, expressed
itself primarily through denominational gatherings and
statements.  The World Council of Churches, established
in 1948, issued a number of statements through its Commission of the Churches on International Affairs.  The
National Council of Churches of Christ in the United
States explored in depth a number of international issues, especially through their World Order Study Conferences.  Individual Protestant denominations issued increasingly sophisticated pronouncements.  Pope John
XXIII's encyclical, *Pacem in Terris,* gave prominence to
Roman Catholic concern, which was further expressed at
the Second Vatican Council.  Various Jewish bodies in
the United States also issued statements on current
matters.

The peace movements, especially in the West, also had a
restricted clientele.  The Church Peace Mission worked
predominantly among Protestants, whilst the Catholic Association for International Peace worked amongst Catholics.  By the mid-sixties, the Fellowship of Reconciliation was only just beginning to involve non-Protestants.
The Jewish Dimensions in Peace Conference was a new
initiative.  The Council of Religion and International
Affairs (as the former Church Peace Union was now called)
maintained an inter-faith interest, publishing some significant material and sponsoring small-scale inter-religious dialogues.  The predominant mood of Christian theology in the nineteen-fifties, however, was still suspicious of inter-faith gatherings.

## The National Inter-Religious Conference on Peace

One of the first large post-war inter-faith gatherings
for peace in the USA was *The National Inter-Religious
Conference on Peace* held in Washington, D. C., from 15
to 17 March, 1966, which was attended by almost five
hundred clergy and lay people.

The first steps were taken by three Boston-area clergy-
men: Dr. Dana McLean Greeley, then President of the
Unitarian-Universalist Association; Bishop John Wesley
Lord, then the Methodist Bishop of Boston; and Bishop
John J. Wright, then Roman Catholic Bishop of Worcester.

They were joined by the late Rabbi Maurice N. Eisendrath,
President of the Union of American Hebrew Congregations
of New York.  The first small committee meeting was held
in 1963.  Amongst the early associates were Rabbi Bal-
four Brickner, Mr. Herman Will, Jr., Msgr. Edward G.
Murray, and Dr. Homer A. Jack.  Dr. Jack, a Unitarian
Universalist minister, who was to become a key figure
in future developments, was at that time Director of the
Division of Social Responsibility of the Unitarian-Universalist Association of the USA.  Bishop Daniel Corri-
gan and some others soon joined this initial group.

In January, 1965, an exploratory conference was held at
the church center for the United Nations.  Soon afterwards the organizational form of the conference was con-
ceived.  In addition to Rabbi Eisendrath, Dr. Greeley,
Bishop Lord and Bishop Wright, Bishop John Hines of the
Episcopal Church, and Archbishop Iakovos  of the Greek
Orthodox Church, agreed to become conference co-chairmen.  An executive committee was formed and a secretariat, consisting principally of denominational executives
with special responsibilities in the field of international relations, was set up.  The secretariat met regularly in Washington or New York, and six months before
the conference, an office was established in Washington,
headed by Mrs. Kay Shannon, the administrative secretary.
A number of people agreed to write position papers in
preparation for the conference.  The conference was completely unofficial, sponsored only by the six co-chairmen and other prominent leaders of church and synagogue.

A suggestion that religious organizations might participate officially was found to create difficulties and
was not pressed.  A number of religious groups did, however, contribute to the costs, which, including the
maintenance of the small office in Washington, totalled
under $20,000.  In preparation for the conference, some
of the co-chairmen had a meeting with U Thant, the U.N.
Secretary-General.  He sent a message of greeting, as
did President Lyndon Johnson.

The conference was primarily a working conference—with
three concurrent workshops on "Living with the Changing
Communist World", "China and Conflicts in Asia", and
"Intervention, Morality and Limits".  Members of the
workshops received in advance background materials and
a specifically prepared position paper.  The first two
workshops in general accepted their position papers,
whereas the third considerably changed theirs.  To be
included in the final report, each paragraph or idea in

the paper had to be agreed by at least two-thirds of
the members of the workshop. Another subcommittee prepared a Conference Declaration, which was agreed by the
three-quarters majority required.[9]

The purpose of the conference, as defined by the co-
chairman, was fourfold: "(1) to bring together clergymen
and laymen from all peace-oriented viewpoints to discuss
the relation of religion to peace; (2) to analyze in
depth the basic religious statements on war and peace
and on the moral principles in world order, to find parallel moral principles and to seek approximate guidelines; (3) to discuss current problems from the viewpoint of these principles and proximate norms; (4) to
analyze existing religious programmes in Washington, at
the U.N., on the local level, and in the world community,
and to recommend further co-operation so that organized
religion can play its role in governmental decisions affecting war and peace".[10]

To what extent were these purposes achieved? Dr. Homer
Jack mentions amongst the achievements, "the rich, unin-
hibited, mature dialogue on some prime questions of our
time, communism, China, and intervention", "substantive
recommendations for effecting peace in Vietnam", and
"the experience of working together showed that previous
rigidities have been relaxed". The reports, he claims,
justifiably, "compare favourably with other such statements of policy from governmental and non-governmental
groups". An indirect achievement, he adds, was that the
publicity "about an *inter-religious* conference on peace
raised hopes, not only among members of various denominations and faiths but also among the general public.
Many were inspired that church and synagogue could unite,
however unofficially, to think through some of the deeply ethical problems of our times, ones that cannot be
left solely to governments".[11] Dr. Jack also refers to
the problems that the conference uncovered. Some churchmen were very new to dealing with war/peace issues and
there were deep divisions among participants. Others
felt that church and synagogue had nothing special to
say, although there were signs that some churches were
appointing experts with specialized knowledge in these
fields. A third problem was that some churchmen,
especially evangelicals, refused to attend inter-religious gatherings. It is also true that although called
inter-faith, the conference was predominantly Judeo-
Christian.

Besides the discussion of specific issues related to the

Communist world and intervention in Vietnam, there was
some consideration of the nature of religion's involvement in political matters.  A valuable contribution was
made by Dr. John C. Bennett, who was President of Union
Theological Seminary.  Answering the charge that high
matters of state belong "to the experts or to policy-
makers—who live with the changing details of the problems and who may have access to classified information"[12]
and that religious leaders are outsiders who lack the
competence to speak, he argued that there were at least
six areas in which "persons who combine religious perspectives and moral sensitivity with a careful attempt
to understand the relevant facts, though not specialists
or insiders in the government, have a duty and right to
speak".[13]  First, they should call attention to the immediate human consequences of any policy, even if they
must also consider the possible human consequences of
any change of policy.  Secondly, the determination of
the goals of policy was a matter of moral choice, and
he went on to suggest some such goals.  Another area of
moral concern was the means used to achieve any or all
of these ends.  Fourthly, Bennett suggested that religious groups could help the American people see the
world as it appeared to peoples in other continents.
Another area was in bringing to the fore and questioning the presuppositions of policy, expressed or unex-
pressed.  Finally churches and synagogues should criti-
cize the false uses of religion and morality, in assumptions about "a holy war" or "honour" or "obligation".[14]

Other keynote speakers concentrated on specific issues
or were content with generalities: but at a luncheon
session three leading religious journalists were invited
to speak on "The Limitations and Possibilities of Organized Religion Acting for Peace".  Arthur Moore, editor of the *Methodist World Outlook,* noted that the vast
majority of statements made by religious groups "have
no effect whatsoever except to make the drafters feel
good".[15]  They are not so much scorned as completely
ignored and are usually a waste of time.  Either such
statements are so general—"we are against war and in favour of peace"—or if they try to be specific they reveal deep divisions amongst religious people.  If such
differences are merely papered over, the statement loses
any weight.  There was also the question of authority.
In whose name were statements made?  Moore ended by
saying: "We must begin to realize that it is not our
role to give the world answers that we already possess,
but to join with the world in searching for the answers
—in trying to find the connection between the great

ethical insights that we proclaim and the events, omi-
nous and confusing, taking place in the world today."[16]

It is significant that although the fact that the conference was inter-religious attracted public attention,
those attending were less concerned to congratulate
themselves on meeting than to concentrate on specific
issues.  To some extent, the 1966 conference had still
to assert the right and duty of religious leaders to
have this interest.  Yet the vital question of what impact religious people can in practice have on world affairs was beginning to emerge, and has come increasingly
to the fore with the development of the World Conference
on Religion and Peace.[17]

The suggestion for such a world conference was made in
the declaration of the 1966 conference.  Besides asking
for a national conference on religion and peace, they
asked the co-chairmen to "explore the possibilities for
calling a world inter-religious conference on peace in
1967, encompassing participation of all the world's religious traditions".[18]  1967 proved to be far too soon,
but by October, 1970, such a conference was in session.


## Towards Kyoto

Soon after *The National Inter-Religious Conference on
Peace,* the U.S. Inter-Religious Committee on Peace,
which had been considerably strengthened by the conference, asked Rev. Herschel Halbert, of the Department of
Christian Social Relations of the Executive Council of
the Episcopal Church, and Dr. Homer Jack to visit some
world religious leaders to explore the possibility of a
world conference.  After a major world tour, they reported to the U.S. Committee in April, 1967.  Since 1945,
they said, there had been no large-scale effort to bring
together leaders of the major world religions to discuss
substantively the problems of world peace.  The need to
convene such a gathering was widely felt: but the task
of organizing it was formidable.  It involved at least
the following problems:

1.  Bringing the leaders of the world religions to
    the same stage of readiness to talk substantive-
    ly about issues of the world peace.

2.  Finding a site which would be politically and
    religiously neutral.

3. Securing balanced initial sponsorship so that
   the conference would not be dominated either
   by United States religious leaders or Judeo-
   Christian leaders.

4. Obtaining funds to pay the international travel
   costs of many, if not most, of the delegates.[19]

The exploratory mission suggested that a preparatory
symposium would be necessary to plan the larger world
conference.

Arranging the preparatory symposium called for careful
planning. The sponsorship of at least one non-American
organization was required, as well as a commitment to
attend from sufficient American religious leaders, and
the assurance of adequate finance. The exploratory mission suggested a preparatory symposium be held in 1968,
preferably in New Delhi, with possibly the Gandhi Peace
Foundation as co-sponsor, or in Tokyo, with an *adhoc*
inter-religious committee as a co-sponsor. The U.S. Committee, however, decided to explore further the convening of two, two-nation, inter-religious consultations,
one Japanese-American in Tokyo, and the other Indian-
American in New Delhi. In both Japan and India, there
were already some groups seeking to foster inter-faith
co-operation.

Further explorations were made and interest was expressed
by the International Seminary Subcommittee of the National Committee for the Gandhi Centenary in India, of which
Sri G. Ramachandran was chairman. The Gandhi Centenary
Committee agreed to pay all costs of the Symposium inside India, including board and lodging of the participants. The U.S. Committee agreed to pay other costs,
including one-half the travel costs of non-Indian, non-
American delegates. Several bodies also agreed to second members of staff for the work. Preparations for
the symposium centred on the offices of the Gandhi
Peace Foundation. Dr. Jack joined the staff there in
December.

Meanwhile, a representative delegation was gathered in
the USA by Rev. Herschel Halbert, which included Dr.
Ralph D. Abernathy, Rabbi Maurice N. Eisendrath, Dr.
Dana McLean Greeley, and Bishop John Wesley Lord.
Leaving New York on January 3, 1968, the team made of-
ficial stops at the World Council of Churches in Geneva,
the Vatican in Rome, the Ecumenical Patriarchate in
Istanbul and in Jerusalem. After the symposium in New

Delhi, the American team visited Saigon for four days
and then shared in a Japanese-American Inter-Religious
Consultation on Peace in Kyoto.  The New Delhi symposium itself was held from January 10th to 14th, 1968.
Forty-six participants attended, as well as eight observers and eight additional consultants or speakers.
They came from nine nations and belonged to nine religions.

The symposium began with a Gandhian religious service,
which included liturgical material from several religions.  Dr. Zakir Husain, President of India, welcomed
the delegates and keynote addresses were given by Sri
Jayaprakash Narayan, the veteran Sarvodaya worker and
Bishop John Wesley Lord.  Narayan was scathing in his
comments on religions in India.  "They do not seem to
be even concerned with the questions of peace".[20]  An
important part of the Symposium were papers on the sanctions for peace within the respective religious traditions.  The papers were of an unusually high standard.
Swami Ranganathananda, of the Ramakrishna Mission,
claimed that: "The concept of man upheld in Hinduism is
the most vital source of its sanctions for peace.  The
discovery, by the sages of the Upanishads, of the true
nature of man as the Atman, the immortal divine self,
and its unity with Brahman, the infinite self of all
beings, constitutes the greatest single source of the
universality and humanism of Hinduism and its perennial
sanction for peace".[21]  Professor K. G. Saiyandain explained the limited circumstances in which Islam per-
mitted war and the stringent conditions laid down to
control it.  Rabbi Eisendrath spoke of the passion for
peace in Judaism and was guarded in his comments on Israel.  Dr. Gopal Singh spoke of the Sikh reverence for
truth from any quarter.  He quoted the words of the
third *guru*, Amar Das, "The world is on fire.  Save it,
O God, save it in Thy mercy through whichever door it
cometh to Thee".[22]  John Burt, Bishop Coadjutor  of Ohio,
described the various attitudes within Christianity and
suggested four ways in which Christianity could work
with other religions for peace.  It should join them in
denouncing national idolatry; in suggesting non-violent
ways to overcome poverty, racism and oppression; in developing and using the world's resources for human good;
and in stressing the unity of all men under God.  The
Venerable Baddeeama Wimalawansa Theo, principal of the
Sri Lanka Vidyalaya in Colombo, quoted the tenfold vir-
tues which the Buddha said should be adhered to by every
ruler and indicated their contemporary application.
Bool Chand, who was director of the Ahimsa Shadh-Peeth

in New Delhi, spoke of the teaching of *Ahimsa* in Jainism.  There were talks,too,about Zoroastrian and Vira
Shaivite teaching.

Another session, appropriately as it was the Gandhi Centenary, was devoted to the "Relevance of Gandhi as a Religious Force for Peace". Participants, before the session  had visited Rajghat, the national  shrine  where
Gandhi's body was cremated.  Attention was also given
to what organized religious groups and leaders were already doing for peace.  There was a moving address by
Ralph David Abernathy, the Civil Rights leader.  Angelo
Fernandes, Archbishop of New Delhi, spoke of the work of
the Second Vatican Council, and Msgr. Edward C. Murray,
of work in the USA.  The Rev. Riri Nakayama, of the
Hozenji Buddhist Temple in Tokyo, told of peace work in
Japan, and Jambel D. Gomboev, who was Chairman of the
Religious Board of Buddhists in the USSR spoke of the
position of Buddhists in his country.

Part of the Symposium was spent in three simultaneous
panels, which discussed Social and Economic Development;
Freedom and Human Rights; and Peace-Making and Peace-
Keeping.  Only the third of these moved beyond generalities to specific issues, with, as one result, a note of
dissent and separate proposals from Jambel D. Gomboev,
of the Buddhists of the USSR.  The Symposium Message is
cast in general terms, but agreement by members of so
many religions was itself significant.

An important item was the question of a world conference.
Two sessions were devoted to this.  Dr. Homer A. Jack
outlined some of the pre-war efforts to hold a world
inter-faith peace conference.  He referred to some secular peace conferences and then suggested the major
purposes of convening a world conference on religion
and peace.  "The first purpose would be to acquaint the
leaders of the world religions with the sanctions and
traditions each major religion has within it for world
peace and for more just international relations...we
still know too little about each other's religions....A
second purpose would be to ascertain if, indeed, there
are principles or middle axioms on international relations and peace which we do have in common...and which
would take priority over our differing national entangle-
ments.  Another purpose  would be to discuss several
specific international problems from the viewpoint of
certain provisional, common religious principles in the
effort toward common action.  A fourth purpose would be
to show the world's people that world religions are

indeed alive to the problems of peace in this world, as
well as to the eternal problems of the spirit.  The final purpose of a world conference would be to develop
a corps of co-workers across religious and national
lines, who might be called upon, indeed mobilized, in
any international emergency.  They could take action
for peace, such as issuing joint statements or participating in joint deputations in specific crises, doing
so irrespective of their particular religion or nationality, but from the perspective of their religions".[23]

Dr. Jack then mentioned likely difficulties.  Finance,
and staffing, obviously, but it might be difficult to
secure the co-operation of religious leaders.  The selection of a suitable site, open to all religionists
from any country, would not be easy.  It was dangerous
to be hasty, as the selection of representatives required
tact and great care, but the quickly changing nature of
the political world did not allow delay and could sud-
denly alter the pattern of world events.

After discussion, the symposium backed the idea of a
world conference.  It agreed that an advisory committee
should be formed and the existing Secretariat be invited
to continue the work.  The participants in the symposium
were to interpret its spirit and findings to their own
religious leaders and constituencies; to enlist the organizations and movements within their bodies devoted
to the pursuit of world peace; to seek financial resources and to promote regional and national meetings.[24]
The Interim Advisory Committee met on January 16th, and
Archbishop Fernandes was asked to take the chair.  At
this, it was agreed to work for a world conference in
late 1969 or early 1970.  The Interim Advisory Committee
should, early in 1969, be replaced by a Preparatory Committee.

At the subsequent Japanese-American Consultation on
Peace in Kyoto on January 22, 1968, Japanese Delegates
agreed that it was "opportune to hold a world religions
conference for peace in the second half of 1969 or the
first half of 1970", and that preparations for Japanese
participation should be made.[25]  Japanese participants
did in fact hold several further meetings and decided to
entrust the calling of a national consultation in Japan
to the Japan Inter-Religious Federation, which was already in existence.

Dana McLean Greeley, in his Introduction to the conference proceedings, tries to assess its achievements.  The

mere fact of a meeting of representatives from nine
world religions to discuss substantial issues on world
peace was significant. The dialogue occurred without
syncretism. No attempt was made to hide differences,
although there was genuine toleration of them. Agreement was reached to proceed towards a world conference.
Further a model for national inter-religious committees
on peace had been established, and the work in the USA
and India had been strengthened. Greeley also points
to certain inadequacies, especially in the composition
of the conference. No Shintoists attended and no Muslims from outside India. There was no African nor Latin
American, and only three participants came from the Communist world. Yet, despite these disappointments, an
important step forward had been taken.


Kyoto, 1970

The Interim Advisory Committee, which had been set up
and had first met at the New Delhi Symposium, met again
in Istanbul, Turkey, on February 21-23, 1969. Archbishop Angelo Fernandes was named president, and both Rev.
Nikkyo Niwano and Dr. Dana McLean Greeley as chairman,
with Rev. Toshio Miyake as treasurer. Co-chairman were
to be Dr. R. R. Diwakar, Rabbi Maurice N. Eisendrath,
Professor Mahmud Husain, Bishop John Wesley Lord, and
Bishop John Wright, who subsequently was appointed
Cardinal. The Japanese invited the committee to convene
the world conference in Kyoto in 1970, and this invitation was accepted. A budget of $300,000 was set and a
larger preparatory committee appointed. Dr. Jack was
named secretary-general, with Rev. Shuten Oishi of Japan
and Sri G. Ramachandran of India as joint secretaries.[26]

Following the Istanbul meeting, an international office
was opened in Boston. During this period, further contacts were made with religious leaders. For a time
there was hope that Pope Paul would visit the conference
In the end, the Vatican announced that he would subsequently visit Asia, but only the Philippines and Australia, as careful explorations showed that guarantees
could not be given that his visit to Japan would be free
from student demonstrations. Several Vatican secretar-
iats, however, continued to show interest in the conference. Initial contacts with the World Council of
Churches in January, 1968, when the American mission visited Geneva *enroute* for New Delhi, were disappointing.
The World Council of Churches' attitude however to

inter-faith dialogue was about to change, with the appointment to its staff of Dr. Stanley J. Samartha.    In
any event, Dr. Eugene Carson Blake, the General Secretary, agreed to speak at the conference, and three
staff members also attended, Dr. Samartha, Dr. Leopolde
J. Niilus and Canon Burgess Carr.    Contacts with the
Archbishop of Canterbury were not fruitful.

The full Preparatory Committee, with 22 out of 31 members present, met in Kyoto in December, 1969.   The committee,   eager   to secure a balanced and representative
membership for the conference, approved a quota system
for delegates according to religions and continents.
Early in 1970, the Secretary General made a round-the-
world trip to recruit delegates.   The committee, wanting
to ensure that a message emerged from the conference,
appointed an Interim Message Committee to prepare for
this.   After some debate, it was also decided that each
plenary session would open with a prayer service, and
that each major religious tradition represented at the
conference   would have charge of one session.   Because
the conference hall was a public building, it was decided that the prayers should be public prayers rather
than full "worship" services.   To avoid any suggestion
of syncretism, the prayers were to be strictly of the
tradition offering them.[27]

The Preparatory Committee worked out ways by which the
conference should be self-governing, and plans were made
for adequate press coverage.

The Japanese office for the conference was opened in May,
1970, in the new Fumon Hall in western Tokyo, in space
donated by a relatively new, lay Buddhist group, Rissho
Kosei-Kai.   In June, 1970,   the international office was
opened in the same building and moved to Kyoto only on
the eve of the conference.

The original Exploratory Mission in 1967 had identified
four problems: where to meet, how to ensure that all
delegates were equipped to participate, how to avoid
American preponderance, and where to find funds for the
travel costs of delegates.   The choice of venue was the
easiest.   Japan was politically acceptable to all states,
and the government agreed in advance to give visas to
all overseas delegates validated by the Secretary-General, even if his or her country of origin was not recognized by the Japanese Government.   To help delegates
reach a similar level of understanding of the issues to
be discussed, the Preparatory Committee agreed that a

pre-conference study packet was to be prepared well in ad
vance and be sent to each registrant. U.S. religious
leaders clearly played an important role in preparing
for the conference, but to avoid domination by them,
Indian and Japanese committees were also involved in
the work. The willingness to subsidize travel costs
for delegates from Asia, Africa, and Latin America,
helped to ensure a reasonable balance at the conference
and reduced "cultural imperialism". Finance was largely dependent on the generosity of the Japanese and
American committees. At Istanbul an estimated budget
of $300,000 was agreed. The Japanese volunteered to
raise $100,000 and the Americans offered to do the same.
It was hoped that religious leaders in the other countries could raise the remaining one-third. This did
not happen and the Japanese and Americans became respons
ible for almost the whole cost of the conference. There
were rumors that some of the money came from the CIA or
the Japanese government, but these were denied in the
"World Conference Daily". "This world conference is
being paid for solely by private funds, overwhelmingly
from religious groups. No government or political party has contributed funds".[28]


## The Kyoto Conference

The conference began on Friday, 16th October,1970.
Earlier in the week, several Japanese academic institutions had arranged a Consultation on Inter-Religious
Dialogue, with reference to peace, which some delegates
attended. The opening session, which some 2,000 visitors watched from the galleries, began with Buddhist
prayers and messages of greeting. After an election of
officers, Archbishop Fernandes gave his presidential address. Later in the morning, Sir Zafrulla Khan, at that
time a president of the International Court of Justice
in the Hague, spoke on "The Fundamentals of Peace". In
the afternoon, Dr. Homer Jack spoke on the background
and purposes of the conference. After certain business
matters, participants met in simultaneous groups, according to their religion.

On Saturday morning, addresses were given by Dr. Hideki
Yukawa, a Nobel Laureate in physics, on "The Creation
of a World Without Arms", and by Professor R. J. Zwi
Werblowsky, Professor of Comparative Religion at the
Hebrew University, Jerusalem. Then participants went
to one of three simultaneous commissions (or workshops)
on either disarmament, development, or human rights. In

the afternoon, Dr. Eugene Carson Blake spoke on "Development"—one of the commission themes.  Later, there
was a panel on peace action, in which Dr. Blake, Dr.
Ralph D. Abernathy, President of the Southern Christian
Leadership Conference, and Thich Thien Minh, Vice-Pres-
ident of the Executive Council of the Unified Buddhist
Church of South Vietnam, took part.

Sunday was spent in the respective commissions.  In the
evening some participants met according to nationality.
On Monday delegates went on a day tour to Nishi Honganji
Temple, Tenrikyo headquarters, Todaiji Temple, and Heian
Jinga Shrine.  On Tuesday, the three commissions met for
the last time.  Later there were five panels on more
practical aspects of peace-work.  In the afternoon,
Archbishop Helder Camara of Brazil spoke on "Religions
and the Need for Structural Changes in Today's World".
The three commission reports and the conference message
were given a first reading, but not debated.

On the sixth and final day, October 21st, the commission
reports were debated and approved, although only after
heated discussion on the Middle East.  The conference
message was approved and also the report of the Follow-
Up Committee, which presented plans for a continuing
body.  The Ven. Thich Nhat Hahn gave a closing summary
and critique, which he called "Saved by Man".

Underlying the discussion of specific issues, the question of the practical impact of religion on world affairs kept bubbling to the surface.  Dr. Blake, having
said that traditional religious attitudes sometimes
stood in the way of development, suggested the positive
contribution that religious communities could make.
They could contribute to "the current debate on the
meaning and goals of development—and to the search of
different societies for new cultural foundations and
new ethos".[29]  They should help educate their followers
to be aware of mankind's interdependence and the need
for justice.  Professor Zwi Werblowsky, critical of religions' record in the field of peace, said that the
mere citing of "peace-texts" was of little value.  Inner peace, too, was not enough.  "The salvation of the
world through the transformation of all hearts is an
eschatological concept and not a social programme".[30]
He looked at the possible conflict between justice and
peace and pointed to the variety of social attitudes
within even one religious tradition.  Delegates at the
conference should be clear that they were using the
term religion in a selective and prescriptive sense.

Religionists, he warned, "have to guard against two
subtle dangers: the danger of getting intoxicated with
their own verbiage, and the danger of overestimating
the significance of what they are doing".[31]   There was
also the danger that the nearer religionists came to
the centres of power, "the more they get caught in the
inevitable ambiguities of compromise and of the political game—and generally of walking—like Agag—very
delicately".[32]

"The Kyoto Conference", he went on, "will be more than
a wasteful exercise if instead of producing high-sound-
ing declarations of principles, or beautiful phrases
about peace, brotherhood, freedom, and human rights, or
making the participants 'feel good', it will succeed,
in its group discussions and commissions, in addressing
itself to the task of isolating problem areas, assessing their dynamics as well as the extent to which the
dynamics of religion can impinge on them and interact
with them, and sketching out concrete modes of action
both inside the religious world and in the contact of
the latter with other sectors of society...Ultimately,
it is not to the world but to themselves that religionists have to send a message...The challenge for religionists is not what to say, but how to be".[33]   Dr.
Abernathy, on the other hand, was emphatic on the need
for religious people to speak out in the name of the
poor and the oppressed.   Archbishop Camara, too, hoped
that "If the religions of the world get together to
support Action for Justice and Peace, something that
seems absurd may become possible, what seems utopian
may become a reality".[34]

In the Kyoto Declaration, delegates expressed their
deep conviction that the religions of the world have a
"real and important service to render to the cause of
peace".   They listed convictions that they had in common, such as belief in the unity of the human family
and the equality, dignity, and sacredness of each individual and the profound hope that good would finally
prevail.   Confessing that religious people had often
betrayed their ideals, they referred to the grave problems of the world that had been discussed.   Speaking as
individuals, but in the name of the "powerless whose
voice is seldom heard", they insisted on the fact that
men and all their works are now united in one destiny.
Promising to do all in their power to educate public
opinion in mankind's unity and the futility of war,[35]
they expressed their backing for the United Nations.

The Commissions were more specific. The report on
disarmament outlines the steps needed to reduce the
threat of war. The internationalism and adherence to
non-violence are obvious. The Human Rights commission
pointed to the rights of various oppressed and minority
groups, whilst the report on development is a sensitive
treatment of the issue. In effect, however, they all
see the major role of religions in influencing public
opinion, by spreading information about the real situation in the world and by deepening a sense of human
unity. The Youth Committee said young people "are beginning to get sceptical of conferences which merely
pass pious resolutions without formulating programmes
action. Therefore, to prevent this conference becoming
another high failure, we recommend that the continuation committees immediately draw up programmes of action
which will be implemented immediately".[36] It was indeed,
as we shall see in the work of the Continuation Body
that the conference continued to have an effect. The
achievements of the conference itself, however, were
considerable.

As the long history of efforts to convene such a conference shows, the fact that it occurred at all was a great
achievement. The reports show good-temper, widespread
agreement, a forward-looking attitude to religion, and
real concern for the issues of the day. The religious
leaders who attended were of a high quality and well
balanced. There were over two hundred delegates and
all major world religions were represented. Although
Christians were the largest group, they were not in a
majority. Ninety-six were Christians and one hundred
and twenty belonged to other faiths. Asian and African
delegates (139) easily outnumbered Westerners (77). With
visitors, journalists, and others, more than one thousand people were involved in the conference. Another
achievement, Dr. Homer Jack lists, was the mature facing
of the Vietnam War. He mentions also two by-products.
"One was that religionists in several countries, notably
Japan and India, developed a co-operative relationship
among themselves".[37] The other was a glossary of words
and phrases on international relations for Japanese-
speaking delegates and on Japanese religions for Westerners.

Dr. Jack mentions some disappointments. The fears that
too few Hindus and Muslims would attend came true. Those
who came were often from an academic background, rather
than influential in the life of the faith. This was
partly because funds to subsidize travel were insuffi-

cient and not enough work had been done to identify
delegates. The death of President Nasser of the United
Arab Republic on the eve of the conference may have
stopped Muslims coming from Egypt. It may also reflect
a failure to appreciate the significance of the conference by some Hindus and Muslims. The same may be said
of the lack of Western European Protestants. Twenty-
one West Europeans attended, of whom only five were
Protestant. The Church of England was not represented.
There were too few women and too few young people. No
one came from China, even though deliberately no one
had been invited from Taiwan or South Korea. The fact
that financial backing came almost entirely from the
generous USA and Japanese committees—with small gifts
from the International Association for Religious Freedom, with headquarters at the Hague, and from the Inter
Religious Organization in Singapore—showed a narrow
basis of interest. The lack of worldwide publicity was
disappointing. It received good coverage in the Japanese media, but little elsewhere. Another disappointment was that some delegates "appeared to be of nation-
states first and only second, adherents of a religious
faith".[38]

The Ven. Thich Nhat Hahn, in his concluding critique,
judged the conference a success. Fears that it would
be dominated by Christians and Westerners had proved
unfounded. Nor had it been too political and too little religious. Various peace groups had made useful
contacts. There had been tensions, but none likely to
break up the conference. "Religious discrimination and
ideological conflicts were not considerable, were not
deeply felt".[39] He found the commission reports more
specific and advanced than he had expected. There were
however, weaknesses. There were too few women and
young people, and no one from China. "Also, the sched-
ule is too tight".[40] This, he said, did not allow sufficient time to get to know each other in depth. He
wondered also whether "the Grand Hotel was too chic
for peace workers".[41]

His remarks highlight the tension between the need to
produce documents at such a conference and the desire
to develop individual friendships. Agreed documents
are useful in further "lobbying" on the issues discussed. They can be presented to the U.N., to governments and religious bodies and a response called for.
Their production can, however, dominate the discussion.
I felt at a second conference, held at Louvain, in the
Commission which I attended, that voting on verbal

amendments, in a Commission of some one hundred people,
hindered real discussion of the issue in hand.  There
is, too, the question of how much effect these documents
have.  For many, especially for those not directly involved in ecclesiastical or U.N. politics, the over-
riding memories of a Conference are the friendships
made and experiences enjoyed of a memorable speech or
of a visit to an interesting site.  For such, a more
leisurely programme would be beneficial, but the cost of
meeting is high.  It may be that the need is for smaller
groups and more delegation, but this requires trust.  It
also lessens the spread of representation on a group.
To some extent the emergence of an on-going body and of
local groupings will ease this problem.  Although some
key members of the Kyoto Conference had been working together closely in preparing for the gathering, most delegates came as strangers.  It takes time to develop rap-
port and trust.  The Preparatory Committee was aware of
this and had arranged for delegates to eat together and
to attend some social receptions.  There is also the
difficulty of ensuring that those who come new to the
conference feel involved in the decision-making and
are not just there to assent to the views of
the inner policy making group.  The question of the
style and standard of accommodation is also difficult—
partly because of different expectations by people from
different backgrounds and partly because it is often
only the more expensive hotels which have facilities
for the numbers involved.

Several of these difficulties are inherent in any large
conference—the more so in one which was international
and inter-religious.  They in no way lessen the sucess-
ful achievement of Kyoto, which has had a sustained influence both through the people who were present at it
and through the continuing organization which emerged
from the conference.

## After Kyoto.  The On-Going Work of WCRP

The Kyoto Conference voted that its work should be continued by forming a new inter-religious world body to
be called the World Conference of Religion for Peace.
This was to engage in at least four programmes:

> (a)  To initiate inter-religious seminars and con-
>      ferences at all levels in order to create a
>      climate for the peaceful resolution of dis-
>      putes among and within nations without violence.

(b)    To encourage the establishment of national and
       regional inter-religious committees for peace.

(c)    To develop an inter-religious presence at the
       United Nations and other international confer-
       ences, whereby the influence of religion can
       be directly exerted to resolve conflicts.

(d)    To encourage the further development of the
       science of inter-religious dialogue for
       peace.[42]

The officers, headed by Archbishop Angelo Fernandes,
Archbishop of New Delhi, as President, and the Board
met immediately after the Kyoto Conference and agreed
to set up an international office, near the U.N. headquarters in New York;  in the event space was found in
the Church Center for the United Nations, which is opposite U.N. headquarters.[43]  Dr. Homer A. Jack was appointed Secretary-General.

A constitution was soon drawn up.  This allowed for a
corporation of some one hundred members, with a board
of directors and executive committee.  When the corporation met at Louvain, Belgium, on the final day of WCRP
II, Archbishop Angelo Fernandes was re-elected president
and Dr. Jack, secretary-general.[44]  Nine people were
elected to the executive committee: whilst the board of
directors consisted of an additional nineteen members.[45]
A number of religious leaders agreed to become sponsors,
including Archbishop Helder Camara, Mrs. Martin Luther
King, Jr., the Hon. Philip Noel-Baker, and, who have
since died, Lord Sorensen, Professor Malalasekera and
Dr. S. Radhakrishnan.  By establishing a Liaison Committee, WCRP has established links with various bodies
in the field of religion and peace, or inter-religious
dialogue.  These bodies include the Inter-Religious
Organization in Singapore, the Temple of Understanding,
and the World Congress of Faiths.

The average income/expenditure of the body in the years
1970-74, was about $65,000, of which nearly all came
from two sources: the U.S. and the Japanese Inter-Religious Committees.  This allowed for a full-time secretar
general and one office secretary.  The 1976 budget was
slightly lower and this reflected the increasing financial pressures of an inflationary period.[46]

Gradually regional committees have been set up.  After

the Kyoto Conference, the Japanese Committee was reconstituted and the Gandhi Peace Foundation continued to serve as a Secretariat in India. The U.S. Inter-Religious Committee on Peace had already been in existence since 1965, and has become more active since WCRP II. After Louvain, a European Committee has been set up, led by Dr. Maria A. Lücker, and some small national groups, such as the U.K./Irish group, created. The most impressive regional activities have been the Japanese-American Consultation in Hawaii in 1972, and the Asian Conference on Religion and Peace held in Singapore from 25-30 November 1976. Much of the work for this was done by the Japanese Committee, although the hosts were the Inter-Religious Organization of Singapore.[47]

An international and some national organizations have been set up. What has been achieved? It is convenient first to consider the years 1970-1974, then to look at the Louvain Conference, and, before trying to answer the question, to consider some developments since Louvain.

## 1970-1974

Dr. Homer Jack begins his report on the four years from 1970-74 with the words: "One frequent criticism of international conferences is that, once they close, nothing further happens—unless some unspent money is found to publish the proceedings. There is a growing feeling about the futility of world congresses just because their decisions are seldom implemented".[48] He has strenuously tried to see that the resolutions of WCRP should have some effect.

An important part of the work has been at the United Nations. In 1970, WCRP received accreditation at the U.N. through the Office of Public Information (OPI). An application was also made for consultative status with the Economic and Social Council (ECCSOC). In 1973, consultative status in Category II was granted. This is the highest status, by agreement, that religious organizations can receive and it allows WCRP to observe meetings of ECCSOC and its commissions and other bodies, to circulate statements, alone or with other Non-Governmental Organizations (NGOs), and on occasion, to make oral interventions. Part of the work has been to make contact with the U.N. community. In 1971, Archbishop Fernandes and other officers met U Thant, the Secretary-General.

Attempts have been made to maintain an inter-religious
presence at the U.N., although this is expensive. Perhaps the most successful example was the visit of the
Japanese Peace Mission, during the 28th session of the
General Assembly. The mission met with Kurt Waldheim,
the Secretary-General. Dr. Jack has also been active
in working with other NGOs, and has cultivated relationships with many members of the press corps. The WCRP
has been active on several issues, especially human
rights. Sessions of the Commission on Human Rights and
its sub-commission on the Protection of Minorities and
Prevention of Discrimination have been closely observed,
and Homer Jack has made some oral interventions. Disarmament discussions have been observed, and special
communications were sent to each U.N. mission by WCRP.
WCRP was represented at the Non-Proliferation Conference
held in Geneva in May, 1975. In November, 1974, WCRP was
represented at the Rome World Food Conference by Dr.
Jack and a few others.[49]

There have been several special projects. During hos-
tilities in Bangladesh (then East Pakistan), Dr. Jack
visited the area and publicized his observations. He
testified on the massacre before the U.S. Senate Judici-
ary Subcommittee on Refugees. The Indochina War was
another concern. In December, 1970, as a direct result
of WCRP I, an inter-religious delegation from Japan visited South Vietnam. Attempts to hold an inter-religious
consultation at Saigon in August, 1971 had, however, to
be cancelled, mainly because the Saigon government refused to give visas to some of the key participants,
including Dr. Homer Jack.[50]

Efforts have been made with other NGOs to define the
human rights of non-citizens and foreign labourers—
especially after Asian citizens had been turned out of
Uganda. Dr. Jack, out of his experiences in Bangladesh
and Burundi, has also pressed the U.N. to find means to
prevent human massacre. Attempts were also successfully
made by WCRP and other NGOs to reactivate procedures
leading to a declaration and ultimately to a convention
against all forms of religious intolerance.

Many publications have also been prepared in the attempt
to influence both the U.N. and world opinion. The list
of leaflets and documentation in the period 1970-74 runs
to three foolscap pages. Dr. Jack, with some help from
others, has also written articles for a large number of
newspapers and journals.

The Louvain Conference

Although the Louvain 1974 conference did not significantly alter the developing pattern of the on-going
life of WCRP, it was important in strengthening this
work and broadening the outreach of WCRP.  New regional
or local committees, for example, have emerged since
the Louvain Conference.

The pattern of events was similar to that at Kyoto.  An
International Preparatory Committee met at Louvain, or
Leuven, Belgium in March,1974.  Again an international
secretariat was formed.  The budget for WCRP II was
$185,000, half of which was used to subsidize travel
for delegates from Asia, Africa, and Latin America.
The money came from Japan, Western Europe and the United
States.  The choice of Louvain as the site increased
European participation, but only from 35 to 42, although
the number of delegates was smaller.  There were 173
delegates at Louvain,against 219 at Kyoto, although the
number of fraternal delegates increased considerably
from 9 to 31, and the total number of participants was
nearly 600.  At Kyoto the total was over 1,000.  By
continents, Asians were still the largest group with 81
delegates—many from Japan.  Seventy-three delegates
were Christian.  There were some twenty each Hindus,
Buddhists and Muslims.

There were fewer speeches—only from Cardinal Suenens
of Belgium, the Ven. Thich Nhat Hahn, and Archbishop
Angelo Fernandes, as chairman.  Cardinal Suenens, on
the opening day, August 28th, indicated that the conference was not directly for dialogue, but for looking
together at the fundamental need of humanity.  In his
opening address, he stressed both the unity of the
world and its inequalities.  Religions were an inesti-
mably fruitful force for humanizing mankind.  Archbishop
Fernandes also spoke of the many problems facing mankind
and the disappointments of the early seventies.  "The
first development decade was a flop; UNCTAD* III as good as
a failure.    The year 1971 brought in the international
monetary crisis...There has been war and skirmishes".[51]
The conference theme "Religion and the Quality of Life"
was urgent and appropriate, because the current malaise
was "a moral and spiritual one affecting the whole of
man and all of mankind".[52]  "It will have to be a deeper
understanding of religion that can meet today's chal-
lenges: one's prayerful regard for God not turning our
eyes away from worldly tasks but sharpening our vision
of what must be done.  The quality of man's life in the

*United Nations on Trade and Development.

last quarter of the century depends among other things
on whether the spirit of religion, as concretized in
prayer and contemplation,can establish an active link
with life as it is and with the caravan of history".[53]
He then looked at some of the areas of special concern.
Thich Nhat Hahn, in part reiterating his critique at
Kyoto, said, "It is *not* for producing more papers  that
we have come to Leuven.  Documents, even the most perfect ones, are not sufficient to make peace.  It is
our way of life, arising from the spirit of love and
understanding and co-operation, that will make peace".[54]
"We have come to encounter each other, as people, people who have truly lived our religious life"—with the
opportunity at the conference to live the religious
life of others.[55]

Participants spent most of their time in four simultaneous commissions,  on disarmament, development, human
rights and environment; in two working parties, on population and religious freedom; and in six panel discussion groups.  Despite Thich Nhat Hahn's words, a lot of
time was spent in producing documents.  There was time
to meet others over meals and on the day tour which began at Breendonk concentration camp, near Antwerp, then
visited the First World War graves and memorial at Ypres
and concluded with a civic reception at Bruges.  Prayer
services were held again and the conference concluded
with a moving convocation in St. Peter's Church, Louvain
Before this convocation, participants walked for a mile
through the ancient University city to draw attention to
the needs of the flood-stricken people of Bangladesh.
The convocation included various prayers, a message from
the Youth Conference at Taizé, the reading of the Louvain Declaration and closing prayers led by Father S.
Paul Verghese, which began:

> Lord of the Universe!
>
> Lord of all mercy and grace!
> Fountain of all good!
> Ground of all being!
> We invoke Thee by many names,
> Allah, Parmeshwar, Satchidanand,
> Ahura Mazda, Adonai Elohenu,
> God our Father.  Father of us all,
> Thou art good, Thou art all good,
> Thou alone art all good.
> Unto Thee we bow our heads,
> In thy presence we bend our proud necks.
> OM SHANTIH, SHANTIH, SHANTIH,
> SALAM, SHALOM, SHLOMO.[56]

The Declaration began by expressing the hope that the
"long-era of prideful, and even prejudicial, isolation
of the religions of humanity is gone forever. Of all
the things learned at Kyoto, none has marked us more
deeply than the discovery that the integrity of the
commitment of each to his own religious tradition permits, indeed nurtures, loving respect for the prayer
and faithfulness of others. We are resolved henceforth
to serve humanity together each in the way most in keeping with the convictions of his spiritual family and
local circumstances".[57] Calling on governments to stop
the proliferation and increase in nuclear weapons, the
Declaration confessed that "we have not known how to
mobilize religious people so that they might contribute
effectively to the prevention of even limited local or
civil wars".[58] Different views on the use of violence
were recognized, but respect for conscientious objec-
tors was called for. "Liberation Plus Development Equals
Peace" is the heading of a section of the Declaration.
"We have come to see human liberation, economic development and world peace as a dynamic triangular process".[59]
There is concern for basic human rights and a call for
religious bodies to avoid entangling political alliances.

The environment crisis was also discussed and the delegates pleaded "with our religious communities to evoke
among their peoples a fresh sense of awe before the
mystery of existence and a recovery of the values of
humble self-restraint in the conduct of personal and
social life. We appeal to the religious communities of
the world to inculcate the attitude of planetary citi-
zenship, the sense of our human solidarity in the just
sharing of the food, the energy, and all the material
necessities of existence which our generous habitat
provides".[60]

The Declaration is a sensitive document. Whilst concentrating on central and urgent issues, it is self-
critical and avoids the tone of a superior lecture to
the world, which such statements sometimes adopt. The
reports of the commissions are also carefully thought
out.

## After Louvain

After the Louvain Conference, the continuing work
of WCRP was similar to that of the period 1970-1974.
WCRP was represented at the World Food Conference held
in Rome in November, 1974; has made its views known

on various matters to the relevant U.N. committees; and
regional organizations have been strengthened.

The officers and board of directors, meeting at Singapore in December, 1976, accepted the recommendation of
the Secretary-General that in future all of his reports
should carry the caveat that the views expressed in the
report are not necessarily those of WCRP and agreed that
reports on human rights and other sensitive issues oc-
curing in individual countries should be made by inter-
religious teams.[61] These sensible decisions show the
difficulty of speaking in the name of "world religions"
or even, in a more restricted way, in the name of WCRP.

The most important event for WCRP in this period has
been the First Asian Conference on Religion and Peace
held in Singapore in November, 1976, attended by three
hundred representatives of the over ten different religions from seventeen Asian countries. The participants
felt that they had achieved amongst themselves their intention to "promote a creative and critical awareness of
the Asian situation, to revitalize the Asian heritage in
pursuit of peace, to motivate religious people of Asia
towards concrete efforts for peace and to study and
evaluate prospects and programmes for world peace from
an Asian religious perspective".[62] They determined to
promote similar objectives amongst the people of Asia.
They called for continuing inter-religious dialogue so
that a code of ethics could be worked out to regulate
the relationships between religions, and suggested that
inter-religious meditation could help to develop inter-
religious fellowship. They called for greater participation by women and young people in work for peace, and dr
attention to the problems of religious education in mult
religious societies. They advocated the establishment o
a permanent Asian centre for inter-religious co-operatio
The commission discussed "peace, security and human dignity in Asia", "new international economic order and in-
tegrated national development" and "development services
through inter-religious co-operation".

The conference also decided on practical action and
launched the Boat People Project. The Ven. Thich Nhat
Hahn became director of the project. The Japanese committee of WCRP gave an immediate grant, and further
money came from religious and secular sources. At the
same time WCRP asked several Western governments to increase their immigration or refugee quotas to help these
new refugees who were drifting on the China Sea.[63]

In February, 1977, however, the board of the project
decided to relieve the director and associate directors
of the project of their positions.  It was also decided
to terminate the project when passengers from both
chartered ships had disembarked and had been given permanent homes.[64]  By the autumn, homes had been found
for many of those on the ships and the board was able
to announce its formal termination, although certain
commitments of the project continued.[65]

In a frank editorial, Dr. Homer Jack comments on this
"Flawed Project":

"WCRP participated in a very flawed effort: the Boat
People Project.  In an era where "cover-up" appears the
reflex of both private and public organizations, ACRP
and WCRP have chosen to reveal the unfortunate turn of
the Boat People Project.  About the only positive aspect
WCRP could save from its involvement in this project is
a determination to tell the truth, however organization-
ally unpleasant....

"The project was badly administered from the start.  In
retrospect, the Ven. Thich Nhat Hahn and his aide, Dr.
Cao Ngoc Phuong, should never have been asked to ad-
minister the project.  As Vietnamese refugees, they were
too emotionally involved with the refugee problems of
the former Indochina.  Their administration of the Project was disastrous....

"Did the project do any good?  It did, in the end, publi-
cize the plight of Boat People to the world community,
but only as a by-product of continuing news of a very
flawed project....

"No agency, public or private, is meeting this need of
rescuing these people at sea.  Yet ACRP/WCRP can no
longer respond to this continuing challenge.  We tried.
We failed".[66]

The failure of almost the first practical inter-faith
relief project is sobering.  It should be added that
the problem is sought to face has now become a major
international concern, partly through the publicizing of
the Boat People's plight by the WCRP.  It seems that
more thought and consultation was required before it was
set up.  It shows also the lack of expertise of religious
people in such fields.  Yet the project was a pioneering
effort and similar attempts at practical action will have
to be made in the future if religious people are to

translate their high words into deeds.

## Princeton

WCRP III met at Princeton, New Jersey, from 29 August to
September 7, 1979.  Forty-seven countries, ten major and
some miscellaneous religions, and a broad spectrum of
"fraternal delegates" from similar organizations were
represented by 354 participants.  Among the notables who
addressed the gathering were Jimmy Carter, President of
the USA; Andrew Young, U.S. Ambassador to the U.N.; and
Kurt Waldheim, Secretary-General of the U.N.  For the
first time, there were delegations from the USSR and the
People's Republic of China.  Princeton was unquestion-
ably the most representative meeting yet held by the
WCRP and demonstrates its viability as a speaker's
platform upon which the religions may address the po-
litical-economic needs of the world.

The published *Findings* summarize the work of its three
commissions and three seminars: Commission I: Religion
and International Economic Justice; II: Religion and
International Security; III: Religion and Human Dignity,
Responsibility, and Rights; Seminar A: Religion, Education, and Peace Commitment; B: Strengthening the Spiritual Dimensions; C: Multi-Religious Dialogue and Action
in Conflict Situations.

The contents of the *Findings* demonstrate two significant
developments within the WCRP: its continuing politicisa-
tion and its initial exploration of religion *per se*, or
"our common spiritual foundations in the formulation and
formation of world community." (p. 27).

"The Princeton Declaration" (7 September, 1979) encapsu-
lates especially the political and economic conclusions
of WCRP III: a strong stand was taken against arms proliferation, especially nuclear, with this pacifist-
sounding resolution: "A global, moral, and religious
campaign which will say NO to ANY KIND OF WAR BETWEEN
NATIONS OR PEOPLES is our call to governments, religious
groups, and all men and women of conscience and faith."
Equally strong statements were made in favor of human
rights; against religious intolerance; for religious
education for peace; against sexual and racial discrimination and apartheid; for a new, just and equitable
economic order; for the rights of conscientious objec-
tors to military service; and for conservation of natura
resources and "a style of human life in harmony with all
of nature."

A theme of approval of and correspondence to certain
ethical concerns of and resolutions pending before the
United Nations runs throughout the Declaration, indicating the degree to which the WCRP increasingly plays
the role of the unofficial religious arm of the U.N.

## The Achievements

After two international conferences and with nearly ten
years experience in the work, Dr. Homer Jack in 1975
tried to sum up the particular approach of WCRP. He
described what it did not try to do: "We have learned,
often the hard way, not to try to create a one-world
religion. We do not want a merging of all religions.
It is not even desirable to create a new artificial
religion. Thus we cannot rightly be accused, as some
still do, of promoting a kind of syncretism. We have
also learned not to dwell, at least for too long, on
the sources of peace in each of our religious traditions.

We have learned that each religion has rich scriptural
resources emphasizing peace. But we have also learned
that there are severe limitations to the number of
times each person can talk about sanctions for peace
in his or her religion. Also we have learned not to
discuss primarily 'religion'—or theology. Inevitably,
conversation gets around to what we believe about prayer
or meditation, about God or the source of being. Again,
we have learned that the discussion of comparative religion is not our particular way. If we of the WCRP
movement", he continued, "have learned three things not
to do or discuss, have we learned anything positive?
We have. We have learned, in using our religious and
ethical insights, to leap over theology and discuss the
next steps for human survival which tend to parallel the
agenda of the United Nations. This has been the unique
contribution of WCRP, and it has been how we have ordered our two world conferences".[67]

In an address given in December, 1975, to the Arya Samaj
in New Delhi, he again reflected on what had been
learned. It had become recognized that religion was
only one among many institutions which had to be mobilized if there is to be peace and justice. Also it has
been found that even if religions can find strong support for peace in their scriptures, many have not been
in the habit of working for peace and justice. Thirdly,
religions working together is not a new religion. "Dialogue is not for the purpose of creating a synthetic,

unifying religion. We want each religion to maintain
its own identity, and to cherish its own traditions.
The world needs differences, richness".[68] Fourthly,
religions must emphasize their social rather than their
personal role in working for peace. In the light of
these discoveries, the role of religion in the quest
for world peace and justice is "to develop moral, ethical, religious influence wherever and whenever policy is
made. It is to take political action and become effective in taking it. This is to be done internationally,
nationally, and locally".[69] This involves acquiring
expertise, not just preaching sermons. "It is not
enough for religion to mean well—hardly a compliment—
but religion must do well, act effectively".[70]

It must be emphasized that WCRP is still young and that
it faces the difficulties of any voluntary body trying
to bring moral influence to bear on those who wield political and economic power. The problems, too, with
which it is concerned are the major problems facing mankind. The resources of WCRP are very slender. The
World Conferences may sound impressive, but the continuing organization is small. That so much has been
achieved both in creating and maintaining an organization and in bringing the influence of WCRP to bear on
the U.N. and on world affairs, is largely the result of
the astounding energy, ability and dedication of the
Secretary-General, Dr. Homer Jack.

It is notoriously hard to assess the impact of public
opinion on events. Politicians are reluctant to admit
that they have been influenced by it. Yet it is clear
that reports to and contacts at the U.N. have been of
value. It is also difficult to get religious people to
agree on specific matters. WCRP has challenged religious leaders to translate their high ideals into recommendations concerned with particular world problems. It
has shown that members of different religions and continents can agree on issues of urgent human concern.
This has been of encouragement to many who wonder about
religions' impact in the world today.


Religious Workers for Lasting Peace

An apparently similar effort has been started in Moscow,
where the World Conference: Religious Workers for Lasting Peace, Disarmament and Just Relations Among Nations
was held in June, 1977.[71] In fact, there are significant differences.

In 1973, the World Council of Peace convened in Moscow
the World Congress of Peace Forces. At this, more than
three hundred representatives of religion met at the
Orthodox Seminary at Zagorsk. They expressed the wish
for further meetings. Two years later, at a meeting of
representatives of churches and religious associations
in the Soviet Union, His Holiness Pimen, Patriarch of
Moscow and all Russia, suggested the holding of an international conference of the followers of different
religions to discuss the contemporary aspects of peace.
A preparatory committee was formed, under the chairmanship of Metropolitan Juvenaly of Tula and Belev. At an
enlarged meeting of the preparatory committee in Moscow
in March, 1976, the date, place and name of the world
meeting was decided, an International Preparatory Committee formed, and an Appeal to Participants was issued.
The appeal, which was fairly general in tone, ended
with these words:

> We are convinced that new light will dawn
> above the world when all believers together
> with all people of good will and peace-
> loving forces of all the world direct their
> energy service of peace all the world round.

The conference itself met from June 6th to 10th, 1977.
It was attended by about six hundred and fifty representatives from over one hundred countries. There were
Buddhists, Christians, Muslims, Jews, Hindus, Shintoists and Sikhs. Observers came from a number of world
religious organizations, including the Holy See, the
World Council of Churches, and the World Muslim League.
The list of participants shows that Orthodox Christians
and Muslims were well-represented. There was a good
selection of representatives from Africa, many delegates
from the Soviet Union and Eastern Europe, but very few
from North America.

The conference was opened by Metropolitan Juvenaly,
Chairman of the International Preparatory Committee.
After silent prayer, he delivered the opening address.
Various messages were read, a Working Presidium was
elected, an address given by Ven. Mufti Ziyautdinkhan
ibn Ishan Babakhan of the Muslim Board of Central Asia,
and papers read on the themes of the three working
groups. Two days were spent in the working groups,
which were on "For Lasting Peace", "For Disarmament",
and "For Just Relations Among Nations". There were
also workshops of the various religious groups represented. The plenary, at the end, adopted two documents:

"An Appeal to the Governments of All Countries in the
World" and "An Appeal to Religious Leaders and Believers
throughout the World".

The contents of the appeals tend to overlap.  They are
fairly general, but cover a range of subjects, including
Detente, World Disarmament Conference, SALT II, Fascist
Dictatorial Regimes, Torture, Religious Beliefs, Population, Nuclear Power, and Non-Governmental Organizations.

The question about the conference is how far it was
genuinely independent and how far it reflected the views
of the Soviet government.  This is not easy to answer.
There does not appear to have been overt pressure.
Rather, the possibility of any real clash with the
Soviet government was avoided.  This was partly because
few delegates from the Western world were invited and a
number of those who came were sympathetic to Soviet
policies.

Only eight people attended from the United States.  It
is also true that the Russian Orthodox Church, whilst
genuinely seeking peace, accommodates itself to the
Soviet government.  Indeed, many members of the church
no doubt sincerely approve Soviet policies.  For the
Soviet government, this conference was useful in show-
ing that there is religious freedom in Russia and is
gaining some support for its attitudes.  The appeals
include some favourite themes of Soviet foreign policy
of the period.  Oppression in Chile and South Korea are
mentioned, but there is no reference to Cambodia or
North Korea.  Human rights are scarcely mentioned.

The relation of religious bodies to the government in
the Soviet Union is different to that in the West and
is a subject in itself.  It is essential, however, if
their work is not to be suspect, that religious leaders
are and are seen to be independent.  It would be tragic
if, instead of bridging the gulf, there were to be,
using the term in an ideological sense, rival Eastern
and Western religious conferences for peace.  This is
why the structure of such conferences is important and
also the source of funds.  WCRP receives no money from
governments and most delegates have to find their own
expenses.  At the Moscow conference, delegates' air
fares and board and lodging were paid.  This is not to
impugn the sincerity of any of those taking part in
the Moscow conference; however, it is important to
recognize that governments also have political interests bound up with progress towards religious unity.

CHAPTER FIVE

CHURCH INITIATIVES

As relationships between members of world religions grow, some religious bodies are seeking official contacts with members of other religions. Christian observers have been invited to some international Islamic conferences. In 1969 Patiala University in the Punjab invited scholars of all faiths to an International Seminar on Guru Nanak. Many religious bodies now invite speakers of other religions. The Christian Church has attempted to put its approach to others on to an organized basis. In 1964 the Vatican established its Secretariat for Non-Christians, and in 1971 the World Council of Churches (WCC) set up a sub-unit on Dialogue Between Men of Living Faiths and Ideologies. Some denominations also have small committees for inter-faith matters. Clearly these confessional bodies are quite different in intention and structure from inter-faith organizations, but some understanding of their work is relevant to the overall picture of the development of interfaith relations.

## The Vatican Secretariat for Non-Christians

The Second Vatican Council's Declaration on the Relationship of the Church to Non-Christian religions marks the beginning of a new approach of the Catholic Church to members of other religions. Not that its thinking was entirely new, but the sensitive approach suggested by some Catholic thinkers was given official approval.

The preparation of the Declaration had a chequered history. It began with Pope John XXIII indicating to Cardinal Bea that he wished the Council to make a statement on the Jews. Originally this was to be included in the Decree on Ecumenism, as chapter four, with chapter five on religious freedom. At the second session of the council, the first three chapters on the schema of this decree were voted, but the other two were held over for lack of time. Between the second and third sessions, some Cardinals made clear that they thought Jewish-

Christian relations were outside the topic of ecumenism,
whilst others indicated their fears that any statement
about Jews would offend Arab countries, where Christians
were a tiny minority.

Before the third session, a draft text became known to
the world in various newspapers; but when the Council
Fathers returned to Rome, they were not presented with
this text, but a new one, from which the rejection of
the charge of deicide had disappeared and added attention had been given to Muslims.  The Declaration was
very fully discussed by the council and, after some
amendments, approved by a large majority.  Even if, in
the light of the original draft, there was some disappointment with the Declaration, it is a significant document.

The Declaration stresses what human beings have in common.  "For all peoples comprise a single community".[1]
It is recognized that from ancient times, "there has existed among diverse peoples a certain perception of that
hidden power which hovers over the course of things"[2]
and reference is made to the contemplation of the divine
mystery in Hinduism, to Buddhism's acknowledgement of
the "radical insufficiency of this shifting world",[3] and
to other religions.  "The Catholic Church", the Delcara-
tion continues, "rejects nothing which is true and holy
in these religions.  She looks with sincere respect upon
those ways of conduct and life, those rules and teachings, which, though differing in many particulars from
what she holds and sets forth, nevertheless often reflect a ray of that Truth which enlightens all men.  Indeed she proclaims and must ever proclaim Christ 'the
way, the truth, the life' (Jn 14.6), in whom men find
the fullness of religious life, and in whom God has
reconciled all things to Himself. (cf. 2 Corinthians 5.
18-19).  The Church, therefore, has this exhortation
for her sons; prudently and lovingly, through dialogue
and collaboration with the followers of other religions,
and in witness of Christian faith and life, acknowledge,
preserve and promote the spiritual and moral goods found
among these men, as well as the values in their society
and culture".[4]  Then follow separate sections on the
Muslims and the Jews.  Finally all forms of discrimination are condemned.

Although the Declaration recognizes a search for God in
other religions and mentions dialogue and collaboration,
no attempt is made to define it.  It is set within the
context of the search for human unity and the assumption

that such unity is ultimately to be found in Christ, to
whom the Church is called to witness. Whilst the approach to members of other religions is to be by way of
friendship and co-operation, the Declaration does not
imply any alteration of the Church's self-understanding,
and, indeed, should be read in the light of the Dogmatic Constitution on the Church (*Lumen Gentium*). The
underlying missionary intention of the Church is clear,
too, in the work designated for the Vatican Secretariat
for Non-Christians.

Following the Second Vatican Council, Pope Paul estab-
lished the Secretariat, with Cardinal Marella Paolo as
President and Fr. Humbertclaude  and Fr. Rossano as
Secretaries. In a discourse to the Sacred College, the
Pope explained its purpose:

> Moreover we have decided to create a separate
> Secretariat for Non-Christians, so that there
> shall be a means of coming to some kind of
> dialogue, both considerate and faithful, with
> all those *who still believe in God and adore
> him*. With the help of this initial step and
> of yet others, we intend to make a clear dem-
> onstration of the *Catholic dimension of the
> Church* which, at this time, and in this con-
> ciliar atmosphere, not only embraces in the
> bonds of understanding, friendship and fratern-
> al consideration, those who are inside the
> Church, but once more looks outside to find
> some basis for dialogue and contact with all
> souls of goodwill.[5]

It was made clear from the beginning that the creation
of the Secretariat did not mean that Mission had been
replaced by Dialogue. "The preaching of the Gospel",
wrote Fr. Humbertclaude, "remains still the most important way of achieving the task assigned by God to his
Church, that of making the nations aware of the Good
News of Salvation".[6] The word "mission", however, had
been abused and misunderstood and respect for the liberty of the soul had at times been infringed. Various
new difficulties faced missionary work, including the
fact that Christianity was almost always the religion
"attributed to the old colonists and so to the old op-
pressors".[7] Equally the Church had become "far more
clearly aware of the universal brotherhood of man in
God and of the new universal redemption by Jesus—diversity of religion or the absence of any belief can no
longer be opposed to this brotherhood of man. If other

religions are no longer moving towards her, the Church
must take the first steps to bring herself to them.  It
must strain itself to the utmost to gain as wide a contact as circumstances allow".[8]  The Secretariat's particular task, Fr. Humbertclaude continued, "is to prepare
the ground, in order to make it capable of receiving
the seed, and then to leave it to germinate quietly and
peacefully".[9]  The Secretariat was more concerned with
whole groups than with individuals.

Dialogue was possible because there was a certain common
ground among men—"examples of religious feelings, of
patience, of assiduity in work".[10]  Moreover people had
compl mentary qualities.  Fr. Humbertclaude distinguishe
between pre-dialogue,which aimed "to create conditions
which are necessary for strict dialogue-mutual understanding, the beginnings of a conversation, the establishment of contact".[11]  "As to dialogue considered in
its strict theological sense, which itself presupposes
a certain amount of confidence and sympathy, as well as
the admission that the truth which another possesses is
worth discussing, this will be limited to start with to
disentangling the genuine main principles of others from
all errors of interpretation, all the prejudices, and
from all the elements, historical and otherwise, with
which they have been falsely coloured.  This supposes
that the partners in dialogue are capable and, as far as
possible,representative".[12]

"With a doctrinal basis firmly established, we have come
to a mutual agreement as to what are common or converging elements, and what are the opposing elements.  If
the opposing elements are considered afresh,it will be
seen that some of them, even if they do not seem to be
converging already, could perhaps converge after a more
detailed study.  In this way the area of basic agree-
ments will continue to grow.  In this situation, however
absolute truth, or what at least appears to be absolute
truth, can never be sacrificed.  In the case of those
elements which are irreducible, since truth can only be
one, recourse must be had once again to research to try
to discover what exactly is true.  When this is done,
what is true must be adopted, and what is false rejected
using as a basis the light which has been mutually
agreed upon from the beginning".[13]

This article is valuable as it makes clear the Secretariat's understanding of dialogue, which is seen as complementary to the Church's overall mission of proclaim-
ing the Gospel.  The view that other religions have

"saving significance" is expressly rejected and the salvation of non-Christians is seen as a secret dialogue
between God and the individual soul.[14]  Dialogue, rather
like the Church's educational work in a previous generation, is a *preparatio evangelica* to remove hostility and
misunderstanding and to make communication possible.
This explains the two main aspects of the Secretariat's
work.  The first is diplomatic: the attempt to build up
relationships with other religious groups.  The second
is study: the attempt to assess honestly other traditions so as to see where there is agreement and disagreement.

At the diplomatic level a considerable number of religious leaders, including the Dalai Lama, a group of
Shinto priests, and a delegation from the Supreme Council for Islamic Affairs of Cairo, have been invited to
Rome and received by the Pope or members of the Secretariat.  In receiving the Ambassador of Iran, the Pope
made reference to Zoroaster, and when he himself visited
the Far East in 1971, he specifically addressed the non-
Christians of Australia and of the Philippines.  Cardinal Pignedoli, since he succeeded Cardinal Marella Paolo,
has also invited several religious leaders to Rome.

The other main aspect of the Secretariat's work is reflected in its publications, such as the Guides for relations with non-Christian religions: *Meeting with
African Religions, Guidelines for a Dialogue Between
Islam and Christianity, Meeting with Buddhism* and *Meeting with Hinduism*.  These aim to give a clear statement
of the religion concerned and to show where they agree
and disagree with Catholic truth.  A similar approach is
seen in *Religions: Fundamental Themes for a Dialogistic
Understanding,* edited by R. Caspar, P.B.  Useful as they
are, they seem to predetermine the Catholic position in
approaching those of other faiths.  In fairness, however,
it must be said that increasingly in the *Bulletin,* members of other faiths are asked to contribute, and in 1972,
non-Christian professors were invited to address the
regular meeting of consultants.

A further aspect of the Secretariat's work which is
clear from copies of the *Bulletin* is its effort to maintain contact with dialogue meetings taking place in
various parts of the world.  There are several reports
of meetings arranged by the Commission for Dialogue of
the Catholic Bishops Conference of India and of the situation in African and Asian countries.  The Catholic
Church too has been represented at gatherings of the

Temple of Understanding and the World Conference on Religion and Peace.

In some twelve years work, the Vatican Secretariat has
made numerous contacts and acquired a wealth of knowledge.  It provides a central point for the wide-ranging
contacts of the Catholic Church with members of other
religions.  Yet whilst many members of the Catholic
Church are in open dialogue with others, it is not
clear how much more the Secretariat itself can be than
a central "clearing-house" and source of information.
For there is an inherent difficulty in structured official dialogues.  Even so, there is great value in the new
friendly relations which the Catholic Church has with
those of other faiths and there is the possibility of
joint action on social and human concerns.

## The World Council of Churches

In this decade, with the creation of a Sub-Unit on Dialogue Between Men of Living Faiths and Ideologies, the
World Council of Churches has become increasingly interested in inter-faith dialogue.  This is not an entirely
new interest.  Christian Study Centres, especially in
India and other parts of Asia, have for some time arranged dialogues with members of other faiths.[15]  The
Ecumenical Institute at Bossey has held meetings involving people of different faiths and ideologies.  As
early as 1956, a study project, *The Word of God and the
Living Faiths of Men*  was approved by the World Council
of Churches Central Committee meeting at Galyatetö,
Hungary.  Various consultations were held in connection
with this study, notably one at Kandy, Ceylon, in 1967,
which brought together for the first time Protestant,
Orthodox, and Roman Catholic theologians to consider the
relationship between Christians and men of other faiths.
There was some discussion of the subject at the New
Delhi (1961) and Uppsala (1968) assemblies.

The subject, however, was given special attention at
the meetings of the Executive and Central Committees of
the World Council of Churches at Canterbury in August,
1969.  Various factors made it clear that this was a
subject requiring greater attention:

    (1)  The World Council of Churches was receiving

with increasing frequency invitations to take
part in inter-religious gatherings.  In 1969
it was invited to the Temple of Understanding
Conference at Geneva and the World Conference
on Religion and Peace at Kyoto.

(2) In many countries, there was a demand that
Christian communities should co-operate rather
than compete with other religious groups.

(3) Migration was creating a multi-religious situation in countries where this had not previously existed.  Some young people were turning
away from Christianity to these new religions.

(4) The need had already been recognized to give
serious attention to the underlying attitudes
of faith that help or hinder programmes of development in pluralistic situations.

(5) In several parts of the world there was hostility or conflict between different religious
communities.

"These situations", wrote Dr. S. J. Samartha, "demand
that, where necessary, the World Council should co-operate
with other World Religious Organizations to enlist the
resources of all faiths to tame political passions, reduce tensions, and to bring about conditions that help
to restore peace and harmony".[16]

The Central Committee discussed this matter and passed
the following resolutions:

"Believing that Christian Mission and Faithfulness to
the Gospel imply a respect for men of all faiths and
ideologies, the Central Committee

(a) Welcomes the increased emphasis on dialogue with
men of other faiths and secular ideologies.

(b) Encourages the Department (on Studies in Mission
and Evangelism) to study further the relation
between dialogue and mission, as well as the relation between our common humanity with other
men and our new humanity in Christ.

(c) Approves the plan for an Ecumenical Consultation
on Dialogue with Men of Other Faiths in March,
1970 in Beirut".[17]

Three aspects of the World Council of Churches' involvement can be distinguished.  Bilateral consultations,
some of which will be considered later, multi-lateral
consultations and the continuing debate about the Christian
theology of dialogue.

Two multi-lateral consultations have been held at Ajaltoun (Beirut) in March, 1970, and at Colombo, Sri Lanka
in April, 1974.  At Ajaltoun, forty people from 17 countries took part and men from four major faiths, Hindu,
Buddhist, Christian and Muslim, were brought together for
the first time under the auspices of the World Council
of Churches.  "The key note of the consultation was the
understanding that a full and loyal commitment to one's
own faith did not stand in the way of dialogue.  On the
contrary, it was our faith which was the very basis of
and driving force to intensification of dialogue and a
search for common action between members of various
faiths".[18]  The Colombo meeting was attended by fifty
people from five religions and from twenty-two countries.
Compared to the Ajaltoun gathering, Jews were invited to
this conference.  It had been jointly planned by a group
consisting of members of all the faiths concerned.
Christians, although the largest group, were in a minority.  The theme was  *Towards World Community,* and the
group made a sober analysis of the problems and possible
contribution of religions.  The meeting called for further exploration of dialogue and of the means of co-
operation for social justice.

Not all Christians have been happy about the World Council of Churches' involvement in dialogue, and considerable attention has been given to the Christian theology
of dialogue.  This was the theme of a consultation at
Zurich in 1970.  The reflections of that meeting and
the experience of the Ajaltoun consultation were considered at the Central Committee meeting at Addis Ababa in
January, 1971.  It was there decided to set up the Sub-
Unit on Dialogue Between Men of Living Faiths and Ideologies, with Dr. Stanley Samartha, an able and experienced theologian from India, as secretary.  The committee
also accepted an *Interim Policy Statement and Guidelines.*
This, firstly, recognized dialogue with people of living
faiths and ideologies as one of the major current concerns of the ecumenical movement.  Commenting, Dr. Samartha says, "Given the great difference in the cultural
backgrounds and theological traditions of the members of
the Central Committee, it is remarkable that such a statement was accepted at all".[19]  Secondly, the statement
acknowledged that dialogue must take place in freedom

and involved living relationships, not just talking.
Dialogue offered to Christians the promise of discovering new dimensions of understanding their faith.  It
required respect for the integrity of partners in dialogue, but the Christian started from his standpoint
of faith in Jesus Christ.  Thirdly, some guidelines to
the churches were suggested.

Reactions to the statement were received from churches
in several countries.  Analyzing these, Dr. Samartha
suggested that certain significant issues emerged:

(a)  The approach to or the meeting point of dia-
     logue, particularly as it touches the ques-
     tion of Truth.

(b)  The theological basis of dialogue with dis-
     cussion swirling around 'Christo-centric' and
     'Theo-centric' standpoints, leading inevitably
     to questions of the work of the Holy Spirit in
     the world.

(c)  The place of 'mission' and 'witness' in dia-
     logue; pushing the discussion beyond the
     alternatives of seeing dialogue either as a
     'betrayal of mission' or 'a new tool for mis-
     sion' in the post-colonial era.

(d)  The motivation, purpose and possibilities of
     dialogue with people of certain ideologies,
     e.g. Marxists, Maoists, secular humanists,
     etc., recognizing the need to take this dis-
     cussion beyond the intellectual confines of
     Europe and also noting that 'religion' and
     'ideological' questions are closely related.

(e)  The possible contributions dialogue can make
     towards the quest for spiritual resources for
     living in community, supporting personal and
     social life in an age of science and technol-
     ogy.

(f)  The place of worship and prayer in the living
     context of dialogue between people of living
     faiths as they struggle to seek the meaning
     of the transcendent in the contemporary world
     dominated by things and machinery and imper-
     sonal forces that seem to be relentlessly
     marching along devouring their own crea-
     tions".[20]

The Nairobi Assembly

Much has been written about the theology of dialogue.
The different attitudes came to the fore at the World
Council of Churches 1975 Assembly at Nairobi in the debates of Section III on "Seeking Community".  "Asian
Christians spoke almost as one and gave witness to
their experience of life in a pluralist society, of
their existence as a minority among great masses of
Hindus, Buddhists and Muslims.  They told of various
levels and densities of community and dialogue, within
daily contacts of living together, in working together
for nation-building, in sharing moral and human concerns and ideals, in shared prayer to God and meditation on the holy scriptures and the holy men of various
traditions.  They told of how such experience of community at the religious and theological level in particular had given them new insights into the Bible, had
deepened and strengthened their Christian faith, en-
hanced their world view and freed them from many fears
they had inherited from missionaries, and from narrow
clannish conceptions of God and his Christ".[21]  They
were supported by Africans and a few Europeans; but
were strongly opposed by "Evangelicals from Scandinavia,
Western Germany and England" who argued that Christ "is
present only in the Word and Sacraments".[22]

Because of the opposition to dialogue, the section's
report was amended by the assembly in a conservative
direction.  This upset many Asian and African theologians, who "were surprised and shocked at the summary
way in which some of their deepest Christian experiences were dismissed and discarded on very flimsy theological grounds.  They asked themselves: 'Is every
Christian experience and every theological initiative
which is not North Atlantic invalid, inadmissible and
unworthy of a hearing?'".[23]

The commission was chaired by Metropolitan Paulos Gregorios (Paul Verghese) and had some two hundred and
fifty members, although attendance was erratic.  The
commission divided into three sub-sections on Faiths,
Cultures and Ideologies.  When the report was presented
to the Assembly, it was attacked by several speakers
who thought it would be understood as spiritual compromise or rejection of the Church's missionary obligations.
The attack was led by Dr. Per Lønning of the Church of
Norway, and Bishop Michael of the Russian Orthodox
Church.  Metropolitan Paulos Gregorios offered to draft
a supplementary page to cover the points made; but Dr.

Zonning felt that the objections were so serious that the Assembly should see a revised version before voting. By a large majority, the report was referred back to the section for reconsideration.

Although this vote showed that a number of delegates were unhappy about dialogue, it was also an expression of frustration at conference procedures by some who felt that real decisions were not made by the Assembly but by the World Council of Churches' "managers". In any case, the Sub-Unit on Dialogue had been a focus of attack by those evangelicals who for some time had been critical of developments in the World Council of Churches. Feeling that the World Council of Churches had stressed social action at the expense of proclamation of the Gospel, they saw the interest in dialogue as a further betrayal of the Church's missionary obligation. It was this cumulative criticism that was voiced by Dr. Per Zonning. The debate was dominated by opponents and Asian speakers were not called, although twelve more people had indicated their wish to contribute.

The revised text of the section report has added to it a Preamble, which deserves to be quoted in full:

1. We are all agreed that the *skandalon* (stumbling block) of the gospel will always be with us. While we do seek wider community with people of other faiths, cultures and ideologies, we do not think there will ever be a time in history when the tension will be resolved between belief in Jesus Christ and unbelief. It is a tension that divides the Church from the world. It is a tension which also goes through each Christian disciple, as each is unable to say that his or her faith in Jesus Christ is perfect.

2. We should also make a proper distinction between the division created by the judging Word of God and the division caused by sin.

3. We are all agreed that the Great Commission of Jesus Christ which asks us to go out into all the world and make disciples of all nations, and to baptize them in the Triune Name, should not be abandoned or betrayed, disobeyed or compromised, neither should it be misused. Dialogue is both a matter of hearing and understanding the faith of others, and also of wit-

nessing to the gospel of Jesus Christ.

4. We are all opposed to any form of syncretism,
   incipient, nascent, or developed, if we mean by
   syncretism conscious or unconscious human attempts to create a new religion composed of
   elements taken from different religions.

5. We view the future of the Church's mission as
   full of hope, for it is not upon human efforts
   that our hope is based, but upon the power and
   promise of God.[24]

The Introduction begins by affirming that the Christian
Gospel creates community, but it is recognized that
there is an urgent desire to seek a wider community.
"Whether we like it or not, we find ourselves thrown in
with all humanity in a common search for peace and
justice".  Such wider community must be sought "without
compromising the *skandalon* of the gospel".  All agreed
that they were linked to others as "fellow-creatures of
God—although in a fallen creation, sin and unbelief divide.  Many of us believe and some witness to the actual
experience of a common ground far beyond our common humanity.  They have found that Christ sets them free to
explore a community under God with men and women of
other faiths.  We believe that in this, as in all matters
the gifts are different.  Some seem to be called to bold
pioneering, adventures and risks beyond the confines of
present ecclesiastical and theological structures.
Others acknowledge an equally exacting calling to deepen
the time-honoured understanding of the community that is
ours in Christ".[25]

The section on Faith and the Search for Community suggests that the term "wider ecumenism" should be avoided
and "inter-religious" used instead, although the "wider
community is one of people with people, not of religions
with religions or systems with systems".[26]  Paragraph
sixteen asked whether there was a theological basis on
which Christians should seek community with their neighbours of other faiths and convictions, and mentioned several answers.  "Many stressed that all people have been
created by God in his image and that God loves all humanity.  Many believed that in a world broken by sin it
is the incarnation of God in Jesus Christ which provides
the basis for the restoration of the creation to wholeness.  Others would seek this basis for community in the
trinitarian understanding of God.  Still others find
theological meaning in the fact that history has removed

and is removing geographical and cultural barriers
which once kept us isolated and so is moving us towards
one interdependent humanity.  In all this discussion we
encountered the question of a possible double basis for
our search for community.  Christians have a specifically theological basis for such a search.  Is there also
a common basis which should be mutually acceptable to
people of differing faiths and ideologies?  Considerable
difficulty was experienced about this and no agreed conclusion reached.  It would appear, however, that in
practice in particular situations men and women of various cultures, faiths, and ideologies can enter into
community together, although their own understandings
of their motivations will vary".[27]

"The question was discussed", paragraph 17 continues,
"whether we can posit that Jesus Christ is at work among
people of other faiths.  Here opinions differed.  Some
stated as their conviction that Jesus Christ as Saviour
is not present in other religions, although they accepted the idea of a natural knowledge of God.  Others acknowledged the presence of *logoi spermatikoi* (scattered
seeds of truth) in other religions but stressed that
only in Jesus Christ do we receive fullness of truth
and life.  Others gave first-hand testimony that their
own faith in Jesus Christ had been greatly deepened and
strengthened through encountering him in dialogue with
those of other faiths.  The point was also made that the
Spirit works among people outside Israel and outside the
Church, and that this Spirit is one with the Father and
with the Son".[28]

The next paragraph recognizes that one can only talk
about each specific religion, not religions in general,
and that the influence of Jesus may act as a ferment beyond the Christian Church.

Many in the section stressed the importance of dialogue.
"It should not be seen as an alternative for mission
and it should not compromise our faith".[29]  The variety
of situations and the nature of the partners affect the
way dialogue is understood and undertaken.  "Depending
on the partners and the situation, a dialogue might
sometimes start with common concerns in society and ways
of working together in tackling problems: sometimes theological issues would be the basis for dialogue.  Very
often these are interrelated".[30]  "The terms 'spirituality' and 'sharing'," the report continues, "need clarification in the context of dialogue.  'Sharing in spirituality' need not mean entering into common worship.

For some, it implies seeking to understand with empathy
the dimensions of worship, devotion and meditation in
the religious tradition and practice of the partners".[3]

The sections on "Cultures and the Search for Identity",
"Ideologies and the Search for Community" and "Recommendations to the Churches" do not make any fresh contribution to the discussion of dialogue.

The whole report is indecisive and describes various
views within the section, because clearly there was not
a common mind. Dialogue is not rejected nor is it en-
dorsed: but the impression given is that it is subservi-
ent to the Church's evangelistic task. The primary community is the Christian Church and the search for a
wider community is based on a common humanity rather
than any "religious" link. There is no suggestion that
the saving power of God may extend beyond the Church.

When the revised text was presented to the Assembly,
Principal Russel Chandran, of the Church of South India
said that the report was weak and uncommitted and the
new preamble made it still more cautious. He therefore
felt bound on behalf of many others to ask for a more
definite endorsement of the dialogue approach.

> In this debate not only the first-hand
> experience of those who have lived and
> moved with people of other faiths but also
> the deeper theological understanding of
> the gospel, Jesus Christ, the Holy Spirit,
> the doctrine of the Trinity and the mean-
> ing of revelation led many to modify or
> abandon the Kraemerian approach and to
> adopt the approach of dialogue. It was
> this development which led to the estab-
> lishment of the World Council of Churches'
> Secretariat on Dialogue following the Up-
> psala Assembly. The Second Vatican Coun-
> cil also led the Roman Catholic Church to
> establish a secretariat for relations with
> other faiths...
>
> This development is not simply the conse-
> quence of human considerations of tolerance,
> religious harmony, and peace. On the con-
> trary, it is deeply rooted in our confes-
> sion of Jesus Christ as Lord and Saviour
> and our commitment to the Trinitarian faith.

The theology of creation affirms the presence and work of God in all cultures. Our
confession of Christ as Lord is an affirmation that he is Lord, not only of Christians
but of all peoples. He is the Logos who
holds all things together. He is the light
which lightens everyone. It is in him all
things and all peoples are to be united.

We also need to acknowledge that we have not
yet fathomed the depths of the unsearchable
riches of Christ and our knowledge of him
must never be absolutized or identified with
the fullness of the reality of Christ. It
is the Holy Spirit who leads us into all
truth. He does this by interpreting Christ
to us and by helping us to learn from one
another's experience of Christ. In a genuine sense, our knowledge and experience of
Christ is enriched by the response of the
people of other faiths. Witnessing to
Christ is, therefore, a two-way movement of
mutual learning and enrichment.

The Church which evangelizes is also evangel-
ized in the sense that its knowledge and experience of Jesus Christ and his gospel is
deepened by the response of those to whom the
gospel is proclaimed...

We would like our brethren who are concerned
about the commitment to the great commission
of our Lord and the dangers of syncretism to
be willing to listen to the testimony and
insights of those who have more intimate
knowledge of other faiths and are in no way
less committed to Jesus Christ and his mission.[32]

Dr. Lynn A. de Silva, a Methodist from Sri Lanka, who is
Director of a Study Centre, also stressed the value of
dialogue:

1.   Dialogue does not in any way diminish full
     and loyal commitment to one's own faith, but
     rather enriches and strengthens it. Many have
     borne testimony to this fact.

2.   Dialogue, far from being a temptation to syn-
     cretism, is a safeguard against it, because

in dialogue we get to know one another's
faith in depth. One's own faith is tested
and refined and sharpened thereby. The real
test of faith is faiths-in-relation.

3. Dialogue is a creative interaction which
   liberates a person from a close or cloistered
   system to which he happens to belong by accident of birth, and elevates him to spiritual
   freedom, giving him a vision of wider dimensions of spiritual life by his sharing in the
   spirituality of others.

4. Dialogue is urgent and essential for us in
   Asia in order to repudiate the arrogance, ag-
   gression and negativism of our evangelistic
   crusades which have obscured the gospel and
   caricatured Christianity as an aggressive
   and militant religion...

5. Dialogue is essential to dispel the negative
   attitude we have to people of other faiths,
   which makes proclamation ineffective and
   irrelevant. [33]

Other criticisms of the report as both too cautious and
incautious were raised, but the motion to commend the
report to the churches for study and appropriate action
was carried.

At the subsequent meeting of the Central Committee in
Geneva in 1976, the continuing work of the Unit was
agreed to, although it will be restricted by the financial cuts which are affecting the whole World Council of
Churches' organization. The development of a Christian
theology of dialogue is likely to occupy as much attention as actual dialogue, although the consultations
with Judaism and Islam are an on-going programme, and
member churches are likely to arrange inter-religious
meetings.


Chiang Mai

At the Consultation at Chiang Mai, in Thailand, in Apri
1977, progress has already been made. The theme was
"Dialogue in Community" and was intended to point to
the living context in which dialogue occurs. There is
dialogue within a community, which involves growth in
mutual care and understanding. There is also dialogue

between communities for the sake of a wider community
of peace and justice. This can happen at a local, national or international level. By relating dialogue
within the community to dialogue between communities,
the statement links the search for Christian unity to
the wider search for human unity. It also sets dialogue
in the context of Christian service. "We see dialogue",
the statement says, "as a fundamental part of our Christian service within community".[34] It is therefore in
no way a secret weapon of "aggressive Christian mili-
tancy" but "a means of living out our faith in Christ
in service of community with our neighbours".[35] Seen
also as sharing in the *missio Dei,* the statement affirms
that the relationship of dialogue gives opportunity for
authentic witness.

The Consultation was aware of the tension in the relation of the Christian community to the community of hu-
mankind. The term "world-community" was avoided, partly
because people in Asia, Africa and Latin America are
suspicious that it really implies the imposition of a
"secular Western Christendom", and partly because people
in the West thought it suggested "a creeping syncretism
that might lead to one religion for the world".[36] Instead "the vision of a world-wide 'community of communities' commended itself to us as a means of seeking community in a pluralistic world. The vision is not one
of homogenous unity or totalitarian uniformity, but it
is for Christians related to the kingly rule of God
over all human communities".[37]

It was recognized that engaging in dialogue in community
raised penetrating questions about the place of peoples
of other faiths and ideologies in the activity of God in
history; but these were not answered, only preliminary
considerations being outlined. There was also discussion of the various ways in which the word "syncretism"
is used.

The Consultation was clearly an important event. Dr.
Samartha has described it as "a step forward because it
overcame some of the difficulties and tensions manifested
in the Nairobi debate of Section III".[38] Monsignor
Rossano, leader of the Vatican observers, commented
"that from now on we will speak of 'Before Chiang Mai'
and 'After Chiang Mai'".[39] Part of the importance, besides soothing some of the disagreements of Nairobi,
lies in the consultation linking dialogue so closely
with the search for community. This relates it to the
search for peace and justice and is perhaps appropriate

if organizations are to engage in dialogue with each
other. It leaves questions of Truth unanswered.

Insofar as the World Council of Churches speaks for
Protestant, Anglican, Orthodox and other churches, it
suggests that the Christian church is still ambivalent
in its attitude to other world religions. Indeed the
variety of opinions expressed at The World Parliament
of Religions in Chicago in 1893 is still prevalent.
Evangelical churches which are not members of the World
Council of Churches are clear in their opposition to
dialogue. The fundamental issue is whether other religions have a place in God's purposes and are channels
of his love. Dialogue in its fullest sense presupposes
a mutuality which is accepted by the inter-faith organizations; whereas the Christian Churches, with the exception of some individuals, are still committed to a
missionary relationship to others based on claims of a
unique revelation. The suspicion of those of other
faiths that Christian interest in dialogue is only a
new, more polite form of evangelization is therefore
difficult to disprove.

It may be necessary to make clear, as is implicit in th
Chiang Mai Consultation report, that the Churches' concern for dialogue is primarily related to its concern
for justice, peace and world order, in which it co-
operates with all who seek similar ideals. Dialogue,
in the deeper sense, of searching together for a Truth
that transcends differences of religious belief, may
have to be left to individuals, as it requires a disinterested freedom which organizations seldom display.

CHAPTER SIX


CHRISTIANS AND JEWS:   OVERCOMING
PREJUDICE AND MISUNDERSTANDING


The primary purpose of some inter-faith organizations
is to promote peace and good community relations.  This
is especially true of attempts to foster Christian and
Jewish co-operation, because the relations between these
two religions have been marked by hatred and bloodshed.
Attempts to build bridges of understanding between
Christians and Jews have therefore a special character
and reveal particular problems for inter-faith dialogue.
Some of these special features will become clearer by
considering the development of the Council of Christians and Jews and its international counterpart; by
looking at the situation in Israel, where religious
differences exacerbate political tensions; and by
sketching the development of "official" dialogue between representatives of Judaism and the Churches.


## The Council of Christians and Jews

It was in the period between the two World Wars that
the relationship of Jews and non-Jews began to come to
the fore.  Christians began to see the need to combat
anti-semitism and to relieve the sufferings of the Jews.

The common background was the violent anti-semitism of
Tsarist Russia from 1881 onwards, which had important
effects on the Jewish people, the majority of whom
lived in Eastern Europe.  This led to an immense dis-
persion of Eastern European Jews into Western Europe
and the United States.  It created an uneasy relationship between the remaining Eastern European minorities
and the new states which emerged after 1919—leading to
further anti-semitism between the wars.  It also
strengthened the Zionist dream of creating a centre of
Jewish life in the ancient Homeland.  At the same time,
the Christian church had become more socially and politically conscious.[1]

The beginnings of organized Jewish-Christian co-

operation go back to 1923, when the Federal Council of
Churches of Christ in America set up a Committee on
Good Will between Jews and Christians. This was in-
tneded to counter the growing influence of the Ku Klux
Klan, with their new slogan "America for the Americans".
It soon became clear that a more comprehensive body was
needed. So, in 1928, a National Conference of Christians and Jews was launched as a joint organization of
Protestants, Catholics and Jews. Based on a belief "in
a spiritual interpretation of the universe", the purpose was "to promote justice, unity, understanding and
co-operation among Protestants, Catholics and Jews, and
to analyze, moderate and finally eliminate intergroup
prejudices which disfigure and distort religious, business, social and political relations, with a view to
the establishment of a social order on which the religious ideals of brotherhood and justice shall become
the standards of human relationships".[2] The work of
the National Conference, under the guidance of Everett
Clinchy, was in the broadest sense educational, including speaking tours by teams consisting of a Protestant,
Roman Catholic and Jew, research projects and the na-
tionwide organization since 1934 of a Brotherhood Week.
The National Conference explicitly rejected charges of
indifferentism. "It strives" (said a statement adopted
in 1949) "for brotherhood in those ways which are acceptable to Protestants, to Catholics, and to Jews—
not on the basis of removing religious differences".[3]
The conference "acknowledges the freedom of the Catholic or the Jew or the Protestant to hold that his faith
is the one true faith. It does not affirm such a holding by any one of the three, for it could obviously do
so only at the expense of the other two—but neither
does it disaffirm. It is not indifferentist, therefore,
it is simply as it must be, non-preferential."[4]

The statement declared that the National Conference did
not sponsor joint worship, exchange of pulpits, or
common observance of Christian and Jewish holy days,
nor did it disapprove such practices on the part of
those who in good conscience participated in them. It
was not an "inter-faith" organization, but rather a
"civic agency" seeking "to promote affirmative co-operative action among Protestants, Catholics and Jews in
areas of common civic concern".[5]

In Britain the story goes back to 1924, when the Social
Service Committee of the Liberal Jewish Synagogue,
feeling that "in spite of serious differences of belief,
Jews and Christians were at one in their desire to bring

nearer the Kingdom of God on earth", consulted some
other religious bodies, set up an organizing committee
and convened a conference intended to provide an opportunity for "Jews and Christians to confer together on
the basis of their common ideals and with mutual respect for differences in belief".[6]  This conference,
on *Religion as an Educational Force,* was held in November, 1924, and aroused so much interest that the *ad
hoc* committee was given a more permanent status and
eventually, in 1927, a Society of Jews and Christians was
established "to promote fellowship and understanding
between Jews and Christians".[7]  The society arranged
various lectures and meetings and a selection of these
were published, under the title *In Spirit and In Truth,*
in 1934.  The activities of the society were viewed
with some suspicion by those who thought they tended
towards religious indifferentism, and there is a defensive note in some of the papers.  Whilst asserting
that there is common ground and that Christians and
Jews need each other, Hewlett Johnson, the then Dean of
Canterbury, in his introduction, made clear that his
Christian commitment was not compromised:  "Christianity is the central point in the wide circle of light
which shines forth from a heavenly Father...I long to
commend to others what I see".[8]  The Christians who
took part were liberal scholars, such as Oliver Quick,
B. H. Streeter, W. R. Matthews, C. C. M. Webb, Charles
Raven and John Oman.  The Jews too were liberal or re-
form, and included Rabbi Mattuck, Rabbi Reinhart,
Claude Montefiore, Lily Montagu, and Herbert Loewe.

Tragic events on the Continent were soon to demand more
than scholarly discussion.  Hitler came to power in
1933 and began to implement anti-semitic policies,
whilst the situation in Palestine was becoming increasingly difficult.  Refugees from Germany started to make
their way to Britain and some Christians tried to help
them, especially the Society of Friends, and a Church
of England committee for non-Aryan Christian Refugees,
set up by George Bell, the Bishop of Chichester.  It
was he who took the lead in setting up the Christian
Committee for Refugees from Germany and Central Europe,
which at first was given hospitality in Gordon Square
by the Save the Children Fund.  It then moved to 20
Gordon Square and, at the beginning of 1939, to Blooms-
bury House, which had formerly been the Palace Hotel.
Jewish organizations were finding it increasingly difficult to cope with the flood of refugees.  Until 1938,
they had not asked about the religious affiliation of
those who came to them for help.  They were aware, how-

ever, that some fifteen per cent of them, while of Jewish birth or descent, were Catholic or Protestant by
religion. In 1938, they approached the churches to
help those who were Christian by religion, and at a
meeting in the Jerusalem Chamber at Westminster, leaders of the Anglican, Free Church and Roman Catholic
churches agreed to support the Christian Council for
Refugees. The Rev. W. W. Simpson was asked to become
an organizer. Lord Baldwin launched a national appeal
on behalf of all refugee organizations.

"Bill" Simpson was at that time the Methodist minister
of Amhurst Park in North London. It was an area which
included much of the Orthodox Hassidic Jewish community
of Stamford Hill. His interest in Judaism had
been aroused earlier. Conscious as a school boy of
Jewish boys who did not fit in, entrusted with the Mandate for Palestine in an inter-school mock Assembly of
the League of Nations, making a close friend of a Jewish student whilst at Cambridge University, the decisive step for him was in 1933.

The authorities of the Methodist Church encouraged him
to devote two years to the study of contemporary Jewish
problems. During the period he was a part-time visiting student at Jews College, a rabbinic seminary in
London. He also made some study of traditional Christian approaches to Jews through missionary societies.[9]
He was well-prepared for his work with the Christian
Council for Refugees and soon afterwards with the Council of Christians and Jews.

Early in the war, Mrs. Kathleen Freeman, a prominent
Anglican lay-leader, and one time president of the
National Council of Women, visited Rabbi Mattuck of the
Liberal Synagogue to discuss ways in which Christians
could promote good relations with their fellow Jewish
citizens. She talked also to Dr. James Parkes, an An-
glican priest and outstanding scholar in the field,
and to Bishop George Bell. They, with the Rev. Henry
Carter, a Methodist who was chairman of the Christian
Committee for Refugees, approached Archbishop William
Temple, who gladly agreed to call together Jewish and
Christian leaders whose support would be necessary.

As a result, in March 1942, a Council of Christians and
Jews was set up "to check and combat all forms of religious and racial intolerance; to promote mutual understanding and goodwill between Christians and Jews in
all sections of the community; to promote fellowship

between Christian and Jewish youth organizations in
educational and cultural activities; and to foster co-
operation between Christians and Jews in social and
community service".[10]   It is significant that the aims
make no reference to anti-semitism.  This was deliberate, because those responsible for setting up the Council took the view that anti-semitism is only one of
many expressions of racial and religious intolerance
which are symptomatic of deeper disorders.  The task of
the Council was to try to remedy these disorders, and
it has devoted itself to the long-term educational
task of removing prejudice.  In this, the journal *Common
Ground* has been especially valuable.  Cardinal Hinsley,
the Archbishop of Canterbury, the Moderator of the
General Assembly of the Church of Scotland, the Moderator of the Free Church Federal Council, and the Chief
Rabbi became the joint Presidents.[11]   This gave the new
body official approval and backing—confirmed later by
the willingness of the Queen to become its Patron.
William Simpson, who had been active in the initial
work, was asked to become Secretary of the new organization.

By the time the Council of Christians and Jews was established, there were similar bodies in South Africa
and Canada.  The South African Society of Jews and
Christians came into existence in the thirties, and
quite independently in 1939 began to publish a journal
called *Common Sense*.  This was intended primarily "to
combat anti-semitism and to foster better understanding
and good will between the Jewish community and its
Christian neighbours", but it soon became clear that
anti-semitism cannot be isolated from other forms of
prejudice and from the economic and social problems of
society.  *Common Sense* therefore developed into a journal devoted to "the combatting of all forms of racial
and group prejudice, the promotion of inter-faith and
inter-cultural education and the fostering of constructive thinking on South Africa's major problems".  After
a time, the publication of this journal became the Society's main work, and eventually even the journal had
to cease publication because of lack of support and a
climate of opinion hostile to its purposes.[12]

Soon, several Jewish-Christian bodies were in existence
and late in 1944, the National Conference of Christians
and Jews in the United States suggested an international conference.  The idea was welcomed by the Council of
Christians and Jews in Great Britain.  Accordingly, a
conference was convened at Lady Margaret Hall, Oxford,

in August,1946, to which all the existing bodies were
invited to send representatives.  To ensure as wide a
representation as possible, individuals from other European countries were also invited.  Eventually 120 people
attended, drawn from 15 countries.  These included
France, Denmark, Czechoslovakia, Palestine, South Africa
and Australia.  Permission was also obtained to allow
Germans to enter the country for the conference.  The
theme chosen was "Freedom, Justice and Responsibility",
and a considerable amount of preparatory work was done
for the conference.  Most of the time at the conference
was spent in six commissions which discussed:

(1) Group Tensions.

(2) Fundamental Postulates of Christianity and
    Judaism in Relation to Human Order.

(3) Religious Freedom.

(4) Justice and its Claims.

(5) Mutual Responsibility in the Community.

(6) Education and Training for Responsible
    Citizenship.

In addition, during the conference, a youth commission
was formed.  The Commission's reports were published; a
resolution was sent to the Paris Peace Conference, and
a Continuation Committee established.

Besides the long term task of strengthening the existing organizations and building up an international council, the committee soon arranged an emergency conference
on the problem of anti-semitism, particularly at the
level of ordinary personal relations.  This was held at
Seelisberg in 1947, and it issued a report—widely known
as the "Ten Points of Seelisberg"—which attracted considerable attention, and which, because of its continuing importance, deserves to be quoted in full.  It
shows the extent to which work in this field has had to
concentrate on clearing away prejudice and misunderstanding.


The "Ten Points"

1.  Remember that One God speaks to us all through the
    Old and the New Testaments.

2.  Remember that Jesus was born of a Jewish mother of

the seed of David and the people of Israel, and
that His everlasting love and forgiveness embraces
His own people and the whole world.

3. Remember that the first disciples, the apostles and
the first martyrs were Jews.

4. Remember that the fundamental commandment of Christianity, to love God and one's neighbour, proclaimed
already in the Old Testament and confirmed by Jesus,
is binding upon both Christians and Jews in all human relationships, without any exception.

5. Avoid distorting or misrepresenting biblical or
post-biblical Judaism with the object of extolling
Christianity.

6. Avoid using the word JEWS in the exclusive sense of
the enemies of Jesus, and the words THE ENEMIES OF
JESUS to designate the whole Jewish people.

7. Avoid presenting the Passion in such a way as to
bring the odium of the killing of Jesus upon all
Jews or upon Jews alone. It was only a section of
the Jews in Jerusalem who demanded the death of
Jesus, and the Christian message has always been
that it was the sins of mankind which were exemplified by those Jews and the sins in which all men
share that brought Christ to the Cross.

8. Avoid referring to the scriptural curses, or the
cry of a raging mob: HIS BLOOD BE UPON US AND OUR
CHILDREN, without remembering that this cry should
not count against the infinitely more weighty words
of our Lord: FATHER, FORGIVE THEM, FOR THEY KNOW
NOT WHAT THEY DO.

9. Avoid promoting the superstitious notion that the
Jewish people are reprobate, accursed, reserved for
a destiny of suffering.

10. Avoid speaking of the Jews as if the first members
of the Church had not been Jews.[14]

In 1948, a further conference was held at Fribourg, and
by now there were joint groups in France, Italy, and in
the American Zone of Germany.

Some of the American leaders were now, however, interested in a broader organization to promote world-wide

fellowship and peace.  In the summer of 1950, they
launched *World Brotherhood*.  A side effect of this was
that instead of an international council of Christians
and Jews developing, international contacts had for the
time being to remain on an informal and unofficial basis.  W. W. Simpson did much to maintain such links and
in 1962, the time was ripe to form an International Consultative Committee of organizations concerned with
Christian-Jewish co-operation.  This group was largely
responsible for convening another international conference at Cambridge in 1966—twenty years after the Oxford conference.  The conference "unanimously condemned
in the most forthright terms all forms of racial and religious bigotry in all parts of the world and stressed
the need for the utmost vigilance and action in the
fields of legislation and education".[15]  The conference
also strengthened the links with the councils in the
USA and Canada, and with the Inter-Faith Committee in
Israel.

The International Consultative Committee has now become
the International Council of Christians and Jews, of
which Mme. Claire Huchet-Bishop is the chairman, and
the Rev. W. W. Simpson, OBE, is secretary.  Member organizations are in Austria, Brazil, Canada, France, Germany,
Holland, Israel, Italy, Luxembourg, Switzerland, Britain, and the USA.  The most recent conference was held
in Jerusalem in June, 1976.

This was a very significant occasion, marking the thirtieth anniversary of the Oxford Conference and being
the first meeting in Jerusalem.  The year before in
mid-June, 1975, a "Holocaust Conference", had been held to
mark the thirtieth anniversary of the freeing of the
concentration camps.  At this, the International Council
of Christians and Jews agreed, in describing the lessons of the Holocaust, that:

    1.   Such carnage must not be allowed to happen
        again, even in a world where violence and
        bloodshed are taken for granted.

    2.   Jews and Christians must speak out in protest
        against any possible recurrence of the Nazi's
        persecutions of the Jewish people.

    3.   Israel, as an independent state in the Middle
        East, must be safeguarded as the most important,
        constructive alternative of the past half-dozen
        years.[16]

The delegates decided that the 1976 meeting in Jerusalem should focus on "Israel: Significance and Realities".

The Jerusalem conference which lasted ten days allowed
considerable opportunity to get to know the country
and its people.  Delegates, for example, visited a reception centre for Jews from the Soviet Union, went to
*Nes Ammim,* a Christian kibbutz, and met the Khadi from
Acco.  There were a number of receptions and addresses,
but delegates spent most of their time in working
groups.[17]

Perhaps the lasting significance of the conference,
meeting for the first time in Israel, was its commit-
ment of the International Council of Christians and
Jews to the existence of the State of Israel.   The
Palestine issue had been carefully avoided at the 1946
Oxford conference, which was attended by Zionists, non-
Zionists and anti-Zionists.  At the Jerusalem conference, there was no doubt about Israel's right to exist,
although as Rev. W. W. Simpson put it, "We vary from
150 per cent pro-Israel to 75 per cent pro-Israel".
The significance of coming to terms with the reality of
Israel was underlined by Dr. Shamaryahu Talmon, of the
Hebrew University, in his address on the final afternoon.  He said that no genuine Christian-Jewish dialogue
was possible without a complete understanding of the
meaning of the experience of Israel.  This experience
was not only of a new national state in the company of
the World's nations, but of a people with a newly
emerged culture with a revivified Judaic content, which
was a unique phenomenon of the twentieth century.

Clearly, Dr. Shamaryahu Talmon was right to say that no
Christian-Jewish dialogue, anywhere in the world, can
be unaffected by the existence of Israel: but the primary emphasis of the various councils of Christians and
Jews has fallen on combatting prejudice  and
uprooting anti-semitism.  Much has also been done to
help both Christians and Jews understand more of each
other's beliefs.  Yet, this has not required of those
involved any assessment of the religious significance
of the other religion, thus allowing orthodox members
of both to share in the work.  Nor has an ideological
commitment to the existence of Israel been required,
thus making possible the participation of those  of
varied political views.  To the extent that the work
of the Council has been to remove prejudice, this is
strictly a necessary preliminary to dialogue, not

dialogue itself.  Not that the aims of the Council of
Christians and Jews are confined to combatting religious and racial intolerance.  They include working
positively together in religious and social fields.
Many of those too involved in the work have also moved
on to dialogue and the Cambridge conferences in particular have been occasions for this.  Even so, because
of the bitter legacy of Jewish-Christian relations, the
task of removing misunderstanding has been dominant.
Many Christians and Jews, who might have been hesitant
about inter-faith activities, have seen the value of
this and there has been evidence of wider support from
orthodox Christians and Jews for this work than for
other inter-faith bodies.


## Inter-Faith in Israel

If Christian-Jewish dialogue everywhere is affected by
the existence of Israel, the situation in Israel must
be seen in its own terms.  Inter-faith activities there
are related to and coloured by the political tensions
and uncertainties.  They are also linked to efforts to foster inter-communal understanding.

Israel, because its population is religiously very mixed
seems an obvious centre for inter-faith dialogue: but
developments have been restricted by features peculiar
to the situation in the country.  "At the beginning of
1975", writes Dr. Spicehandler, of the Hebrew Union College, "there were some 360,000 Jews in Jerusalem—drawn
from over sixty communities from Harbin to San Francisco
from Bokhara to Melbourne; 60,000 Moslems of various
persuasions; and 20,000 Christians representing dozens
of Christian confessions, Roman and Greek Catholic,
Protestants of almost every denomination, Armenians,
Ethiopians, Copts, Greek and Russian Orthodox".[18]  Despite this variety, "It must be admitted that the Holy
Land is an underdeveloped area in matters of inter-
faith and ecumenical relations", writes Dr. Coos Schoneveld, who is Theological Adviser in Jerusalem to the
Netherlands Reformed Church and is Secretary of the
Rainbow Group and the Ecumenical Theological Research
Fraternity.[19]

There are many factors which inhibit dialogue.  Relations between religious groups were formalized and defined by the *millet* system, which derives from the time
of the Arab conquests of the Holy Land.  Whilst the
Arabs reserved a privileged position for themselves,

they allowed a degree of independence to the religious
minorities under their rule.  This was not limited to
matters of liturgy, but included personal and family
rights.  The British, during the Mandate, continued the
system.  The State of Israel, from its inception, established a Ministry of Religions to aid, protect and safeguard the rights of various communities.  Each community
appoints its own ministers, rabbis, or imams, administers
its own property and exercises jurisdiction over its members in matters of marriage, divorce and maintenance.
The system, whilst preserving a limited autonomy for the
communities, also isolates them from each other.  Fr.
Dubois describes the relations of the heads of the communities, Bishops, Rabbis, Imams and Ministers of Government as consisting of "exchanges of courtesy, relations
of strict justice, defense or recognition of rights according to the *status quo*, whose norms Israel has accepted; all this is in short mutual respect and respect
for what Claude Levi-Strauss would have called the syn-
chronistic system with all that makes up tradition and
immobility".[20]

Orthodox Jewish rabbis are not willing to enter into
dialogue with others, although their opposition to dialogue has decreased over the years.  Many Jews came from
Oriental countries, where they escaped Christian "oppression" and have only a peripheral interest in Christianity.  Other Jews, especially from Eastern Europe,
who knew Christian oppression, are glad at last to work
out their own destiny free from Christian pressures and
their primary concern is to give political and social
expression in Israel to the Biblical imperative.  These
other concerns leave little time or energy for dialogue,
and, in any case, only a minority of the population are
religiously observant.  The Jews who are involved in
dialogue are scholars.  Professor Shamaryahu Talmon, of
the Hebrew University, says their "theological involvement is of a nature which more often than not does not
express itself in pastoral activities.  Their motivation
to participate in the dialogue arises out of a historical cultural consciousness, no less, and sometimes more
than out of their religious persuasion".[21]  Mostly they
are of West European or American background.  Their interest springs partly from a desire to ensure that
Christians are aware of the roots and dangers of anti-
semitism and to help gain friends for Israel, and partly
from a historical concern with the origins of Christianity in relation to Judaism.  Hardly any see any relevance of Christianity to their own faith commitment, although a few have a real appreciation of the person of

Jesus. Some Jews are also involved in dialogue more as
social-community workers concerned to build bridges of
understanding between different groups.

Scarcely any Muslims have wished to involve themselves
in inter-faith dialogue. Arab-Israel hostility does
not allow the necessary atmosphere of trust. Indeed,
East Jerusalem Arabs are reluctant even to meet socially with Jews.[22] There is little Muslim leadership.
After the 1948 flight of many Arabs from Israel, "Israel was left with a considerable Arab population, but
an Arab population without intellectuals, because among
those who had left were all the intellectuals".[23] A
new generation of Israeli Arab intellectuals, mostly
born in Israel and educated in Israeli schools and universities, is now growing up, but because of their educational background, they are not in the continuity of Arab
intellectual tradition. Some of these may be willing to
enter into dialogue, but on social and educational,
rather than religious, issues.[24] There is no such possibility amongst Arabs of the occupied territories. In
any case it needs to be remembered that Jerusalem has
not been a centre of Islamic scholarship.

Arab Christians, who are a majority of the indigenous
Christian population, are also reluctant to share in
dialogue. As a minority amongst a minority, they do
not wish to draw attention to what separates them from
their Muslim Arab brothers. They have no history of
dialogue and mostly lack the theological sophistication
of those who would be their partners in dialogue.
Leadership of the churches is seldom in local hands. In
addition, the *lingua franca* for dialogue is English in
which they are not at home. Fr. Elias Chacour, speaking
as an Arab Oriental Christian, observed that English was
only his fourth foreign language and that his mentality,
logic, style, and approach to reality was different to
those who took the lead in dialogue.[25] Even amongst
Western Christians, those who adopt a missionary stance
towards Judaism, have not entered into dialogue. Dr.
Schoneveld says, for example, of the Ecumenical Theological Research Fraternity in Israel that "it has kept
aloof from all who were filled with a missionary zeal
towards the Jewish people".[26]

Only a limited circle of people therefore are engaged
in inter-faith dialogue. The Bahá'ís and the tiny
handful at home in Eastern religions do not make any
noticeable contribution. Dr. Spicehandler is justified
in saying: "Those active in the inter-faith movement

are mainly Western European and American Christians and
Western European and American Jews".  He adds, "The
Christians are almost all clergy, while the Jews are
laymen or non-orthodox clergy".[27]  There are a few exceptions, but this is largely true of the religious
dialogue, although there is a slightly broader base to
the attempts to encourage cultural inter-community
meeting.  Yet despite all these limitations, the inter-
faith dialogue taking place in Israel is varied and of
a high standard, and many warm personal friendships
have been developed.

## Inter-Faith Activities

*The Israel Inter-Faith Committee* was established in
1957 and is composed of representatives of religious
bodies in the country: Jews, Christians (Catholic, Orthodox, Protestant), Muslims and Druze.  The inaugural
meeting was attended by about 100 people.  Professor
Mazar, then President of the Hebrew University, took
the chair.  Greetings were received from many religious
leaders and an address given by Mr. Moshe Sharett.  In
a statement of purposes the group said that "Since the
establishment of Medinat Israel, the question of the
relations between the adherents of Judaism and the adherents of other religions has attained an unprecedent-
ed degree of moral and social significance".  Mentioning the holy places and the moral obligations thereby
imposed on the Israeli government and people, the
group went on to say, "The relations between the majority in Israel and members of other religions in this
sensitive area, constitute a probestone of the human
and spiritual content of Israel's sovereignty and are
likely to have an influence on ties between Israel and
the nations of the world—as well as between Jews and
non-Jews in other countries...The aim of this Council
is to cultivate fellowship and tolerance between religious groups by means of broad educational endeavours
which face up to existing difficulties and which seek
to pave the road to mutual confidence.  The council
will seek to create contacts with similar organizations
abroad".[28]

The movement did not at first make much headway, except
for occasional publications and reception-lectures.
There was no ongoing programme.  Early in the seventies
the committee was reactivated, largely through the
initiative of Professor Werblowsky.  The organization
has a council of some fifty members and a smaller

executive committee and some subcommittees.  There is
an energetic full time secretary, Mr. Joseph Emanuel,
who has some voluntary help.  Finance comes mainly from
supporting religious bodies and from some five hundred
individual members.

There are two main areas of work: amongst inhabitants of
Israel and with visitors to the country.  In Israel the
committee helps to arrange meetings between members of
the various communities.  Those in Jerusalem are more
theological, those in Galilee mainly on cultural matters.
In Tel Aviv there is an affiliated local group, which is
mostly of Jews and Christians, although efforts are being made to involve Muslims.  In Haifa and Acre there
are community centres aimed at social and cultural exchange between Jews and Arabs.  The Haifa centre was
started by and is supported by the municipality.  The
centre in Acre was started by the Inter-Faith Committee.
It is now supported jointly by the municipality and the
government, whilst the Inter-Faith Committee remains a
consultant.  A new centre was opened at Lydda in 1977.

The committee also helps visitors to be aware of the
contemporary religious situation in Israel, by making
arrangements for visiting groups to hear speakers from
the various faiths.  It has arranged, sometimes with
other bodies, important consultations.  In November,1970,
for example, an international colloquium was held on
"Religion, Peoplehood, Nation and Land".  In May,1972, a
congress was held in Jerusalem on "Black Africa and the
Bible", involving African Christians and Jewish and
Christian scholars in Israel.  In 1976,seminars were arranged for clergy and scholars from Spain and, again,
for clergy from Africa.  Increasingly the committee has
become related to growing official international Jewish-
Christian consultations.  In 1970, a Jewish Council in
Israel for Inter-Religious Consultation was formed, to
which all Jewish members of the Inter-Faith Council belong.  Some members of this Jewish council are members
of the International Jewish Committee for Inter-Religious Consultation.  This body is now having regular
meetings with members of the Vatican Commission on Religious Relations with the Jews and of the World Council
of Churches' Committee on Churches and the Jewish People.
In October,1976,a similar meeting was arranged with some
representatives of the Greek Orthodox Church.  In 1976,
consultations with both Vatican and World Council of
Churches  representatives took place in Jerusalem.
These were separate meetings, although the groups came
together informally for a weekend at the religious

Kibbutz Lavi.  Part of the responsibility for the arrangements fell on the Inter-Faith Committee.  Indeed
there is some feeling that its international responsibilities may detract from its local activities.

In 1965, a private group of Jewish and Christian academicians, called the *Rainbow Group,* was established with
Professor Fwi Werblowsky of the Hebrew University as
chairman and Canon Peter Schneider, an Anglican, as
secretary.  Professor Werblowsky has described it as "a
private closed club of self-confessed, unrepentant  intellectuals who meet for theological, intellectual labour, and the Inter-Faith Committee very deliberately
has no intellectual pretensions".[29]  It is composed of
equal numbers of Jews and Christians—making up an
elected and restricted membership, which does not exceed
twenty-five or thirty.  Each month throughout the academic year, theological papers are read, followed by
lively and sometimes controversial discussions.  Some
of the subjects are contemporary, such as *Modern Medicine and Morality.*  The group, writes the present secretary, Dr. Coos Schoneveld, "has come beyond the academic
level and has evolved as a circle of friends, in which
genuine confidence has been reached, so that most discussions no longer divide on merely Jewish and Christian
lines but rather on the particular religious and social
issues involved.  This has, however, not been achieved
because political and other sensitive issues were
shunned.  Rather, the opposite is true.

Difficult crises in Jewish-Christian relations, such as
followed the *Yom Kippur* War, have been overcome within
the Rainbow Group by a completely open and frank discussion of the issues involved".[30]  The membership is varied, including both Orthodox and Liberal Jews of different political viewpoints and Catholics, Protestants and
a Christian Arab.  Relationships are friendly and the
level of discussion is high.  The group is a good example of the possibilities for inter-faith dialogue where
a number of people of similar cultural and intellectual
background, albeit of different faiths, meet regularly
over a period of years.

In addition to the Inter-Faith Committee and the Rainbow
Group, there are a number of Jewish or Christian bodies
much engaged in dialogue, as well as other efforts to
promote understanding between different communities in
Israel.

In 1966, *The Ecumenical Theological Research Fraternity*

*in Israel* was established.  The minutes of the first
meeting show that its objectives were:

  (1) To draw together personnel into a theolog-
      ical fraternity.

  (2) To help the Christian church to understand
      itself in the new situation created by the
      emergence of the state of Israel.

  (3) To deepen the Christian relationship with
      Jews, Judaism and Israel.

It is an ecumenical group, including members of many
Christian denominations, who usually are already  engaged in other ways in Jewish-Christian relations.
Working for a new relationship with Judaism, the group
rejected traditional missionary approaches and saw as
fundamental conditions for its work "a deep respect for
Jewish self-understanding, an attitude of openness towards the spiritual values of Jewry and Judaism in its
new setting in Israel and a preparedness to listen and
to learn".[31]  The fraternity began by using the lecture-
discussion format, with a theme chosen for the year,
such as *The Interpretation of Prophecy*.  In 1973, a
review of the work was held and it was felt that the
meetings had become too much like public lectures.  It
was decided to limit membership, to stress the element
of theological research and to arrange the meetings more
as seminars.  It was decided also to continue to concentrate on Jewish-Christian relations and not to extend to
the study of Islam.  Jewish scholars are often invited
to address the meetings.  The fraternity performs an important service in publishing twice yearly the journal
*Immanuel,* which aims to keep English readers abreast of
current writing in Hebrew on the Hebrew Bible, the New
Testament and Judaism of that period, Jewish-Christian
relations, past and present, and Contemporary Religious
Life and Thought in Israel.

The fraternity relates to the work of the World Council
of Churches Committee on the Church and the Jewish People.  It has issued public statements on important current issues.  During the *Yom Kippur* War, an appeal was
sent to churches around the world.  An eight-page document was prepared in response to the United Nations
resolution which equated Zionism with Racism.  An appeal
has been presented to the government of Israel about
Jewish-Arab relations in Galilee.  The fraternity also
supports a *Student Christian Forum,* to orientate Chris-

tian students, both from Israel and abroad, to religious
and political life in Israel.

There are a number of Christian denominational bodies
concerned to build new relationships with Jews. *St.
Isaiah House,* founded by Father Bruno Hussar, is a centre for Jewish and Israeli studies. The present superior, Fr. Marcel Dubois, lectures at the Hebrew University. *The Swedish Theological Institute, The American
Institute of Holy Land Studies,* the  Fathers of Zion at
*Ratisbone* monastery, *Dormition Abbey* on Mount Zion, and
*The Ecumenical Institute for Advanced Theological Study*
at Tantur are amongst Christian institutions concerned
with this field. *The United Christian Council,* whilst
mainly designed to promote Christian unity, has also
addressed itself to the churches' relationship with
Judaism.

On the Jewish side, the Hebrew University of Jerusalem—
*Martin Buber Centre for Adult Education*—arranges lectures or seminars for visiting Christian and ecumenical
groups. With the Sisters of Zion, it promotes language
courses for Jews and Arabs in the Old City and elsewhere.
The centre itself has become a place of social intercourse. The *American Jewish Committee's* Israel office
helps to arrange conferences for Jewish and Christian
visitors and is active in increasing communication between American and Israeli citizens, in the hope that
this will contribute to peace and reconciliation. *The
World Zionist Organization* (External Relations Department) deals with non-governmental and non-Jewish bodies
abroad, providing systematic information on all aspects
of Israeli life to interested church and inter-faith
groups. The *Hebrew Union College,* a branch of the main
institution in Ohio, which trains students for the Reform or Progressive Rabbinate, has been the setting for
a number of inter-faith seminars.

There are various bodies concerned to promote intergroup understanding. Religious dialogue may not be
their primary aim, but in Israel, religious affiliation
is part of a group's self-identify. *Meditran,* started
in 1971, brings together a diverse membership to show
that Jewish, Muslim  Christian and other communities of
Jerusalem can work together culturally, socially and
economically. There are language courses in Hebrew,
Arabic and English, in which students learn each other's
languages and meet as people. Visits are arranged which
help people to learn about others' ways of life—perhaps
to the home of an Arab family or of a native Sabra. At

the time of the *Yom Kippur* War, forty *Meditran* members
met at a branch of the International Red Cross in the
Old City to donate blood for use by both injured Israeli and Egyptian prisoners.  They then made history
by visiting the wounded of both sides who were recuper-
ating in two Israeli government hospitals.[32]

*Neve Shalom* is intended to be an inter-faith community.
The esssential  idea, as formulated by the community in
November, 1975, is "to be a group of persons:

    (a) Coming from all social strata in Israel and
        neighbouring areas.

    (b) Desiring to live together, either permanently
        or for a limited time, in mutual respect and
        understanding, and in brotherly love.

    (c) Having as purpose:
        1) to participate in the effort of those
        who are working for peace;
        2) to offer a place and to form an environ-
        ment where members as well as guests will
        enrich each other through the diversity of
        their skills, characters and spiritual
        heritages".[33]

The society, which is inspired by Fr. Bruno Hussar, was
registered in 1970.  Some land was leased on a long-
term basis near Latrun from the Trappist Monastery
there.  During the past three years a number of people
have "tried to live the idea" on the site but facilities
are minimal and residents have only been temporary.  It
is hoped, however, that a more permanent settlement will
soon be begun.

At Ein Karem, a suburb of Jerusalem, a *Terra Sancta
Youth Lodge* was set up in 1970 to provide wholesome accommodation for students, with the hope that living together would enable trans-cultural exchange and unstructured communication.  In the summer, in recent
years, Hope Ecumenical Seminars have been held at Ein
Karem to provide an inter-faith experience, primarily
for those from abroad.  In 1977, a series of weekly
lectures and residential weekends were arranged for
local people to foster inter-faith understanding.

At Abu Gosh, *The Society of Friends of the Youth of Abu
Gosh* brings together Jews, Muslims and Christians to
provide facilities for young people in the village and

to promote extracurricular activities. Lessons in Hebrew and courses in folklore and music are provided in
the village and educational visits arranged to many
parts of the country. Activities with Jewish youth in
the neighbourhood are also organized. The *Spaffords
Childrens' Playground* in the economically deprived
Saadieh quarter of the Old City has a board of directors
which includes Jews, Christians and Muslims. Besides
providing play facilities in the area, field trips to
other parts of the country are arranged. Within the
*Histadruth* (trade unions), too, there are various activities which bring together Jews and Arabs.

At *Nes Ammim*, near Haifa, a Christian village was formed
to seek to identify with Israel. Its aim is "to serve
Israel with investment, economic initiative and techni-
cal know-how. The desired outcome of this project, in
human and moral terms, should be the experience of Israelis that there exists a genuinely Christian attitude
of goodwill, service and profound respect for Jewry and
Judaism; and a more concrete experience by Christians
of the realities, values and problems of Jewish life
and creative efforts in Israel".[34] When it started in
1963, there were ten adults and two children. Now there
are over eighty, many from Holland. The day of rest is
the Sabbath and the pattern of life is closely related
to the Jewish. At first there were objections. Nearby
villagers wanted the land and water. Religious Jewish
organizations feared proselytism, but a definite guaran-
tee was given that missionary work would not be allowed.
This, in turn, brought objections from conservative
Christian groups. The village, however, thrives and
contributes to the economy particularly by its rose-
growing for the European market. It also provides lectures for many visiting groups. It has difficulty in
attracting residents willing to stay for a long period
and seems still a little isolated from the life of
Israel

Another group, *Aktion Sühnezeichen*, consists of young
Germans working in Israel to atone for Nazi crimes. Led
by Pastor Michael Krupp, they engage in charitable projects.

In Galilee, at *Lavre Netofa* is a hermitage, founded by
Albuna Ya'akov Willebrands. Fr. Willebrands aims to
bring about an appreciation of Judaism, Christianity
and Islam amongst Arabs and Israelis and to revive Eastern monasticism. Fr. Murray Rogers in 1972 transplanted
his ashram *Jyotiniketan* from India to the Old City of

Jerusalem and has made his home, in an informal way,
another inter-faith meeting point.  Through his evenings
"Facing East", he has helped to introduce some awareness
of Indian religions to the Israeli inter-faith scene.

Quite different is *Yat Shimonah,* set up by millenialist
Christians from Finland, who see in the in-gathering of
the exiles a sign of the End.

It is clear that many inter-faith gatherings and meetings across community boundaries and involving visitors
from abroad are taking place in Israel.  They occur at
various levels; some with a high degree of theological
sophistication, some for the simple enjoyment of meeting people from different backgrounds.  All in their
own way help to build up human understanding which is
a necessary prerequisite for lasting peace.  No one
knows, however, whether international politics will allow time and space for what is still a tender plant to
grow and blossom.  Because encouraging as is all the
work of dedicated people, the limitations to inter-community meeting are still very real.  On a few occasions,
some from various communities have come together to
pray for peace, but there is still need for considerable
growth in understanding and trust before much common
action is possible.


The Issues

Jewish-Christian dialogue in Israel is conditioned by
two events.  The tragedy of the Holocaust and the re-
birth of the Jewish nation.[35]  "The first impetus",
writes Professor Shemaryahu Talmon of the Hebrew University, "to initiate inter-faith meetings between Jews and
Christians was given in the early post-second world war
years by the experience of the Holocaust.  The perpetra-
tion of the most horrible crimes in all history propelle‹
Jews and Christians into an endeavour to analyze the
psychological, social and theological factors which had
made possible the indescribable events of the war years.
Jews had to discover for themselves to what degree a
meaningful, renewed co-existence with Christians was yet
possible.  Their endeavour was complemented by the heart‹
searching of conscientious Christians in the western
world, who on their part scanned their own past as individuals and analyzed basic tenets of Christianity in the
attempt to diagnose the theological-historical roots of
anti-semitism, aiming at conceiving ways and means of
interpretation and self-education, which would safeguard

Christians and Jews—indeed safeguard humanity—from the very possibility of another such hellish debacle".[36] "The founding of the state of Israel in 1948", he continues, "introduced a new dimension into the dialogue situation. For many Jews and Christians, the major issue of dialogue soon became                     on the Israeli Jew and on Jewry in the State of Israel. This shift could best be discerned in the direction which the dialogue took in post-war Germany. Wittingly or unwittingly, the Christian-Jewish encounter became pinpointed on the encounter of the new, or supposedly new, Germany with the sovereign State of Israel".[37]

It was nearly two decades after the war before the Christian churches began to make official pronouncements about relations with the Jews.  Those individual Christians, however, who made the first approaches to dialogue with Jews in Israel were indeed conscious of the burden of Christian guilt for anti-semitism, which had so recently and so violently expressed itself.  The sense of guilt seems to have been more strongly felt by Christians with a Continental, rather than an Anglo-Saxon, background.  If some of these pioneers may have tended to over-compensate, they had also to justify their attempts to build a new Christian theology of Judaism to their fellow Christians.

Jewish confidence in Christian repentance was almost destroyed by the Six Day War.  The silence of Christians during the war and their seeming unconcern over Israel's fate disillusioned Jewish partners in dialogue.  The experience, however, convinced those Christians who were involved that the question of the Land was central to Jewish self-understanding.  They had previously tended to think of Judaism as a "religion" which could be separated from the political realities.  "What we all supposed at first to be an essentially religious undertaking, i.e. the renovation of the Jewish Christian relationship," wrote Canon Peter Schneider at the time, "has become in the post-1967 Jerusalem situation of a significant Arab-Christian and Arab-Muslim minority a challenge to engagement in the Arab-Israel conflict".[38] Dr. Hartman, a Jewish scholar, put it like this: "Christianity could have come to terms with the existence of the Jewish people in Tel Aviv—Tel Aviv could be disposed of as a manifestation of Zionist, secular, political nationalism.  But when the Jews came back to Jerusalem, Judaism was back as a living force in history".[39]

The silence of Christians outside Israel at the time of

the *Yom Kippur* War was another disillusionment to Jewish
partners in dialogue, eased a little by support from
some Christians within Israel.  Yet even most Western
Christians within Israel tended to adopt a mediating position, in the hope that they could be go-betweens and
agents of reconciliation, whereas Jews noticed that
Christians in other Middle Eastern countries identified
themselves with their governments' policies.  The experi
ences of the Six-Day and *Yom Kippur* Wars leave Jewish
dialogue partners unconvinced of the depth of Christian
concern for Israel and suspicious that anti-semitism may
still be latent.  To Christians of a younger generation,
especially from outside Europe, who do not feel person-
ally guilty for the Holocaust, Jewish insistence upon it
may be counter-productive.  They ask, "How long must we
feel guilty?", and may suspect that it is being used to
gain political capital for the State of Israel.  They
are impatient for the past to be forgotten.  Yet forgiveness cannot be compelled, but must be awaited with
patience.  Besides, as Ezra Spicehandler says, "the bitter memories of centuries and the recent memory of the
Holocaust, have deeply scarred the Jewish mentality and
the scar cannot be removed in one generation".[40]  The
theological task, however, of how still to believe in a
righteous God in the face of such evil, remains—and it
is a task which will require thinkers of both faiths to
share their deepest insights.

For Christians in Israel it was a new experience to find
themselves in a minority in a Jewish State—even if in
world terms, they were still part of a large majority.
The rhythm of life is articulated by the Sabbaths and
the great Jewish festivals.  Most Christians from abroad
came to visit the holy places and on the whole they
took little interest in contemporary inhabitants of the
land.  Others were concerned to learn more of Christian
origins and of the Bible which took shape in the Holy
Land.  They found themselves sharing scholarly interests
with Jewish academics.  For some, the continued existence
of the Jewish people was a theological anachronism, but
others have become involved in Jewish-Christian dialogue
Other Christians again have been primarily concerned to
work out a new Christian theological understanding of
relationships to Israel and Judaism.[41]

In the attempt to do so, they have had to take seriously the significance of the Land of Israel in Jewish
self-understanding.  To the Jews, the existence of a
Jewish state in Israel is obedience to the promise of
God.  "Israel", says Dr. Hartman, "is not only the

creation...of twentieth century Zionism...Israel is the
creation of hundreds of generations of Jewish mothers
who taught their children to dream of Jerusalem".[42] The
people may have been exiled from the land, but never
abandoned it. Throughout the centuries a remnant remained on the soil. The in-gathering is incomplete but
there is a strong sense that the historic existence of
Israel has more significance than mere survival and
self-preservation.

The importance of the land to Jews bears upon Jewish-
Christian dialogue, because Christians until recently
have tried to approach Jews solely as adherents of a
religious faith—and dialogue experience with Diaspora
Jews might confirm this. Jews in Israel resist this,
insisting that their dialogue partners recognize the
national dimension of their identity. Professor Talmon,
for example, has said that his faith commitment cannot
be separated from his Jewishness, and that commitment
to the land of Israel is a component of his Jewishness.
Yet once this issue is raised, Christians begin to
think in political terms and to discuss possibilities
for a peaceful reconciliation of the Middle East conflict. The significance of the land for Jews, however,
is prior to questions of boundaries and government policy. As Dr. Spicehandler explains, Christians must be
ready to recognize the right of a Jewish state and a
Jewish people to exist. This recognition, he adds,
"does not mean that anyone should be obliged to give a
blanket approval to the Israeli government and agree
with all its political decisions, right or wrong".[43]

Whilst most Christians in Israel would now recognize
the right of Israel to exist, their enthusiasm may be
less wholehearted than their Jewish partners would wish.
Partly this is because the universalist tendency of much
Christian thought makes it unsympathetic to nationalism.
Partly it results from the ambiguity of Jewish-Israeli
identity. To what extent is Israel a Jewish state? In
some ways the issues would be clearer if it were either
a religiously orthodox Jewish theocracy or an entirely
secular state. In accepting the religious significance
of Israel to a Jew, a Christian has to think in a way
to which he is not accustomed. Christians may also have
difficulties because of their concern for human rights.
If they express sympathy for Palestinian aspirations
and express criticism of Israeli military occupation,
this may be heard as anti-semitism.

There is therefore an unevenness in the dialogue situa-

tion, as the partners meet with different concerns and
expectations.  As Rabbi Henry Siegman, of America, has
said, Christians cannot avoid the truth question posed
by the continued existence of Judaism, whereas the Jew
is interested "because of obsession with history and
concern for present and future survival".[44]  As scholars
Christians and Jews may work together on historical,
linguistic and Biblical studies; but when contemporary
issues are treated, this is still a time of explanation
which, it is hoped,will lead to mutual trust and understanding.  Jewish partners are conscious that only very
few Christians have begun to enter into Jewish self-
understanding,whilst the Christians who are involved
have still to work out a theology of Judaism.  Those
who recognize the continuing validity of God's covenant
with the children of Israel enable Jews to know that
they are accepted as equals.  This provides a basis
for common exploration and action.  Many Christians,
however, who are concerned with Jewish relations are
primarily concerned with this as a Christian theological
issue, which means that Jews remain actors in someone
else's salvation history.  The development of international official Christian-Jewish discussions may in
fact serve to polarize Christians and Jews, whereas the
participation of both in multi-faith meetings—insofar
as this is possible—may allow them to discover their
common,God-given humanity.  Members of the same family
sometimes behave better when friends are present.  In
Israel itself it may be unstructured,informal meetings
and the growth of genuine friendships across religious
divisions that offer more hope than "organized" dialogue, in which vested ecclesiastical and political interests may inhibit freedom and openness.


## International Consultations

     Jewish Structures.  The development in the last dec-
ade of official international contacts between Judaism
and the churches has been rapid.  This has necessitated
the creation of a special Jewish structure for this purpose.  No such structure existed in 1965,at the time of
the first Jewish-World Council of Churches (WCC) meeting
and it was felt that Jewish representation at the meeting was limited.  In 1969,the World Jewish Congress and
the Synagogue Council of America agreed to co-operate
and act jointly in the field of Jewish-Christian relations vis-à-vis representative bodies of the Christian
churches.  They formally established the International

Jewish Committee on Inter-Religious Consultations
(IJCIC) and invited other bodies to join.  The American
Jewish committee accepted the invitation in March, 1970,
while the B'nai B'rith Anti-Defamation League and, shortly afterwards, the Jewish Council in Israel for Inter-
Religious Relations formally became members of the International Committee in 1973.  It is this body, IJCIC,
widely representative of world Judaism, which relates
to the Vatican, the WCC, and to Christian denominations.

The World Council of Churches.  Already at its
first general assembly in Amsterdam in 1948, the WCC,
meeting in the aftermath of the second World War and
the Holocaust, showed its concern for the Jewish question.  It declared that "to the Jews our God has bound
us in a special solidarity linking our destinies together in His design".[46]  It condemned all anti-semitism
as unchristian.  "We have failed to fight with all our
strength the age-old disorder of man which anti-semitism
represents.  We call upon all the churches to denounce
anti-semitism as absolutely irreconcilable with the
Christian faith.  Anti-semitism is sin against God and
man".[47]  Individual churches only acted gradually on
this and the condemnation of anti-semitism was repeated
at subsequent assemblies of the WCC at Evanston (1954)
and New Delhi (1961).

The Amsterdam Assembly, meeting just after the emergence
of the State of Israel, also referred to the Middle East
situation.  It spoke of Jews as neighbours and contem-
poraries and encouraged Christians "to pray and work
for an order in Palestine as just as may be in the midst
of our human disorder".[48]  Detailed study of current
anti-semitism and of Jewish-Christian co-operation in
civic and social affairs in relation to the State of Israel was called for.  This was of greater concern to
Christians in Europe and North America than to many in
Asia or Africa who did not see that contemporary Judaism
was of much significance to the Christian faith.  If
anything, they tended to be hostile to Israel, seeing
it as an extension of Western imperialism.

In 1962, informal discussion began between some Jewish
leaders and members of the WCC about the possibility of
a joint consultation.  This was eventually arranged at
the Ecumenical Institute at Bossey in August, 1965, and
was jointly organized by the WCC and the Synagogue
Council of America.  Discussion centered on common social concerns, rather than theological problems.  The
general theme was *The Situation of Man in the World*

*Today.* The report emphasized that "the Jewish people
have often preserved truths of the revelation of God
through the Old Testament to which Christians have often been blind. In particular Judaism has an abiding
message for the Church in its stress on the revelations
through the Law and the Prophets, that God is Lord over
every realm of life, material as well as spiritual". [49]

Despite intentions expressed at the consultation, there
was no quick follow-up. The WCC's interest, however,
was shown in the study on *The Church and the Jewish
People,* jointly undertaken by the Faith and Order Commission and the Committee on the Church and the Jewish
People. This study said that "Christians and Jews are
rooted in the same divine history of salvation" and
that on-going encounter with Jews could mean a "real
enrichment of our faith". Christians were encouraged
to take every opportunity of social co-operation and
theological discussion. The word "dialogue" with Jews
was used for the first time in a WCC document and was
defined. "Such conversation", the study says, "should
be held in a spirit of mutual respect and openness,
searching together and questioning one another, trust-
ing that we together with the Jews will grow into a
deeper understanding of the revelation of the God of
Abraham, Isaac and Jacob. What form this further understanding may take,we must be willing to leave in His
hands, confident that He will lead both Jews and Christians into the fullness of His Truth". [50] This so-called
"Bristol" document was not discussed at the Fourth Assembly of the WCC at Uppsala.

Even so, in June,1968, representatives of Jewry and of
the WCC met again in Geneva for a consultation. It re-
viewed the development of Christian-Jewish relations
since the 1961 assembly and tried to define areas of
common concern in such fields as economic and social
justice, international peace and security,and human
rights. It was agreed that such meetings should take
place periodically and that there should be a permanent
exchange of views. A small group was asked to plan and
arrange for future consultations.

Another consultation was held at Geneva in May,
1969. The main issues considered were Jerusalem in Jewish and Christian traditions and religious education and prejudice. A report was given on a
meeting of some Christians and Muslims. The next consultation was again at Geneva in February,1970, with
emphasis on current issues. It was agreed to put

the consultations on a more permanent basis and a small
steering committee, with five Jews and five Christians,
was set up.  In October of the same year, a consultation
on *The Quest for World Community: Jewish and Christian
Perspectives* was held in Lugano.

In April, 1972, a smaller group met to prepare for the
next consultation, held at Geneva in December, 1972.  At
this the topic *Quest for World Community* was pursued
and the papers were subsequently published.  Current
issues, such as racism in Southern Africa, human rights
in the Soviet Union, and the Middle-East conflict were
also raised.  The pattern of alternating smaller and
larger meetings has since continued to a two-year cycle.
In 1975, a meeting was held in London on *The Concept of
Power in Jewish and Christian Traditions*.  In 1976, the
WCC-IJCIC meeting was in Jerusalem, a significant venue.
Rather than discuss a specific topic, time was spent in
evaluating the past decade of co-operation.  A report
on the WCC Nairobi assembly was given and there was relief that the WCC had not followed the UN in equating
Zionism with racism.  Jewish members expressed disappointment that the WCC had not published guidelines
similar to those of the Vatican.  The difficulties of
such an enterprise were explained.  It was suggested
that future exploration might centre on *Christian and
Jewish Traditions about Creation in Relation to Science
and Technology.*

The WCC has also been concerned about the Middle East
political situation, partly through the Commission of
Churches on International Affairs as well as through
the Committee on the Church and the Jewish People. From
1971 to 1974, a study on *Biblical Interpretation and its
Bearing on Christian Attitudes Regarding the Middle East*
was conducted.  To prepare for the discussion of this,
a pre-consultation was arranged by the Ecumenical Theological Research Fraternity in Israel, so that the views
of Jewish scholars and Arab Christians could be heard.

Some Jewish scholars have also been invited to take
part in multi-lateral consultations arranged by the WCC.
Three Jews from Israel attended the gathering in Sri
Lanka in 1974.

   Roman Catholics.  The Second Vatican Council, and
in particular its decree *Nostra Aetate* of 1965, marks the
beginning of a new relationship of the Roman Catholic
Church with the Jewish people.  In September, 1960, Pope
John XXIII, moved by the secular sufferings of the Jews

and by the share of responsibility of Catholics in
those sufferings, asked Cardinal Augustine Bea, President of the Secretariat for the Unity of Christians,
to prepare a text on relations between the Church and
the Jewish people for submission to the Ecumenical
Council. The text, which came to be included in the
Declaration on the attitude of the Church to non-Christian religions, met with considerable opposition and
underwent various changes, which weakened it, before
it was passed. Even so, it marked the beginning of a
new era.[51] For it recognized the Church's relationship
to its Jewish origins, declared that the Jews should
not be presented as rejected by God or accursed, asked
for care in Christian teaching and decried all hatred
and displays of anti-semitism.[52] It said nothing about
Judaism or the State of Israel and did not express pen-
itence for the Church's share in the sufferings of the
Jews.

Despite the decree, the Vatican still does not give *de
jure* recognition to the State of Israel. This is partly because of a general policy to avoid recognition of
a state which is at war or whose frontiers have not received international approval. There is also a concern
for churches in Arab states and for relations with the
world of Islam. The Vatican, too, continues to have
theological reservations, even if these are not openly
expressed. "Following religious sources, as tradition-
ally expounded", writes Fr. Marcel Dubois, "the Church
cannot recognize the Return to Zion. This is further
complicated by the problem of the refugees. And oddly
enough, the conservatives in the Church are here at one
with radical leftist movements".[53]

Even so there is a measure of *de facto* recognition.
Pope Paul visited the Holy Land in 1964, although the
visit disappointed Israeli hopes. After the Six Day
War, he sent a special emissary, Msgr. Angelo Felici,
to discuss with the Israeli authorities the status of
the Holy Places and of the Christian communities. Yet
when Fr. Pierre de Contenson, Executive Secretary of
the Commission for Judaism, said in Jerusalem in 1976
that the frequent contacts amounted to a "kind of recognition", his remarks were quickly repudiated by the
Vatican.

Although Vatican relations with the State of Israel are
still unresolved, there has been growing Vatican contact with world Jewry. In 1969, an informal meeting
with some Jewish scholars was held near Rome. Early in

1970, Pope Paul VI set up a liaison committee, which has had a series of meetings with IJCIC. Yet at first,because of lack of relations with Israel, the little Hebrew speaking church in Israel was not even told of the existence of the committee. Catholic-IJCIC meetings have been held at Marseilles (1973), Antwerp (1974), Rome (1975), where Jewish delegates were received by the Pope, and, very significantly, in Jerusalem in 1976.

In October, 1974, the Pope established the Vatican Commission on Religious Relations with Judaism, with Cardinal Willebrands as president and Fr. Pierre-Marie de Contenson, O.P., as secretary. Interestingly, within a month of his appointment, Fr. de Contenson visited Israel. In December of the same year, the commission issued *Guidelines and Suggestions for Implementing the Conciliar Declaration 'Nostra Aetate'.*

Eighteen months before, in an important development, the French bishops had issued a declaration on Relations with Judaism, which went some way beyond *Nostra Aetate*. Recognizing the importance to Christians of the continued existence of the Jewish people, it affirmed the significance of *Nostra Aetate,* which should be looked upon "as a beginning rather than an end".[54] The Jewish people could not be regarded as one religion amongst the "world religions". It was through the people of Israel that monotheism became the shared legacy of Judaism, Christianity and Islam. "Even if, for Christianity, the Covenant is renewed in Jesus Christ, Judaism must be regarded by Christians as a reality that is not merely social and historical, but primarily religious, not as a relic of a venerable antiquated past, but as a living reality for all time".[55] This forces Christians to ask "What is the precise mission of the Jewish people in the Divine plan?"[56] The Declaration urges Christians to stop picturing Jews in terms of old clichés and says it is wrong to hold the Jewish people responsible for the passion and death of Jesus Christ. "It is a fallacy to set Judaism as a religion of fear against Christianity as a religion of love".[57] Contrary to widely held opinions, it must be asserted that the doctrine of the Pharisees is not the reverse of Christianity".[58] In the fifth section on *Teaching a Just Understanding of Judaism,* Christians are encouraged to acquire a true and living knowledge of Jewish traditions. It goes on to say that, "Beyond the legitimate diversity of political options, the universal conscience cannot deny the Jewish people, which has undergone so many vicissitudes in the course of its history, the right and the means to its

own political being among the nations",[59]—even though
the process of return has left some others the victims
of serious injustice. The Declaration then urges a
better understanding of Judaism and respect for the Jew
at all times, "whatever his way of being a Jew". Encouraging dialogue, it says that "the Jewish people, as
a nation, was the object of an "Eternal Covenant" without which the "New Covenant" itself would have no being
Therefore, far from envisaging the disappearance of the
Jewish community, the Church realizes itself as in ques
of a living link with it. Whilst recognizing the present validity of both Israel and the Church, the Declara
tion suggests they are bound together in God's ultimate
plan.

The Declaration had a mixed reception. Warmly welcomed
in some Jewish circles, it was attacked by some Roman
Catholics. Like *A Short Statement to our Fellow Christians,* prepared by an ecumenical study group of America
theologians in 1973, or the *Declaration of the Synod of
the Archdiocese of Vienna on Christian Attitudes to
Jews and Judaism,* it asserted that the Jewish people
had not been deprived of its election by the New Covenant even if it did not spell out the nature of Israel's
continuing vocation.

The Vatican Guidelines are more cautious. Referring to *Nostra Aetate* as an "important milestone", they
underline the condemnation of all forms of anti-semitisr
and discrimination. Because the two religions are so
closely linked, Christians "must strive to acquire a better knowledge of the basic components of the religious
tradition of Judaism, they must strive to learn by what
essential traits the Jews define themselves in the
light of their own religious experience".[60] The first
section deals with dialogue, which "demands respect for
the other as he is, above all respect for his faith and
his religious convictions".[61] Yet a missionary intention remains, even if it is subdued. Friendly talks
and mutual study are encouraged and the possibility of
praying together is envisaged. The second section
treats of liturgy and the approach to Biblical and
liturgical texts and the continuity of the Christian
faith with the earlier Covenant is stressed. The third
section deals with teaching and education and discour-
ages wrong views of Judaism and its relationship to
Christianity. The fourth section discusses joint social
action and the conclusion encourages bishops to see how
best to implement the guidelines and mentions the creation of the Commission for Religious Relations with the

Jews, joined to the Secretariat for Promoting Christian
Unity.

The Guidelines were an important subject of discussion
at the Catholic-IJCIC meeting in Jerusalem in 1976.
The consultation started under a cloud, because at a
recent Catholic-Islamic consultation in Libya, the Vatican delegation consented to statements on Zionism, the
Palestinians and Jerusalem that were resented in Israel.
The Vatican subsequently dissociated itself from these
statements; and after explanations by the Catholic partners, the consultation continued according to the agenda that had been previously agreed.  Time was spent in
reviewing ten years of Catholic-Jewish relations.  Rabbi Siegman, in welcoming the Guidelines, said that the
theological dimension of the Jewish relationship to
the Land of Israel had still not been dealt with nor
the Christian responsibility for anti-semitism acknowledged.  Yet in the "condemnation" of anti-semitism in
all forms, in the call for fruitful co-operation in social action, in recognizing that Judaism  did not end
with the destruction of Jerusalem, and in the admission
of the viability and vitality of Jewish tradition, the
document marks an important advance on *Nostra Aetate.*


## Conclusion

1976 is somethong of a watershead in Jewish-Christian
relations.  Both the WCC and Catholic delegations met
with the IJCIC in Jerusalem  for the first time, the
International Council of Christians and Jews held their
conference there and the IJCIC held their first meeting
with representatives of the Orthodox Churches.  A structure for regular consultations is now established.

The discussions of each group have their own characteristics.  The ICCJ  was free from the restrictions which
necessarily had to be imposed upon the official discussions of established bodies.  The meetings were in public, with attendances of over one hundred; whereas the
official discussions were limited to quite small groups
held in private.  There is a difference also between
the WCC and Catholic groups, as Professor Talmon has
explained.  "The WCC, because of its heterogeneous composition, cannot proceed in the same way as the official
representatives of the Roman Catholic Church.  Yet, besides these structural differences, I have come to realize increasingly of late that representatives of the
WCC are assuming an ever-more pronounced political

stance. The concept of liberation theology, and a new
interest in social problems, which inevitably acquire
a political orientation, and above all, the white race's
sense of guilt towards the Third World, introduce a tone
which is quite distinct from that of discussion with the
Roman Catholic Church".[62]

Christians seem to be moving towards certain agreed positions. There is almost universal condemnation of
anti-semitism, although sometimes seen as a particular
evil, sometimes as one manifestation of the abuse of
human rights. In varying degrees,Christians from the
West accept their share of responsibility for the hor-
rors of the Holocaust and insist that Christian teaching in the future must avoid condemnation of the Jews,
who are not to be held guilty of deicide. The Jewish
roots of the Christian faith and the fact that Jesus
was a Jew are recognized.

There is growing acceptance of the right of the State
of Israel to exist. Much time has been spent at consultations in Christians trying to come to terms with the
Jewish self-understanding of the significance of the
Land. It is recognized that the desire for a Jewish
state is integral to Judaism. The principle has, however, to be related to political realities. There is
the particular problem that the Vatican does not recognize the State of Israel. Most Christians are sensitive to the aspirations of the Palestinians, to the sufferings of the refugees, and to the fear of further conflict in the Middle East. Jews in Israel perhaps accept
the political necessity of the use of force a little
more easily than do many Western Christians today. Less
creditably, the churches may also be subject to anti-
Zionist pressures in the Third World. In effect, whilst
accepting the right of Jews to a Jewish state in Israel
Christians are equivocal in their attitudes to the actual State of Israel and her policies.

Thirdly, there is widespread use by Christians of the
word "dialogue". This at least implies the willingness
to accept the Jew as he is and to listen to his own self
understanding. Does it imply the abandonment of any
missionary hope to convert the Jew? The International
Council of Christians and Jews' conference said that
"dialogue must be based on unqualified respect for the
integrity of the other party, free from any proselytizing intention and directed solely towards improving
mutual understanding".[63] The Vatican Guidelines, having
said that "dialogue demands respect for the other as he

is; above all, respect for his faith and his religious
convictions", continues: "In virtue of her divine mission and her very nature, the Church must preach Jesus
Christ to the world (*ad Gentes 2*). Lest the witness of
Catholics to Jesus Christ should give offence to Jews,
they must take care to live and spread their Christian
faith while maintaining the strictest respect for religious liberty in line with the teaching of the Second
Vatican Council (Declaration *Dignitatis Humanae*). They
will likewise strive to understand the difficulties
which arise for the Jewish soul—rightly imbued with
an extremely high, pure notion of the divine transcen-
dence—when faced with the mystery of the incarnate
Word".[64] It is not surprising, therefore, that "Jews
are still on their guard against the possibility that
Christianity still assumes that missionary purpose which
we know is part and parcel of the Christian heritage".[65]

The ambiguous use of the word "dialogue" reflects the
debate within Christianity on its relation to other
world religions and the unresolved theological issue of
its understanding of Judaism. Professor Zwi Werblowsky,
in an address to the Council of Christians and Jews in
London in 1973, suggested that there were three dominant approaches. "There is one which denies any special
status to the Jews. Judaism *post Christum* has no special claims, and should be viewed theologically (which
is not the same as historically) like any other non-
Christian, or possibly like any other monotheistic, religion. Others would claim a very special character
for the Jewish-Christian relationship, but this is still
a far cry from asserting equal validity for a complemen-
tarity of covenants. Moreover, confusion easily arises
between a historical uniqueness and dignity attributed
to the Jews (e.g., as God's originally chosen people,
the original recipients of the promise and the blessing,
the people from which Christ came according to His humanity) and a theological affirmation of the continued
validity of Judaism. Others, again, would even go so
far as to speak of equal and complementary covenants",
a view associated, especially in England, with the name
of James Parkes.[66] Those who see Judaism as one amongst
the world's religions will adopt a missionary or dia-
logical position, depending on their view of the relationship of Christianity to other religions. The second
group, who recognize a special relationship, believe
that the former Covenant will eventually be absorbed by
or perfected through the new Covenant. Whilst perhaps
eschewing a missionary approach at the present time,
the hope that in God's time the Jews will recognize

Jesus as Messiah is retained.  The third group, which
speaks of equal or complementary covenants, would suggest that one Word of God to Jews became Torah and to
Christians became flesh.  The two religions are as sisters with, until the eschaton, their own vocations.

Whilst the Christian theological understanding of Judaism is unresolved, the Jewish attitude to dialogue will
remain defensive.  The Jewish interest is far more
practical and immediate.  As Professor Talmon has said,
"The main interest for us as Jews must lie in the fact
that our Christian partners become channels for us to
reach out to Christian authorities and to Christian
communities on all levels, so that they may communicate
to Christians how Jews want to be identified, and make
them sensitive to our problems and concerns".[67]  The
chief Rabbis of Israel, in a new move of receiving WCC
and Vatican delegations, made clear that dialogue must
be on a human and not a theological level.  Yet the
stress on practical concerns can make inter-faith activities appear to serve the public relations interests
of the State of Israel.

In a discussion, Fr. Bernard Dupuy, Secretary of the
French Bishops' Committee for Religious Relations with
the Jews, said, "Jews rightly demand of Christians that
they come to an adequate understanding of Jewish identity, of the significance of Jewish peoplehood, of the
return to the Land, and so on.  On the other hand, we
Christians are engaged in dialogue because we have the
same roots as the Jews and we seek to return to those
roots.  Our demand on the Jews would be not to keep at
such a distance from our search".  To this, Dr. Franz
von Hammerstein of the WCC commented, "We should not
think in terms of demands, but rather of a common search
for a new spirituality.  As Jews and Christians we
should engage in studying together issues of common concern".[68]  These remarks highlight the fact that Jews
and Christians have entered into discussions with different concerns and expectations.  This is now being
recognized, and in a decade of meetings a great deal
more has been learned about each partner, although there
is still more to learn.  The question for the future is
whether there is a desire to seek together for common
goals.  Whilst there may not be a desire to search together for a deeper spirituality or pursue theological
questions, there seems to be the wish to continue historical studies and together to combat prejudice and
face common social issues.  On social and moral matters,
besides the exchange of views, there are the beginnings
of common action.[69]

# CHAPTER SEVEN

# CHRISTIANS AND MUSLIMS

The relationship of Christians and Muslims has at times, especially during the Crusades, been as bitter as that of Christians and Jews. In this century, scholars have helped members of both religions to a truer understanding of each other. In the last decade, there has been the beginning of official discussions between Muslims on the one hand and representatives of the Vatican or the World Council of Churches on the other.

The first Christian-Muslim meeting, initiated by the World Council of Churches, was held at Cartigny, near Geneva, in 1968, in which twenty-two people took part. The aide-mémoire, prepared at the end, stressed the need for Christians and Muslims to meet, discussed what the two religions have in common, looked at the questions which the modern world poses for both religions, and considered the nature and tasks of dialogue.

Although Christians and Muslims both took part in the multi-lateral dialogue at Ajaltoun in 1970, the next bi-lateral meeting was not until 1972 at Broumana. Forty-six people attended, almost equally from the two religions. They came from twenty countries. The memorandum, after mentioning the reasons for meeting and considering the hopes for and guiding principles of dialogue, summarizes what was discovered at the meeting. The responsibility of Christians and Muslims to achieve inter-racial, inter-cultural and international community, and to be concerned for society was agreed. It was felt that the concept of revelation in both religions should be studied more carefully.

The question of sharing in each other's devotions, which is not often mentioned in reports, was also discussed. "Where Muslims and Christians meet together we are not only listening to each other, but we are listening to God. On occasion, therefore, Christian and Muslim individuals or groups may also express their mutual understanding and trust in opening themselves to each other's devotional idiom, notably of *dua*, of supplication and

143

meditation. Though conscious of our real and imagined
differences in such actual or vicarious spiritual part-
nership, and though anxious to avoid misleading others,
some of us felt that it was feasible to attempt this
kind of interpenetration of mutual recognition and re-
sponsiveness to God".[1]

The reports of two regional gatherings, one held at
Legon, Ghana, in July, 1974, and the other at Hong Kong
in January of the next year, are particularly interesting, as they are more detailed and specific. The Legon
meeting was the first Christian-Muslim meeting on an
African regional basis and was marked by a desire for
mutual awareness and caring. "Christians should be
willing", the report says, "to share with their Muslim
neighbours those facilities and opportunities for religious, educational, social and economic advancement
which Christians happen to possess. A similar spirit
may be expected from the Muslim side".[2]

Examples of concrete, local collaboration are given.
Joint prayers for the welfare of a whole community,
goodwill messages on each other's feast days and the
exchange of information about important events in each
community are suggested. In schools, religious instruction should be provided for all religious groups represented. "Christian and Muslim schools should be open
to the principle of providing teachers and educational
materials for the respective religious communities".[3]
The discussion of mixed marriages is very sensitive and
insists that the primary duty of both religions is to
help the individuals concerned. "It is a matter of
widespread concern that religions should not attempt
to impose conditions on people whose emotional involvement, of which marriage is the natural climax, makes
them ready and prepared to cross religious barriers,
particularly when such conditions pertain to children
as yet unborn.

Religious leaders should never try to exploit the emotional vulnerability of such people for their own narrow confessional interests, but must instead help these
people to fulfill their potential and discover for themselves what is true for them. Where religious counsel
is requested from one or the other religious tradition,
such help must be given, with the welfare and harmony
of the people concerned as the over-riding consideration
It is unhealthy both for a normal family life and for
the spirit of dialogue that religious competition should
be extended into the field of family life and responsi-

bility".[4] Any suggestion that medical care should be
conditional on religious confession is also condemned.

At the Hong Kong meeting, those present affirmed that
their faiths enjoined a loving relationship with each
other. They believed both religions had a responsibility to work together for political and social harmony
and should defend each other's interests. They deplored
"the deliberate and unnecessary multiplication of com-
petitive charitable organizations and social agencies",[5]
and, by contrast commended the Inter-Religious Co-operation for Community Organization in Indonesia, which
tried to meet direct human need in the country's big
cities. Like their fellows at Legon, they argued that
"schools providing religious instruction for children
from different religious communities should arrange to
have such instruction given by qualified persons belonging to the respective communities".[6] They rejected the
view that because an educational institution had a religious foundation, it should only teach that religion.

Following the Nairobi assembly of the World Council of
Churches, a consultation was held at Chambésy in Switzerland, in June, 1976, to study the Christian concept of
mission and the Muslim understanding of *da'wah*.[7] In the
autumn, a meeting was arranged at Cartigny to plan together the next steps in Christian-Muslim dialogue. At
this, it was agreed that preparation and sympathy for
dialogue needed to be encouraged at all possible levels
within both communities. The report says that whereas
dialogue is usually thought of as conversation, it is
often part of people's daily experience. Three areas
of encounter—education, family life and prayer—were
discussed in detail. Clarification on certain socio-
political issues was required in the future, namely
"Faith and Politics in Islamic and Christian Thought",
Social Justice and Development" and specific situations
such as Lebanon or Muslims in Europe, need attention.
On theological matters, revelation; inter-religious attitudes; faith, science, technology; the future of humanity and Christian mission and Islamic *da'wah* are
mentioned as deserving further study.

During this same period there have been the beginnings
of official contact between the Vatican and the Muslim
world. The most important event was the Islamic-Chris-
tian Dialogue held in Tripoli in February, 1976, although
it proved to be a controversial occasion and did not go as
planned. It arose from a visit to Cardinal Pignedoli by
Dr. Shehati, Secretary for Foreign Affairs of the Libyan

Socialist Union.  In prior discussion, the purely religious nature of the gathering was stressed.  It had
been intended that the delegations should each consist
of twelve members and that a few observers should be
invited.  The Catholic delegation was taken aback to
find some five hundred guests were present.  Throughout,
the Catholics were given generous hospitality, but the
Muslim delegation "carried out its 'dialogue' by system-
atically attacking the Catholic delegation".[8]  It was
in preparing the final declaration that difficulties
occurred.  The declaration included two paragraphs (20
and 21), which attacked Zionism as "an aggressive ra-
cialist movement", affirmed "the national rights of the
Palestinian people and their right to return to their
lands" and "the Arab character of the city of Jerusalem
and demanded the liberation of all prisoners in occupied
Palestine and of all occupied territories".[9]  The Cardinal, on hearing the declaration, made known the Catholic
disagreement with these paragraphs, which the Vatican
repudiated.

The other sections of the Declaration are unexceptional
and show quite a measure of agreement and understanding.
In reflecting on the meeting, the report in the *Bulletin*
says that despite the final episode, the gathering
showed the necessity and urgency of dialogue with Muslims.  It also showed the difficulties.  "There is a
discrepancy of history, of culture, of social evolution,
of religious mentality, which only now we fully realize"
"The most concrete result of the days in Tripoli and the
most valid methodology for dialogue seem, for the moment
to be meeting and personal welcome:  to feel and call
each other brothers in the name of the same God".[11]
The conference also shows, despite the assurances asked
for by the Catholics that it would be purely religious,
how easily dialogue can be perverted for political purposes.

The growing number of Muslims in Europe is stimulating
Christians there to a greater concern for good community
relations and for inter-faith understanding.  The World
of Islam Festival in London created some interest and
prompted some reflection on Christian attitudes to Islam.[12]  Recently, in February,1978, the Conference of
European Churches arranged a consultation in Salzburg,
for representatives of churches in East and West Europe
and for representatives of specialized organizations to
consult with Muslim lecturers and specialists.  The reports of this gathering are largely descriptive, but
stress the need for further action.[13]

Jews, Christians and Muslims
─────────────────────────────

Muslims and Christians, like Jews, look back to Abraham,
as the father of the faithful.  Because of their common
semitic origin, some have felt there should be a special
relationship between these religions, and this desire
is expressed, for example, in the Standing Conference
of Jews, Christians and Muslims in Europe.

It was early in the sixties  that some young Jews and
some young Germans began to develop a curiosity about
each other.  Rabbi Lionel Blue and Rabbi Dow Marmur made
contact with Pastor Schoneich and Pastor Maechler, and
arranged the first interchange between an English synagogue and a German church.

The unsettled situation in the Middle East made both
Jewish and Christian participants aware of a third religion, Islam.  Already, too, there was a considerable
Muslim community in Europe, about which there was widespread ignorance.  Helped by Bishop Scharf, Pastor
Maechler organized a meeting in Berlin between a number
of Jewish, Christian and Muslim religious leaders and
students.  The meeting took place  at the end of the
war of 1967, not far from the Villa in Wannsee, where
the "Final Solution" was planned.

One meeting led to another, so that trust and confidence
began to grow.  By 1971, it was felt that the time had
come to form a loose organization, known as the Standing
Conference of Jews, Christians and Muslims in Europe.
The next year, the first European Conference was held in
London, in February—somewhat interrupted by the power
cuts caused by the miners' go-slow.  The subject was
"The Faith of our Fathers - the Fate of our Children".
The main addresses were given by Rev. Michael Hollings,
Dr. M. Navearn, and Rabbi Dr. Louis Jacobs.  A full re-
port of the conference was published.

The second European Conference was held near Haarlem in
Holland in March,1973, attended by some fifty people.
The conference explored the role of religion in a secularized time.  A few accepted a positive,critical function
of secularization, but the majority warned against its
dangers.  The third conference was held at Berlin in
November,1974 on "Violence and its Roots".

Branches of J.C.M. have now been established in Germany,
Great Britain and Holland.  These have arranged a number
of smaller gatherings, interchange of theological

students and lectures.

When the Standing Conference was set up, it was felt
that the existing structure of inter-faith co-operation
mirrored the past, not the present, reality. All over
Europe there were Christian-Jewish councils and friendship organizations set up in the thirties and occasioned
by the rise of anti-semitism. It was difficult to enlarge these to include Muslims. On the other hand,
inter-faith organizations which included all religions
were too general for the dialogue desired between the
"Abrahamic" religions.

The Standing Conference has four main aims; to help educate ministers of religion; to provide better information about the three religions; to encourage religious
minorities in their search for identity in the European
setting; and to improve public relations between religious minorities, the Standing Conference, and society.[1]

There is plenty for Christians and Muslims to discuss
and to do together. In his Preface to *Christians Meeting
Muslims,* Dr. Mulder, who is moderator of the Sub-Unit for
Dialogue, rightly says that "when compared to a history
of many, many centuries of tensions, these ten years
show a remarkable development, a new spirit of co-operation, a real effort towards mutual understanding". He
warns, however, "that ten years is a short period and
that the sapling of dialogue is still very tender and
continually in danger of being uprooted".[15] The danger
comes from those on both sides who, theologically, reject the approach of dialogue and from explosive political and social situations which would wreck the new-
found friendship and trust. "Much goodwill", as Dr.
Mulder says, "on both sides is needed to overcome tensions".[16]

The regained self-confidence of the Muslim world suggests
that dialogue with Islam will be of increasing importance
Yet this very self-confidence, together with an uncritical view of the authority of the Qur'an, can make Muslims
seem inflexible. Certainly few Muslims—except some
Ahmadiyyas—have taken an active part in inter-faith
movements. The Qur'an teaches respect for the "people of
the Book" (Jews and Christians)—and some Muslims have extended this to Hindus and Buddhists: but there is a clear
belief that the message of the Prophet is the final word
of God. Mr. A. K. Borhi, Minister for Religious Affairs
of Pakistan, for example, has said that Islam was not
"just one religion among others", it was "in some sense
the totality of the religious experience of all mankind"

# CHAPTER EIGHT

# THE INDIAN SCENE

The mutual influence on each other of Hinduism and Christianity has been considerable in the last one hundred and eighty years, since the beginning of large scale Christian missionary work. Leading figures of the Hindu Renaissance, such as Ram Mohun Roy, Keshub Chander Sen, Rabindranath Tagore or Dr. Radhakrishnan, were influenced by Christianity. Equally, Europeans, such as the philosopher Schopenhauer or Annie Besant, who became a leader of the Theosophical Movement, were affected by Hinduism.

There have been various inter-faith movements in India, but paradoxically the hospitality of Hinduism has sapped their growth. Leaders of the Hindu Renaissance have affirmed the equality of religions. Swami Vivekananda declared at the World Parliament of Religions that "to the Hindu, the whole world of religions is only a travelling, a coming up of different men and women through various conditions and circumstances to the same goal".[1] Dr. Radhakrishnan, as we have seen,[2] looked for the emergence of a universal religion, of which the various historical religions are the branches.

The view that all religions are really the same and the acceptance of different spiritual paths as equally valid has made for tolerance. It has, however, perhaps made Hindus too tolerant of differences and not especially interested in reconciling or overcoming them. Thus the dynamic necessary to inter-faith work has been lacking. At the same time, to members of semitic religions, the Hindu approach seems to evade questions of truth. For them, it has been unhelpful to be told that all religions really say the same thing, when they are convinced that they do not. Christians have often, therefore, recoiled from the embrace of Hinduism for fear that their integrity might be compromised. Whilst there has been a growing concern that Christianity in India should not appear alien, but be expressed in an Indian idiom, there has been a constant fear lest the particularity of the

Christian Gospel be endangered.  Thus the Hindu asser-
tion that all religions really say the same has led to
an easy acquiescence in difference, so robbing inter-
faith movements of their drive, whilst frightening away
from close contact Christians who have feared that they
might be put in a false position.  Together with this,
the relation of religions has been complicated by political issues.  The desire of many Muslims, during the
struggle for independence, for a Muslim state, led often
to hostility towards Hindus.  Before independence,
Christians were often identified with the alien ruling
power, and since independence have been concerned to
show that they were active Indian citizens.  The Sikhs,
whose homeland was split by partition, had to spend
many years struggling for a Punjabi state.  At Patiala
University, however, they have established a centre for
the study of world religions.

The views of most nineteenth century Christian missionaries were hostile to Hinduism.  An exception was William
Miller, who was principal of Madras Christian College at
the turn of the century.  He believed that Hinduism had
a place in God's plan.  "Future generations", he wrote,
"will see clearly...that Hinduism and the Hindus are em-
braced within the limits of God's plan.  The time will
come when it will be deemed simply foolish to deny that
Hindu thought, as truly as Greek philosophy, or Roman
law, is a factor in the building of the historic fabric
of which the foundation was laid when Abraham was called
and of which the cornerstone is Christ".[3]  He spoke of
Christ fulfilling the aspirations of Hinduism, but also
of Christianity needing to be fulfilled by the contributions of other religions.  As Dr. Kaj Baago notes,
Miller's view and that of Bernard Lucas of the London
Missionary Society, need to be distinguished from the
idea of fulfillment usually associated with J. N. Farquhar and his book, *The Crown of Hinduism*.  "Whereas
Farquhar always maintained that the fulfillment of Hindu
ism in Christianity would happen through a *replacement*
of Hinduism by Christianity, Miller and Lucas expected
the fulfillment to take place through a *development* of
all higher religions, Christianity included, into a
World Religion with Christ as centre".[4]

Miller expressed his support for the World Parliament of
Religions, but, apart from attempts within the Brahmo-
Samaj, and by Keshub Chander Sen in his Church of the
New Dispensation to include material from all religions,
the first inter-faith developments were associated with
Mahatma Gandhi and his independence movement.

Gandhi was guided by five underlying principles in his
discussion of the relation between religions.  First,
*Satya* (Truth) and *Ahimsa* (Non-Violence) served as the
key to unlock the mysteries of all religions.  Second,
the Bhagavadgita was the clue to the Scriptures of the
world.  Third, the principle of equi-mindedness enabled
him to look for agreement, rather than differences, between religions.  Fourth, the experience of the seeker
served as the final norm of judgment about truth and
the validity of a religious doctrine.  Finally, a religion had to be studied through the writings of a known
votary of that religion.  He believed that all principal faiths constitute a revelation of Truth, but, as
they are expounded by fallible men, they are all affected by imperfections.  Beneath the differences of the
actual religions, he proclaimed a religion of humanity
that underlay them all.  He never tired of pointing out
to adherents of different religions that they all believed in one God.  Addressing Hindus and Muslims, he
said, "We believe in one and the same God, the difference of nomenclature in Hinduism and Islam notwithstand-
ing".[5]  He thought of the underlying religion or *dharma*
as a "belief[6] in the ordered moral movement of the universe",[6] and in personal terms as the search for truth.

He appealed to the adherents of different religions to
recognize their underlying unity.  "The need of the moment", he wrote in *All Religions are True,* "is not one
religion, but mutual respect and tolerance of the de-
votees of different religions.  We want to reach not
the dead level, but unity in diversity.  Any attempt to
root out tradition, effects of heredity, climate and
other surroundings, is not only bound to fail but is
sacrilege.  The soul of religion is one, but it is en-
cased in a multitude of forms..God is one,whatever the
name given him".[7]  In the spirit of *swadeshi* (acceptance of our immediate situation) he recognized the particularity of each religion to which an adherent should
remain loyal, but he pleaded for harmony and mutual
understanding.

Gandhi, on the basis of his own experience, made various
suggestions for relating one religion to another.  The
first step to effect understanding was a serious and
reverent study of other scriptures, with an impartial
mind, from the standpoint of their adherents.  Equally
important was the willingness to live together with
people of other faiths.  This was not so much geographical or spacial proximity, as a social relatedness, which
rejected the predominant caste and communal mentality.

"I hold", he wrote, "that believers who have to see the
same God in others that they see in themselves must be
able to live amongst all with sufficient detachment.
And the ability to live thus can be cultivated not by
fighting shy of unsought opportunities for such contacts,
but by hailing them in a spirit of service".[8]  As a
further step, he suggested active participation by all
religious communities in constructive programmes of
nation-building.  Understanding between religions re-
sulted from their adherents actively sharing in such
constructive ventures as the improvement of village
sanitation, education of villagers, or the removal of
untouchability.  "The edifice of unity", he said, "can
rest on constructive work alone".[9]  This is an important insight, as too often inter-faith meetings have
been all words and no action.

In an atmosphere of mutual tolerance, he thought each
religion should be ready to adopt and adapt good things
in other religions.  Equally, each religion should work
for the good of others.  "Our inmost prayer should be
that a Hindu should be a better Hindu, a Muslim a better Muslim and a Christian a better Christian".[10]  He
opposed the efforts of missionaries to win converts,
although when pressed by C. F. Andrews, he admitted
that on occasion  an individual, for his spiritual
growth, might wish to change religions.

Gandhi was particularly concerned to reconcile Hindus
and Muslims and opposed the partition of India on independence.  He attracted members of various faiths to
his movement and at his Ashrams, devotions included
readings from the scriptures of the world.  He was not
particularly concerned with theological differences,
but wished to see members of all religions working together for the development of the nation.

A number of Christians joined the Gandhian movement and
formed part of the Gandhian inner circle.  Amongst the
missionaries were C. F. Andrews, Verrier Elwin and Ralph
Richard Keithahn, whilst Indian Christians included
Rajkumari Amrit Kaur, S. K. George, Aryanayagam, Bhara-
tan Kumarappa and J. C. Kumarappa, who wrote *The Practice of Precepts of Jesus*.

We may concentrate on S. K. George, as he was most active in promoting inter-religious fellowship.  In 1932,
when he declared his support for Gandhi, he was compelled to resign his post at Bishop's College, Calcutta.
He had an unsettled life, scratching a living from

occasional teaching jobs and from his writings. He and
his wife espoused a variety of good causes, including
the Inter-Religious Student Fellowship and of The
Fellowship of the Friends of Truth.

The Inter-Religious Student Fellowship was an offshoot
of the International Fellowship. The International Fellowship, of which A. A. Paul was founder secretary,
came into being during the period of the national struggle for independence, with a view to creating mutual
understanding between people of different races and religions in India. It became a forum for inter-religious discussions and international encounters. From
this was born the Inter-Religious Student Fellowship,
with the organization of which S. K. George helped in
the thirties and forties. The aims and basis of the
Inter-Religious Student Fellowship declared that the
religious attitude was of permanent value to mankind and
always deserved reverent recognition. The fellowship
desired to encourage mutual respect, appreciation and
sympathy of religions for each other, and to this end
said "it is absolutely necessary that no member of the
fellowship should claim for his religion any exclusive
and final possession of truth".[11] Further, "we do not
desire to persuade any within the fellowship to our own
religious belief and practice".[12]

This was to renounce the missionary thrust of the Church,
and George believed that Christianity should not seek to
replace Hinduism, but find its place within it, as "a
small shrine adjoining the central Hindu temple existing
side by side with, never seeking to displace, the giant
structure of Hinduism".[13] Hinduism, he held, had "a
place for Jesus among the many leaders and teachers it
reverences as revealers of God to man, nay as incarna-
tions of God in his aspect as the Lover and Redeemer of
men. Its conception of a favourite God, Ishta Devata,
would sanction even an exclusive worship of him to those
who find in such adoration the way to God-realization.
But it would definitely place him in its own setting
among the diverse modes and ways in which the Unfathom-
able and the Eternal manifests itself to mortal minds.
Who can say that this is not the setting in which he
will find his permanent place in the religious heritage
of the race, at any rate in India".[14] It is not surprising that with such views, which for most Christians
would have meant an abandonment of their convictions,
George did not attract many Christians to the inter-
religious fellowship, and with independence achieved,
both the International Fellowship and the Inter-Religious

Student Fellowship went out of active existence.

The Fellowship of the Friends of Truth is also no longer
active in India, having been largely replaced by the
Bhoodan-Gramdan Movement. The British branch, formed
in 1956, however, continues to flourish and holds an
annual conference and other meetings and publishes a
journal.

The Fellowship grew out of the experience of members of
the Society of Friends working and worshipping together
with Gandhi and some of his followers. Horace Alexander
an English Quaker, was walking through some fields in
East Bengal with Gandhi one day in January, 1947. "It
seems to me", Alexander said, "that what the world,
especially India, needs above all today is some religious fellowship which can be joined by adherents of all
the chief religions. I am not now thinking of a 'syncre
tistic' movement...I am thinking of a union of hearts, a
fellowship in which men of each faith...all find themselves at one, because they are seeking together to
practice the truth of God in the world. And I have wondered whether the Society of Friends, the 'Quakers' so
called, could help to provide such a metting ground".
After some thought, Gandhi agreed that the Quakers would
be the best society: "but only on one condition. Are
they prepared to recognize that it is as natural for a
Hindu to grow into a Friend as it is for a Christian to
grow into one?" Horace Alexander replied: "Some would
agree to that condition and some would not. I, for one,
am one of those who would readily accept that position,
not only for Hindus but for Muslims and others".[15] The
Friends, as a society, felt unable to commit themselves
to the idea, but individually a number of them supported
it.

At a meeting held at the Friends Rural Centre, Rasulia,
in 1949, the Fellowship was formed.[16] S. K. George took
a leading part, being at times secretary and editor of
the *Quarterly*. Meetings were held in different parts
of the country and quite a membership was built up.
With the death of George in 1962, the quarterly ceased
publication. For a time, a newsletter was published by
G. Ramachandran, a well-known member of Parliament,
who had founded Gandhigran, which was a rural, social
and educational development in South India, which was
also the headquarters of the Fellowship of the Friends
of Truth.

The specific inter-faith movements, inspired by Gandhi,

may have disappeared in India, but his approach to the
relationship of religions is still influential amongst
those who seek to perpetuate his ideas.  The Bhoodan-
Gramdan movement attracts workers from different faiths.
As we have seen, the Gandhi Peace Foundation acted as
host for one of the preparatory meetings that led to
the Kyoto World Conference on Religion and Peace.[17]
Perhaps the special contribution of Gandhi was linking
inter-faith fellowship and practical action together,
and many of those who came to share his ideas on the
relation of religions were attracted by his work of nation-building.

An Indian Christian, who also hoped that religions could
work together in building the new India, was Chenchiah.
He was a lawyer and rose to be Chief Justice of Pudo-
kottai High Court.  He was an ardent nationalist and was
concerned that Christianity should adapt to the needs
and aspirations of India.  He contributed to the book
*Rethinking Christianity,* and was for a time editor of
*The Pilgrim,* which was concerned with the relation of
Christianity to other religions.  He devoted most of
the March,1950,issue of *The Pilgrim* to advocating "the
desirability of co-operation of religions in the new
national set-up of India".[18]  Where religions had met
in a spirit of brotherhood, they had first discovered
what they had in common, but then became aware of their
differences.  The need now for renewal required a pool-
ing of resources.  His aim,therefore,was "to stress the
importance of the study of comparative religion—for the
formation of a universal faith—and to point out what
common practical efforts religions have tried to draw
together and co-operate".[19]  His mention of some practical attempts at co-operation are especially interesting.  He described the common celebration of festivals
in Madras; he pleaded for a place for common prayers in
every town; he asked Christians to take the lead in suggesting common prayers at times of grave national crisis,
and he mentioned the small groups which he had started,
consisting of Christians and Hindus who joined together
in prayer for the sick.  He spoke, too, of the beginnings
made in the field of common worship.  Criticized by Dr.
Kraemer, Chenchiah made clear that he rejected the
"facile maxim" that all religions lead to the same goal.
Inter-religious co-operation was the story of how "life-
forces of three different religions brought together
are coalescing and producing—a new type of life".[20]

Chenchiah's was a voice in the wilderness.  Although in
the wake of the "fulfillment" theory, Christian mission-

ary scholars had studied Hinduism sympathetically, by th
forties the mood had changed.  The Dutch missionary theo
logian Hendrik Kraemer, who himself had a profound knowl
edge of other religions, argued in his *The Christian Mes
sage in a Non-Christian World* that the Church's primary
task was "the announcement of the Message of God which
is not adaptable to any religion or philosophy."[21]  He
stressed the discontinuity of the Gospel from world religions.  His views were influential, especially at the
International Missionary Conference held at Tambaram,
Madras, in 1937.  The general view of Christian thinkers
in India in the forties, as represented for example by
Dr. Marcus Ward's *Our Theological Task,* was that whilst
it was right to interpret the Gospel in Indian terms,
there was an unchangeable fundamental core of the Christian faith that could not be altered.  At the same time,
the partition of India, accompanied by bloody communal
fighting, had embittered the relation of Hindus and Muslims.  Attention, too, was directed to the problems
facing newly independent India, and Christians were concerned to discover their identity in the new situation.

It was Paul Devanandan, through the newly-formed Christian Institute for the Study of Religion and Society at
Bangalore, of which he became director in 1956, that
Christian attention was again directed to Hinduism. He
was aware of the resurgence of the ancient religions of
Asia and of the cultural influence of Hinduism in the
newly independent India.  He wanted Christians to play
a full part in nation-building.  Through the institute
he arranged occasions for dialogue between Christian
and Hindu thinkers, and also stimulated Christian thinking about the relationship of the Church to contemporary
Hinduism.

One of the first seminars, for example, held at Nagpur
in 1958, took as its theme "The Christian Approach to
Renascent Hinduism". Many of the papers and discussions
at these seminars are recorded in *Religion and Society,*
the bulletin of the Institute.  The debates of the sixties are a preview of the discussions in the World Council of Churches in the seventies.  It can be seen that
gradually there is less fear of compromising the final-
ity of Christ and of the risk involved in dialogue.  Increasingly, dialogue is thought to have its own inherent
value and is not regarded as a new form of evangelization.  It is recognized that as part of his commitment
the Christian has certain beliefs about Jesus and that
he brings these to the dialogue, but the purpose of
dialogue is a common search for truth.  There is some
tension between those who stress common humanity as the

basis for dialogue and those who put emphasis on sharing
religious experience.

Besides the growing openness to dialogue, the seminars
have led to a deepening understanding by Christians and
Hindus of each other's beliefs.  The discussions have
been mainly at an intellectual and doctrinal level and
have generated a considerable literature.  In the group
which centered around Swami Abhishiktananda, and which
included for a time the Swiss Ambassador Jacques Albert
Cuttat and the Anglican priest, Fr. Murray Rogers, the
attempt was made to enter into the spirituality of Hinduism.  The Upanishads were read in a meditative way
"to enter as authentically as possible into the experience which has moulded the religious soul of India".[22]
This search for a spiritual meeting point has become
increasingly influential, as the works of Swami Abhishiktananda have become known outside India.  At the same
time some Roman Catholic theologians, especially Fr.
Raymond Panikkar, were coming to speak of the world religions as the ordinary means of salvation.[23]

The last fifteen years have seen a growing interest by
Christian thinkers in India, both Protestant and Roman
Catholic, in Hinduism.  They study it deeply and have
penetrating discussions with Hindu scholars.  It is un-
certain whether this interest is shared by ordinary
church members, but in the churches there is a concern
that the Christian faith should be expressed in an Indian idiom.  The approach of the theologians is clearly
from a Christian standpoint.  They recognize that they
can learn from this dialogue; but it is dialogue between separate communities, not an inter-faith movement.
Perhaps at an intellectual level there is a friendly
acceptance of each other's religious path and there is
not the need for a body to foster inter-faith meeting.
At a more ordinary level, the Catholic Bishops Conference of India since 1973, under the supervision of
Father Albert Nambiaparambil, has initiated various ex-
periments.  One approach is through "Get Togethers on
Dialogue", with individuals coming together for two or
three days to "study the nature, scope, demands, difficulties, risks, and concrete possibilities of inter-
religious dialogue in that particular region".[24]

Another experiment is through "Live-Togethers", where
participants of different religions come together for
prayer, meditation and shared reflections.  They discuss such topics of common concern as "what my religion
means to me, my attitude towards other religions, prayer and

religious experiences in my life, my religion and my
suffering neighbour", and they consider how to foster
mutual unity and communal harmony.  The Dialogue Commission is in touch with thirteen ashrams, fifteen dialogue centres and eight dialogue groups in India.  Recently it has arranged a number of multi-religious
retreat-prayer sessions, and is now trying to promote
multi-religious evening panels in all major cities on
"Values in a Fast Changing World".[25]

Fr. Albert Nambiaparambil is also active in the Indian
followup group to the World Conference on Religion and
Peace, and attended the Asian Conference on Religion
and Peace.  In the South of India, there is a branch of
the World Congress of Faiths, and the chairman of the
International Committee of the Temple of Understanding,
Mrs. Sarala Birla lives in Calcutta.  In 1974, the
World Fellowship of Religions held an international
inter-faith conference in New Delhi and a similar occasion was sponsored by the Projapita Brehma Kumaris
Ishwariya Vishwa Vidyalaya in 1978.

The Indian religious climate is favourable to inter-
faith co-operation and it is beneficial to those elsewhere if Indians play a full part in world bodies, and
if Christians there contribute their insights to the
world church.  The task in India is, as Gandhi saw, to
translate the friendship and openness that exists between many religious leaders into the promotion of communal harmony and the uplift of the people.

## The Buddhist World

Further to the East, there has been growing Christian
interest in understanding Buddhism.  The approach is
similar to that of the Christian Institute at Bangalore
towards Hinduism.  A consultation on "Buddhist-Christian
Encounter" was held at Rangoon in 1961, attended by
Christians from Burma, Ceylon and Thailand, which encouraged Christians to show deeper concern for Buddhism.[26]
There are also attempts to enter into Buddhist spirituality, as by Father William Johnston in Japan or by
the members of Devasaranaramaya, a monastery village
in Ceylon.[27]

Within the Buddhist world, there is an "ecumenical"
movement, to reconcile Buddhists of different traditions,
and a World Fellowship of Buddhists, with headquarters
in Thailand, has been created.

There are also some local inter-religious bodies, such
as the Congress of Religions in Ceylon, the Inter-
Religious Organization of Singapore, and various inter-
faith councils in Japan, which are doing valuable
work.[28]  They are similar to inter-faith bodies elsewhere.  Unfortunately it has not been possible to obtain detailed information about them.  They are evidence, however, that the desire for inter-religious
harmony and co-operation is felt by many people in
many parts of the world.  The hope must be that such
groups will themselves develop closer links.

# CHAPTER NINE

## CONCLUSION

Many other meetings between members of different religions have been arranged. Those described here are amongst the most important and illustrate the different patterns of and expectations for such meetings. Yet often the purpose of a meeting has been ill-defined and there has been confusion because the term "dialogue" is widely, but loosely, used.

A person can take an interest in a religion other than their own for a number of reasons. It may be to learn more about another faith, so as more readily to win adherents from it to his own faith. Many Christian missionaries, from this motive, have studied other religions and increased knowledge of them. Such studies, however, served a missionary purpose and, even if sympathetic, usually contained a concluding chapter which pointed out how Christianity fulfills the highest aspirations of that other religion. Others have studied another religion because their own did not fully meet their spiritual needs. Some have become converts to that other religion, whilst some are eclectic, drawing spiritual help from various traditions. Some converts totally reject their previous faith, whilst some see it as a pointer to their new beliefs. Amongst the latter, a number have contributed to inter-religious understanding.

Other people have studied religions with scholarly detachment. Their interest may be historical, anthropological, philological, or of another academic discipline. Essentially, they see religions as part of human culture and therefore worthy of study for their own sake. Some scholars have suggested that such studies have a further value, such as the promotion of human understanding, or the advancement of truth, but the justification of this academic study of religions lies within itself. Academic study may provide material for dialogue, but is not itself dialogue.

Others believe that all religions teach the same es-

sential truth and study them to illustrate this belief.
Mme. Helena Petrovna Blavatsky, for example, who founded the Theosophical Society, claimed to teach an ancient
hidden wisdom ("theosophia"), which was the central core
and the teachings of wise men throughout history have a
certain common body of knowledge. Theosophists, and thos
who think like them, have contributed to greater friendship between members of different religions and to understanding of their spiritual teachings, but they give less
weight to the differences between historic religions than
is usual in inter-religious organizations, which insist
that the distinctiveness of each tradition be respected.

By contrast, there are those who work for inter-religious
understanding, without compromising the exclusive claims
to truth of the tradition to which they belong. For them
inter-religious understanding is akin to inter-communal
understanding. In a mixed society, it is important to
respect the freedom of religion and to understand why
others believe and act as they do. Yet, such understanding can be valued without admitting any validity to the
truth claims which others make. Much of the official con
tact between religious bodies is at this level of mutual
respect. Mutual respect and the search for good community relations are important, but it is confusing if this
is called dialogue.

The distinctive character of the main inter-faith organizations is their recognition of both the particularity of
the great religions and their validity. The Declaration
the Louvain Conference of the World Conference on Religio:
and Peace said that, "of all the things learned at Kyoto,
one has marked us more deeply than the discovery that the
integrity of the commitment of each to his own religious
tradition permits, indeed nurtures, loving respect for th
prayer and faithfulness of others".[1] In similar mood,
Bishop Appleton, speaking at the Canterbury Conference of
the World Congress of Faiths, said: "Each relition has a
mission, a gospel, a central affirmation. Each of us nee
to enlarge on the gospel which he has received, without
wanting to demolish the gospel of others. We can enlarge
and deepen our initial and basic faith by the experience
and insights of people from other religions and cultures,
without disloyalty to our own commitment".[2]

Here the historic actuality of the great religious traditions is recognized and affirmed. Their distinct heritag
and view of the world is understood. For a religion is a
complex organism in which different features are closely
related and one aspect cannot be isolated without distor-

tion.  Yet, whilst the distinctiveness of religions is recognized, they are seen as complementary, rather than as rivals.  It is not that one is true and the others false, but that together they point beyond themselves to a richer truth, as yet not fully realized.

Such dialogue in depth can happen only between those who know each other intimately.  This suggests that the work of inter-faith organizations is, in the area of truth-seeking dialogue, secondary.  An organization can arrange meetings and discussions and encourage such dialogue: but it cannot make such mutual sharing happen.  This is the work of the Spirit.  This is why it is so hard to assess the effects of bodies like the World Congress of Faiths and the Temple of Understanding.  The effects are primarily in the enrichment of individual lives which are opened to a fuller awareness of truth:  rather than in the growth of an organization.  The influence on religious education, or the growth of interfaith worship, or indeed the size of membership can to some extent be assessed:  but this is to concentrate upon the external, whereas the organizations exist for a spiritual purpose which cannot be measured.

Where the aims of an inter-religious organization are more specifically concerned with peace and other practical matters, their achievements can be more readily assessed.  There have been hardly any specific inter-religious projects.  The Boat People Project of the World Conference on Religion and Peace was unsuccessful.  In principle, however, members of different religions could act together on relief and humanitarian schemes.  In the more general effort to influence governments and public opinion, religions are only one factor amongst many, although their influence will be greater if they speak with a common voice.  As yet, the attempt of leaders of different religions to speak on specific issues is only at a beginning in the pioneering work of the World Conference on Religion and Peace.  There are many problems as to how religious leaders can do more than speak in very general terms and how they can acquire the necessary expertise to speak about particular situations.  Their goodwill may easily be manipulated for political purposes.

The great difficulty, however, is that many of the adherents of the world religions see themselves primarily as members of their community or nation or religion and identify with its interests.

Dialogue at its deepest is truth-seeking.  It is the

attempt of those nourished in different spiritual traditions to shre the truths they hold in the hope that together they may reach a fuller or convergent awareness
ot the truth.  It does not ask any denial of truths already believed, but the willingness to hope that they
may be corrected and enlarged in the light of truths perceived and valued in other traditions.  Such deep mutual
exploration of the truth requires great trust and openness, and much so-called dialogue is in fact only preparation for dialogue.  Where dialogue in depth occurs,
some will be more intellectual, some more spiritual.  It
may be the attempt to appreciate the truth contained in
the teaching of different traditions on some great matter such as creation, salvation or life beyond death,
and to see how the various insights can be reconciled.
It may be the willingness to share and explore spiritual
disciplines in the hope of deepening awareness of ultimate reality.

Critics regard this as "syncretistic", but it depends
what meaning is attached to this word.  The term was
originally used by Plutarch (*De Fraterno Amore* 19) for
the fusion of religious cults which occurred in the Graec
Roman world.  Genrallly the process was spontaneous, but
sometimes, as in the institution of the cult of Sarapis,
syncretism was the product of official action.  By modern
writers, the term is usually used of an artificial mixing
of religions—the attempt to create a new religion by
fusing elements from various religions.  This would be to
produce an artificial and man-made religion.  This is gen
erally condemned and expressly rejected by the World Congress of Faiths and the Temple of Understanding.  At a
much deeper level, however, religions exert a mutual influence upon each other.  Is this also "syncretism"?

In his report to the Nairobi Assembly of the World Counci
of Churches, the moderator of the Central Committee, Dr.
M. M. Thomas, distinguished between a right and wrong syn
cretism.  A right syncretism for the Christian Church wou
be "Christ-centred": "Is it not legitimate to welcome a
Christ-centred process of inter-religious and inter-cultu
penetration through dialogue.  If you will permit the use
of the word 'syncretism' to denote all processes of inter
penetration between cultures and religions, the only answ
to wrong syncretism, which means the uncritical, superfic
ial, normless mixing of basically incompatible religious
conceptions and cultural attitudes, is a Christ-centred
syncretism which grapples and evaluates all concepts and
attitudes critically in the light of Jesus Christ".[3]   The
Preamble to the report of section III, however, said

expressly: "We are all opposed to any form of syncretism, incipient, nascent or developed, if we mean by snycretism conscious or unconscious human attempts to create a new religion composed of elements taken from different religions".[4]

Confusion about the word "syncretism", however, can blur a significant difference between those who believe that eventually their religion will displace the other religions of mankind and those who believe that from the meeting of religions a more universal religion will emerge.

Whilst inter-faith bodies do not expressly suggest the latter development, this is the logical implication of their position. It makes for freedom and openness in dialogue and a willingness to follow where the Spirit leads, which may be lacking in the official relationships of religions with each other. Because for any religion to suggest that it may grow into something larger, means a radical revision of its claims to truth. Especially is this so for Christianity, as it appears to modify traditional claims for the uniqueness of Christ.

Those who believe that a more universal world faith is being born, hope that with its birth may come a renewal and development of spiritual values appropriate to a world civilization. The coming together of the great religions is therefore a hopeful sign for mankind's future.

If this is the implicit hope of the inter-faith organizations, they need to articulate it more clearly. Part of their weakness has been that their aims, whilst well-intentioned, seem general and diffuse, and they have been unable to attract any large following. If they welcome the coming together of world faiths more enthusiastically and proclaim this as offering spiritual renewal to mankind, they will have a clear appeal. At the same time, they are likely to arouse even stronger hostility from the more traditional members of the world religions. In the past, the inter-faith organizations have perhaps been too keen to dispel this hostility, whereas their development is in fact a challenge to the traditional standpoint of all religions. Only time will tell whether they have rightly anticipated the religious future of humanity.

APPENDIX A

WORLD FELLOWSHIP OF FAITHS
CHICAGO, 1933


In 1933 an inter-religious gathering was again held at
Chicago, in conscious imitation of the 1893 World Par-
liament of Religions. The initiators were Charles F.
Weller and Mr. Das Gupta. Weller, who had been a so-
cial worker since 1896, started in 1918 the League of
Neighbours. This was a body to help alien groups, such
as negroes and foreign born citizens, interpret to American communities their idealism and social spirit. Das
Gupta came to England in 1908, where he found little
understanding of Indian culture and aspirations.
To promote greater sympathy, he organized *The Union of
East and West,* and produced some thirty plays about
Indian life. In 1920 he accompanied Rabindranath Tagore
to the United States. He stayed on and started his
union there. Meeting Weller, they decided, in 1924, to
merge the League of Neighbours and the Union of East
and West to create *The Fellowship of Faiths*. This arranged meetings at which representatives of several
faiths spoke on such subjects as "Peace and Brotherhood".
They particularly favoured the method of appreciation
by which members of one faith paid tribute to another.
For example, at a Liberal Jewish synagogue, before an
audience of some seventeen hundred, non-Christians paid
tribute to Christianity. Activities were developed in
eighteen cities and contacts made with eleven countries.
From 1928 to 1932, a quarterly journal, *Appreciation,*
was published.

In May,1929, the theme of a Chicago Fellowship of Faiths
meeting was "Peace and Brotherhood as Taught by the
World's Living Faiths". This revived memories of the
1893 World Parliament there. After contact with religious leaders in Chicago, the suggestion was made that
a second parliament should be held to coincide with the
Second World Fair, which was being planned for 1933, to
mark a "century of progress".

The next three years were occupied with preparations.

Twenty seven gatherings in Chicago—with the massive
total attendance of 44,000 people—developed the subjects that were to be discussed and the methods to be
used.  These ideas were shared with religious leaders
across the world.  Over three hundred leaders—drawn
from 30 countries and 24 states of the USA—responded
with comments and suggestions.  Many of these were
printed in *Appreciation*.  In New York, preliminary
meetings were linked to a Peace Week from 12th to 18th
May, 1932.  May 18th had already been observed as an
*International Goodwill Day* for seven years.

In June, 1932, the first letters inviting foreign speakers were dispatched, signed by Rabbi Stephen S. Wise.
From November, 1932 to May, 1933, preparations centered
on the New York office.  The National Chairman was
Bishop Francis J. McConnell, of the Methodist Episcopal
Church.  Mr. William H. Short, who was chairman of the
Executive Committee, and who had formerly been leader
of the League to Enforce Peace, was also active, as of
course was Weller, now General Executive of the Fellowship of Faiths.  Some three hundred people agreed to
serve on the national committee.  It was stated that
the World Fellowship of Faiths "is a movement not a
machine; a sense of expanding activities, rather than
an established institution, an inspiration more than an
achievement.  It has never sought to develop a new religion or unite divergent faiths on the basis of a
least common denominator of their convictions.  Instead,
it believes that the desired and necessary human realization of the all-embracing spiritual Oneness of the
Good Life Universal must be accompanied by appreciation
(brotherly love) for all the individualities, all the
differentiations of function, by which true unity is
enriched".[1]

The main meetings—or culminating convention, as it was
called—took place from August 27th to September 17th,
1933.  Fifty sessions were held during these twenty-two
days.  Eight sessions had already been held during the
preparatory period and two more were held in October.
Twenty-three supplementary meetings were held in New
York from October, 1933 to June, 1934, especially during
Peace and Goodwill Week in May, 1934.  In all, at these
eighty-three meetings, two hundred and forty-two addresses were delivered by one hundred and ninety-nine
"spokesmen of All Faiths Races and Countries".  They
are collected and condensed in the book *World Fellowship,*
which was edited by Weller and was published in 1935.
Attendance varied from several hundred at morning and

afternoon sessions to two thousand or more at evening
sessions.  At one evening session the number reached
five thousand, many of whom were visitors to the World
Fair.

Bishop McConnell, the Chairman, said at the opening that
the name "World Fellowship of Faiths" was appropriate.
The gathering was world wide.  It was a fellowship, because there was no synthetic unity, but people were accepted "as they were".  It was a gathering of faiths,
rather than religions.  The congress differed from the
World Parliament of Religions in two ways.  "The first
difference is that, instead of a comparative parade of
rival religions, all faiths are challenged to manifest
or apply their religion by helping to solve the urgent
problems which impede man's progress.  The second difference is that the word 'faiths' is understood to include, not only all religions, but all types of spiritual consciousness or conviction which are determining
the actual lives of significant groups of people.  Educational, philanthrophic, social, economic, national and
political 'faith' are thus included.  The effort is to
help mankind to develop a new spiritual dynamic, competent to master and reform the world".[2]

Judging by the issues discussed, considerable attention
was paid to contemporary problems.  There were sections
amongst others, on economic projects; youth, sex and
race; machines, fear, security, adult education, prohi-
bition and motion pictures; peace, war and *ahimsa;* on
world chaos and the way out, as well as on the situation
in particular parts of the world, and the message of
particular faiths.

Reference was made at the gathering to some other inter-
faith groups.  A message was received from Professor
Wadia of *The International Fellowship of India*.  In the
previous ten years this had established small groups in
several Indian cities to share "Values of Life".[3]  In
India also, in anticipation of the Chicago gathering, a
"Preparatory Fellowship of Faiths" was held at Nasik
for three days in June,1933, at which an *All Faiths
League* was set up.  Dr. Herman Neander, in his talk,
spoke of Rudolf Otto's *Inter-Religious League* and of
proposals for a *World Conference for International Peace
Through Religion*.[4]  This world fellowship also influenced Francis Younghusband, who was present for some of
it, and who convened the World Congress of Faiths, held
in London in 1936.  There does not, however, seem to
have been any real follow-up in the United States itself.

The organizers were satisfied with the gathering.
Throughout the sessions "there was a strong, sustain-
ing sense of spiritual power like a swelling tide lift-
ing the movement forward".[5]  Amongst all the addresses
there "was not one which assumed that the speaker's
faith was the one and only way of salvation".  Indeed
the over-riding atmosphere of unity was expressed in
the first verse of the hymn specially written for the
closing ceremony.

> One Cosmic Brotherhood,
> One Universal Good,
>     One Source, One Sway.
> One Law Beholding Us,
> One Purpose Moulding Us,
> One Life Enfolding Us,
>     In Love Always.[6]

# APPENDIX B*

## A SUMMARY LIST OF
## INTER-FAITH ORGANIZATIONS


*Asian Conference on Religion and Peace.* A conference held by the Asian section of the World Conference
on Religion and Peace, in Singapore in 1976. Office:
Fumon Hall, 2-6 Wada, Suginami-Ku, Tokyo 166, Japan
(Chapter IV).

*British Association for the History of Religions*
(BAHR). The British section of the International Assoc-
iation for the History of Religions. Hon. Secretary:
Dr. M. Pye, The University, Leeds.

*Congress of Religions in Ceylon.* Formed in 1963 to
foster harmony and understanding amongst various religious communities in Sri Lanka. 100 Rosemead Place,
Colombo 7.

*The Council of Christians and Jews.* Formed in
Britain in 1942 to combat all forms of religious and
racial intolerance, and to encourage understanding between Christians and Jews. Publishes *Common Ground.*
48 Onslow Gardens, London SW7. 3PX. (Chapter VI).

*The Ecumenical Theological Research Fraternity in
Israel.* Consists of Christians in Israel concerned for
dialogue with Jews. Founded in 1966. Secretary: Dr.
Coos Schoneveld. P.O.B. 249, Jerusalem. (Chapter VI).
Publishes *Immanuel.*

*Fellowship of the Friends of Truth.* An inter-religious fellowship formed by Friends in India under
Gandhian influence. No longer active in India, but
there is a British branch. Secretary: Ruth Richardson,
52 Green Meadow Road, Birmingham. (Chapter VII).

---

*Where a chapter number is given, it refers to the
discussion of the organization in the text.

*Global Congress of the World's Religions.* The proposal
for this was made at the World Religions Conference
(see below) and is projected for 1981. Contact: Professor Warren Lewis, Unification Theological Seminary,
Barrytown, New York. (Chapter III).

*The International Association for the History of
Religions* (IAHR). Founded at Amsterdam in 1950 to pro-
mote the academic study of the history of religions.
Arranges international congresses. Publishes *Numen*.
(Chapter II). Professor R. J. Zwi Werblowsky, the
Hebrew University, Department of Comparative Religion,
Jerusalem, Israel.

*The International Association for Religious Free-
dom.* A body for free Christians, it now brings together "liberal" members of all religions. Auf dem
Mühlberg 6, D-6000 Frankfurt 70, Federal Germany.

*The International Association for the Study of the
History of Religions* (IASHR). The original name of the
International Association for the History of Religions.

*International Council of Christians and Jews.* Links
national bodies working for Jewish-Christian understanding. Rev.
Dr. Franz von Hammerstein, ICCJ Secretariat, Martin Buber Haus, 6148
Heppenheim/Bergstrasse/W. Germany. (Chapter VI).

*The International Fellowship.* Formed in India
under Gandhian influence to create mutual understanding
between members of various religions. No longer active.
(Chapter VII).

*International Jewish Committee on Inter-Religious
Consultations* (IJCIC). This body, widely representative
of World Judaism, engages in dialogue with Christian
bodies. (Chapter VI).

*Interreligio Netherlands.* The Dutch group of the
World Congress of Faiths. Nieuwe Gracht 27-1, 3521 LC. Utrecht.

*Inter-Religious Co-operation for Community Organi-
zation* (ICCO). A body run jointly by Christians and
Muslims to meet human need,which operates in the big
cities of Indonesia.

*The Inter-Religious Fellowship.* Existed in the
nineteen thirties and was organized by Rev. L. Belton,
then editor of the *Inquirer*.

*The Interreligious Peace Colloquim*. Held in Lisbon in 1977. A group concerned to bring the resources of religion to bear on the imminent problems of the new international economic order.

*The Inter-Religious Organization of Singapore*. Formed in 1949, to encourage tolerance and understanding between religions in Singapore. Acted as host to the Asian Conference on Religion and Peace, 1976. Hon. Secretary: Mr. Mehervan Singh, the Inter-Religious Organization, 5724 Golden Mile Shopping Center, Beach Road, Singapore 7.

*The Inter-Religious Student Fellowship*. An offshoot of the International Fellowship. No longer active.

*Israel Inter-Faith Committee*. Established in 1957 to cultivate fellowship and tolerance between religious groups in Israel. Secretary: Mrs. Joseph Emanuel, 12 Koresh Street, Jerusalem. (Chapter VI).

*Jews, Christians and Muslims*. Formed in 1971 to bring together Jews, Christians and Muslims in Europe. 17 Chepstow Villas, London Wll. 3DZ.

*Malaysia Inter-Religious Organization*. No details available.

*Monchanin Centre*. Founded in 1963 to develop inter-cultural and inter-religious appreciation. 4917 rue St-Urban, Montreal, Canada.

*National Conference of Christians and Jews*. Formed in 1928 in the USA to promote understanding between Christians and Jews. (Chapter VI).

*National Inter-Religious Conference on Peace*. Held in Washington in 1966. Proceedings in *Religion and Peace*, ed. Homer A. Jack. Bobbs-Merrill Co., Indianapolis, 1966. (Chapter IV).

*National Religious Conference for International Peace*. A conference held in Japan, 1931. (Chapter IV).

*New Universal Union*. A body which preaches unity amongst all creeds and faiths. Secretary-General: A. A. Keshavarz, office: Shemran Gate, Malek Avenue, Kheradmandan Street, #111, PO Box 335, Teheran, Iran.

*Rainbow Group*. A private group of Christian and Jewish academicians meeting in Jerusalem. Founded in

1965. A similar group meets in London.

*Religions of the Empire Conference*. Held in London, 1924, to provide knowledge about the religions of the Empire, apart from Christianity and Judaism. Proceedings edited by William Loftus Hare, published by Duckworth, 1925. (Chapter II).

*The Religious League of Mankind (Religöser Menschheitsbund)*. Founded by Rudolf Otto in 1921 as a religious counterpart to the League of Nations. It was proscribed by the Nazis. It was revived in 1956 by Friedrich Heiler, and became the German group of the World Congress of Faiths, but the group became merged in IARF and no longer exists.

*Religious Workers for Lasting Peace, Disarmament and Just Relations among Nations*. A conference to which members of various religions were invited, convened by the Russian Orthodox Church in Moscow in 1977.

*Shap Working Party*. Set up in 1969 to assist teachers of world religions, by advice and the provision of materials. Has produced *World Religions: A Handbook for Teachers*, ed. W. Owen Cole, published by the Commission for Racial Equality. Hon. Secretary Mr. Donald Butler, %West Denton  High School, Newcastle-upon-Tyne, NE5.2SZ. (Chapter II).

*Society for the Study of Religions*. A body formed in the 1930s, which arranged and published lectures on world religions. After the second World War, it merged with the World Congress of Faiths.

*Spalding Trust*. Endowed by H. N. Spalding, to foster study of world religions. Best known endowment is the Chair at Oxford. Secretary: Mr. K. D. D. Henderson, Orchard House, Steeple Langford, Salisburg, Wilts. (Chapter II).

*Standing Conference on Inter-Faith Dialogue in Education*. Formed in 1973, arranges inter-faith conferences concerned with education in school and community. Hon. Secretary: Mr. J. Prickett, Little Brunger, Appledore Road, Tenterden, Kent. (Chapter II).

*Temple of Understanding*. Founded in 1960 by Mrs. Judith Hollister. Has held several spiritual summit conferences and arranged lectures. Publishes *Insight*.

Offices: Wainwright House, 260 Stuyvesant Avenue, Rye, N.Y. 10580. (Chapter III).

*Theosophical Society*. Founded in New York in 1875. Claims to teach the central core of all religions, contained in the "secret doctrine". International headquarters are at Adyar, Madras, India.

*Union des Croyants*. The French group of the World Congress of Faiths. Chairman: M. H. Mavit, 10 Avenue Paul Appell, 7501h, Paris.

*Union for the Study of Great Religions*. Founded in 1951 by H. N. Spalding and others to encourage the study of the religions of the world. Helped to start the journal *Religious Studies*. Mr. K. D. D. Henderson, Orchard House, Steeple Langford, Salisbury, Wilts.

*The Universal Peace Mission*. A group working for peace and harmony amongst religions inspired by a Hindu swami. Arranged World Parliament of Religion and Culture in London in 1976. 24A Mission House, Bhubaneswar 6, Orissa State, India.

*Universal World Harmony*. Attempts to utilize the power of constructive thought to promote the brotherhood of man. 1 St. George's Square, St. Annes-on-Sea, Lancs. FY8. 2NY.

*Vatican Secretariat for Non-Christians*. Set up in 1964 by Pope Paul to engage in dialogue with other faiths. Publishes a *Bulletin*. (Chapter V).

*Week of Prayer for World Peace*. A week held annually in October in which members of all faiths are encouraged to pray for peace. Rev. Gordon Wilson, St. John's Vicarage, 14 Dane Bank Avenue, Crewe, CW2 8AA.

*Wereldgesprek der Godsdiensten*. Dutch branch of the World Congress of Faiths, now called Interreligio Netherlands.

*World Conference on Future of Mankind*. Held in Delhi in 1978, arranged by Prajapita Brahma Kumaris Ishwariya Vishwa Vidyalaya, H. Q. Mount Abu, Rajasthan, India.

*World Conference for International Peace Through Religion*. The title of the proposed inter-religious peace conference for which plans were made in the nine-

teen thirties.  Preparatory meetings were held, but the
conference itself never met.  The story is told in
*Pioneers For Peace Through Religion* by C. S. Macfarland.
Fleming H. Revell Co., New York, 1946.  (Chapter IV).

    *World Conference on Religion and Peace*.  Has ar-
ranged international inter-religious conferences for
peace at Kyoto (1970) and Louvain (1974), Princeton (197
lobbies U.N. delegates and publishes newsletter, *Religio*
*for Peace*.  Offices, 777 U.N. Plaza, New York, N.Y.
10017.  (Chapter IV.)

    *World Congress of Faiths*.  Founded in 1936, by Sir
Francis Younghusband to encourage mutual understanding
and fellowship between religions.  Arranges conferences
and lectures and publishes *World Faiths*.  Offices:  28
Powis Gardens, London W11 1JG.  (Chapter III).

    *World Council of Churches Sub-Unit on Dialogue Be-*
*tween Men of Living Faiths and Ideologies*.  Set up in
1971 to engage in dialogue and to help Christian churche
work out their relationship to other bodies.  W.C.C.
P.O. Box 66, 150 Route de Ferney, 1211 Geneva 20.
(Chapter V).

    *The World Fellowship of Faiths*.  An inter-religious
conference held in Chicago in 1933.  Proceedings edited
by C. F. Weller, published by Liveright Publishing Co.,
New York. (Appendix A).

    *The World Fellowship of Religions*.  An inter-reli-
gious body, of which Baron von Blomberg is a co-presi-
dent, which has arranged conferences in India.  Offices:
12 Rhagat Singh Marg,  New Delhi.

    *World Goodwill*.  Based on the teachings of Alice A.
Bailey, who broke away from the Theosophical Society.
Formed in 1932, it seeks to deal with the world's major
problems by utilizing the constructive power of goodwill
Linked to the Lucis Trust.    Suite 54, Whitehall Court,
London SW1A 2EF.

    *The World Order for Cultural Exchange*.  A plan to
twin children from different countries, with a guardian.
It is hoped to set up peace libraries and to purchase an
inter-faith study centre.  The Provost, Michael Woodard,
%Fr. S. G. Kiddell, The Church Lodge, Wimborne St. Giles
Wimborne, Dorset. BH21.5L.

    *The World Parliament of Religions*.  The first large

scale inter-religious gathering, held at Chicago, in
1893. Proceedings edited by Henry Barrows and published
in Chicago, 1893. (Chapter I).

    *World Parliament of Religion and Culture.* Held at
Caxton Hall, London, in September 1976, organized by
the Universal Peace Mission, P.O. Box 36, Tring, Hertfordshire.

    *World Parliament of Religions for Unitive Under-*
*standing.* An inter-religious conference held in Kerala
in 1971. Address of convener was Sangham House, Quilon-
12, Kerala State, India.

    *World Religions Conference.* Held in San Francisco
in November, 1977, in Boston, 1978 and in Los Angeles,
1979; sponsored by the International Cultural Foundation
of the Unification Movement, %Unification Theological
Seminary, Barrytown, New York 12507.

April 1980

# NOTES

## INTRODUCTION

[1]See K. S. Murty. *Revelation and Reason in Advaita Vedanta*, Andhra University, 1959 and 1961,    *passim.*

[2]Report in the *Times.* 3. 5. 1978.  p. 5.

[3]*The Myth of God Incarnate.* J. Hick (ed.)  S.C.M., 1977; and *The Truth of God Incarnate.* M. Green (ed.) Hodder and Stoughton, 1977.

[4]See, for example, N. Smart.  *Background to the Long Search.*  B.B.C. 1977, p. 292.

## CHAPTER ONE

This account is based on *The World's Parliament of Religions. An Illustrated and Popular Story of the World' First Parliament of Religions, held in Chicago in Connection with the Columbian Exposition of 1893.*

Edited by Rev. John Henry Barrows, D.D., who was Chairman of the General Committee on Religious Congresses of the World's Congress Auxiliary. The account is in two volumes, published by the Parliament Publishing Company, Chicago, in 1893. The speed of publication (and the post) is impressive. The date of the preface to volume one is 8th November, 1893, and the volume was received by Cambridge University Library, England, on 11th December, 1893. The editor's speed in preparing the material for publication is the more noticeable, as, whilst he was at work on it, the death occurred of his eldest son at the age of 13.

[1]The Committee thought that this would be the first attempt ever made to bring together representatives of all major religious traditions. Only in the course of their labours  did they hear of Asoka and Akbar. Dr. Martin, President of the Imperial University of Peking, said that the idea had occurred quite often in literature. A correspondent from Bohemia said that

the idea had been suggested by John Comenius. It was
also discovered that in the eighteen-seventies, the
Free Religious Association of Boston had suggested that
such a Congress might be convened. Yet although the
idea was not entirely new, this was the first attempt
to realize it.

[2]The proposed objects, agreed in 1892, are the
clearest statement of the aims.

(1) To bring together in conference for the first
time in history  the leading representatives of the
great historic religions of the world.

(2) To show men, in the most impressive way, what
and how many important truths the various religions
hold and teach in common.

(3) To promote and deepen the spirit of human
brotherhood among religious men of diverse faiths,
through friendly conference and mutual good understanding, while not seeking to foster the temper of indifferentism, and not striving to achieve any formal and
outward unity.

(4) To set forth, by those most competent to
speak, what are deemed the important distinctive truths
held and taught by each religion and by the various
chief branches of Christendom.

(5) To indicate the impregnable foundations of
Theism and the reasons for man's faith in immortality,
and thus to unite and strengthen the forces which are
adverse to a materialistic philosophy of the universe.

(6) To secure from leading scholars (representing
the Brahman, Buddhist, Confucian, Parsee, Mohammedan,
Jewish and other faiths, and from representatives of
the various churches of Christendom) full and accurate
statements of the spiritual and other effects of the
religions which they hold, upon the Literature, Art,
Commerce, Government, Domestic and Social Life of the
peoples among whom these faiths have prevailed.

(7) To enquire what light each religion has af-
forded, or may afford, to the other religions of the
world.

(8) To set forth, for permanent record to be published to the world, an accurate and authoritative account of the present condition and outlook of religion
among the leading nations of the earth.

(9) To discover from competent men, what light
religion has to throw on the great problems of the

present age, especially and important questions con-
nected with Temperance, Labour, Education, Wealth and
Poverty.

(10) To bring the nations of the earth into a more
friendly fellowship in the hope of securing permanent
international peace.

[3]*The World's Parliament of Religions*, p. 15.

[4] p. 10.

[5] p. 22.

[6] p. 23.

[7] pp. 67-68.

[8] See Chapter five.

[9] p. 93.

[10] It seems to have been remarks about polygamy
which aroused the hostility. This was taken, the
editor says, as an attack on a fundamental principle
of social morality. This part of his speech has been
omitted in the record because, in the editor's words,
it "opened a subject requiring more than a bold statement in five lines to be at all rightly understood".

[11] p. 1,235.

[12] p. 94.

[13] p. 127.

[14] p. 459.

[15] p. 500.

[16] p. 1,314.

[17] See Day 17.

[18] p. 75.

[19] p. 169.

[20] p. 80.

[21]In his reflections on the Influence of the Parliament, Barrows wrote, "The idea of evolving a cosmic or universal faith out of the parliament was not present in the minds of the chief promoters. They believe that the elements of such a religion are already contained in the Christian ideal and the Christian Scriptures". p. 1,572.

[22]p. 101. His italics.

[23]p. 782.

[24]p. 843.

[25]Quoted by Barbara Foxe in *Long Journey Home, a Biography of Margaret Noble* (Nivedita). Rider & Co., London, 1975. p. 18.

[26]*The World's Parliament of Religions*, p. 102.

[27]p. 170-1.


## CHAPTER TWO

[1]*Actes du Premier Congrès International d'Histoire des Religions, Paris 1901*. Ernest Leroux, 1901. From the circular of 12.5.1899, quoted on p. III.

[2]*The History of Religions, 1950-1975*. C. J. Bleeker. University of Lancaster, n.d., p. 2.

[3]Quoted by C. J. Bleeker. *op. cit.* p. 3.

[4]*Ibid.*, p. 4.

[5]*Comparative Religion. A History*. Eric J. Sharpe. Duckworth, 1975.

[6]*Proceedings of the Ninth International Congress for the History of Religions, Tokyo, 1958*. Maruzen. Tokyo, 1960, p. VI.

[7]Eric J. Sharpe. *op. cit.*, p. 271. See also C. J. Bleeker, *The Future Task of the History of Religions*. Numen VII, 1960, p. 221.

[8]*Proceedings. op. cit.*, p. 7 to 22.

    [9]*Faiths in Fellowship.*  M.C.R. Braybrooke, London,
1976, pp. 30-31.

    [10]*Proceedings,*  p. 12-13.

    [11]*Ibid.,* p. 18.

    [12]*Ibid.,* p. 19.

    [13]*Ibid.,* p. 21.

    [14]R. J.  Zwi Werblowsky.  *The Hibbert Journal.*
Vol. LVIII.  Oct. 1959 to July 1960, p. 34.

    [15]C. J. Bleeker.  *The Future Task of the History of
Religions.*  Numen VII, 1960, p. 226.

    [16]*Ibid.,* p. 232.

    [17]Annemarie Schimmel.  *Summary of the Discussion.*
Numen VII.  1960, p. 236.

    [18]*Ibid.,* p. 237.

    [19]*Ibid.*

    [20]*Ibid.*

    [21]*Ibid.,* p. 239.

    [22]*Religions of the Empire.*  Ed. William Loftus
Hare.  Duckworth, London, 1925, p. 3.

    [23]Despite the intention of the organizers, Sir
Francis Younghusband in his opening address voiced the
hope that the religions of the world could work together
for peace.

    [24]*Ibid.,* p. 4.

    [25]*Ibid.,* p. 3.

    [26]*Union for the Study of the Great Religions. Leaf-
let.*  June 1954, p. 1.  The information here is based
on this leaflet, the obituary of H. N. Spalding (1877-
1953) in *The Oxford Magazine* for 21.1.1954 by K. D. D.
Henderson, and the article by the same author, *The Work
of the Spalding Trust and the Union for the Study of the
Great Religions* in *World Faiths,* No. 79, spring 1970,
pp. 1-6.

[27]*World Faiths, op. cit.,* p. 3.

[28]The members included Maulana Azad, Arnold Bake, Basil Blackwell, Framroze Bode, A. C. Bouquet, Reader Bullard, Victor Butterfield, G. Chandra Dev, S. C. Chatterjee, Hishop George Bell of Chichester, D. M. Datta, Sir James Duff, Leslie Edgar, Alfred Egerton, Lynda Grier, William Ernest Hocking, Zakir Hussain, L. P. Jacks, S. K. Maitra, Sir John Marshall, Dean Matthews, Christopher Mayhew, P. D. Mehta, Nathaniel Micklem, Nurul Amin, Lord Pethick Lawrence, Anson Phelps Stokes, Leon Roth, Seebohm Rowntree, Lord Samuel, Greg Sinclair, Wilfred Cantwell Smith, Sidney Spencer, D. T. Suzuki, George F. Thomas, Douglas Veale, Herbert G. Woods and W. P. Yetts.

The co-ordinating committee consisted at first of Sir Richard Livingstone and Charles Raven, Arthur Arberry, K. J. Spalding and T. W. Thackers.
The secretaries were Dr. Mahadevan for India, Itrat Hussain Zuberi for Pakistan, Kenneth Morgan for the U.S.A., W. A. C. H. Dobson for Canada, F. H. Hilliard for West Africa, and Lev Gillett for the Middle East.

[29]*Comparative Religion in Education.* Ed. John R. Hinnells, Oriel Press, Newcastle-upon-Tyne, 1970, p. 109.

[30]The fruit of much of its work is *World Religions: A Handbook for Teachers.* Ed. W. Owen Cole (1976), which builds on the earlier *World Religions: Aid for Teachers,* ed. by P. Woodward (1972). Both were published by the Community Relations Commission, which is now the Commission for Racial Equality. An annual Calendar of Religious Festivals is also produced.

[31]The terms of reference agreed at the first meeting of the Standing Conference on Inter-Faith Dialogue in Education, held at 23 Norfolk Square, London, on 6-12-73. "It shall be the function of the Standing Conference to convene, or encourage the convening, of national and regional inter-faith conferences concerned with education in school and community, including Religious Education, and to circulate or publish reports of the proceedings or findings of those conferences."

[32]*World Religions, Humanists and Religious Education.* John Prickett. *World Faiths,* No. 94, 1974, pp. 24-25.

[33]*Where Two Faiths Meet,* W. W. Simpson, C.C.J.,
1955, p. 16.

[34]*What is the Inter-Religions Organization?* Statement of aims on back cover of *Is Religion Necessary?*
Inter-Religions Organization, Singapore, 1974.


CHAPTER THREE


[1]S. Radhakrishnan. *Eastern Religions and Western
Thought.* Oxford, 1939, pp. VIII-IX.

[2]S. Radhakrishnan. *Religion and Society.* Kamala
Lectures. Allen and Unwin, 1947, p. 55.

[3]S. Radhakrishnan. *Religion in a Changing World.*
Allen and Unwin, London, 1967, p. 133.

[4]S. Radhakrishnan. Fragments of a Confession in
*The Philosophy of Sarvepalli Radhakrishnan.* Ed. A.
Schilpp. Tudor Publishing Co., New York, 1952, p. 62.

[5]The standard biography of Francis Younghusband is
by George Seaver, published by John Murray in 1952, on
which this account of his life relies. The quotation
is from *Francis Younghusband,* p. 14.

[6]*Ibid.,* p. 97 ff.

[7]Francis Younghusband. *Vital Religion.* John Murray, 1940, pp. 3-4.

[8]*Ibid.,* p. 6.

[9]Seaver. *op. cit.,* quoted p. 275.

[10]The titles of his religious books are: *The Gleam,
The Reign of God, Life in the Stars, The Living Universe
Modern Mystics, The Sum of Things,* and *Vital Religion.*

[11]*Vital Religion, op. cit.* p. 7.

[12]*Ibid.,* p. 5.

[13]*Ibid.,* p. 31.

[14]*Ibid.,* p. 17.

[15]Quoted in A. Peacock's *Fellowship Through Religion*. W.C.F. London, 1956, pp. 12-13.

[16]In *Religions of Empire*.  Ed. William Loftus Hare, pp. 18-19.  See above p. 14.

[17]*Ibid.*, p. 19.

[18]Peacock. *op. cit.* p. 11.

[19]See below, p. 53f and Appendix A.

[20]*Faiths and Fellowship*, being the Proceedings of the World Congress of Faiths, held in London, July 3-17th, 1936.  Ed. A. Douglas Millard.  Published for the W.C.F. by J. M. Watkins, London, p. 131.

[21]*Ibid.*, p. 224.

[22]*Ibid.*, p. 422.

[23]*Ibid.*, p. 309.

[13]*Ibid.*, p. 9.

[25]*Vital Religion, op. cit.* p. 93.

[26]*Ibid.*, pp. 97-98.

[27]Quoted by A. Peacock, *op. cit.* p. 21.

[28]Quoted by G. Seaver, *op. cit.*  p. 371.

[29]Erik Palmstierna,*The World's Crisis and Faith*. John Lane, Bodley Head, 1941, p. 24.

[30]*Ibid.*, p. 24.

[31]*Peacock. op. cit.*  p. 27.  See also below p. 59.

[32]Reginald Sorensen.  *I Believe in Man*.  The Lindsey Press, 1970.  *passim* but especially p. 114.

[33]*Ibid.*, p. 120.

[34]*Ibid.*, p. 54.

[35]Reginald Sorensen.  Conference Sermon in *World Faiths*.  No. 77, Autumn 1969, p. 19.

[36]*Ibid.*, p. 20.

[37]*Ibid.*, p. 18.

[38]George Appleton. *Faiths in Fellowship.* In *World Faiths*, No. 101, spring 1977, p. 3.

[39]*Ibid.*, pp. 4-5.

[40]Edward Carpenter. *A Pluralist Society.* The St. Paul's Lecture, 1975.

[41]Yehudi Menuhin. *World Faiths*, No. 101, spring 1977, p. 2.

[42]See also John Hicks' Second Younghusband Lecture. *Christian Theology and Inter-Religious Dialogue. World Faiths*, No. 103, autumn 1977, pp. 2-3.

[43]Until 1961, issue 48, the journal was called *Forum*.

[44]Will Hayes. *Every Nation Kneeling.* Published by the Order of Great Companions, 1954.

[45]Marcus Braybrooke (Ed). *Inter-Faith Worship.* Galliard, 1974.

[46]In 1966 the Service was held at St. Martin-in-the-Fields, but was then moved to a secular building, the Guildhall, in the city of London, because of protests from some Christians. It is now held at Westminster Abbey.

[47]*World Faiths*, No. 48, March 1961, pp. 15-17.

[48]*World Faiths*, No. 73, 1968, p. 24.

[49]B. Cousins. *Introducing Children to World Religions.* CCJ, 1965.

[50]*World Faiths*, No. 62, March 1965, p. 11.

[51]Statement on R E in *World Faiths*, No. 81, 1970, p. 20.

[52]*Ibid.*

[53]*Ibid.*

[54]*World Faiths,* No. 86, 1972.

[55]See above, p. 16.

[56]*What Future for the Agreed Syllabus?* A report of the Religious Education Council, 1976.

[57]There are also Overseas Groups of the Congress in Belgium, India, and in France. The French group is known as L'Union des Croyants.

[58]This is based on a summary of a booklet *Inter-religion—respect for the other one* by Dr. R. Boeke in *World Faiths,* No. 105, summer 1978.

[59]John Hick, *op. cit.* pp. 2-3. See also Dr. Ursula King, *World Faiths,* 106, p. 1 ff.

[60]*Six Days of Hope.* Leaflet of the Temple of Understanding, column 2, undated.

[61]*Ibid.,* column 4.

[62]Some of this information is derived from private letters from Mrs. Hollister.

[63]Speakers were Dr. Lowell R. Ditzen, Director of the National Presbyterian Centre, Washington; Professor John Haughey, S.J., of Georgetown University; Ven. Piyananda Maha Thera, President of the Buddhist Vihara Society in Washington; Dr. Wen Yen Tsao, Professor of Asian Studies at Michigan College; Sri Raja Ram, of the Indian Embassy; Dr. Ali Abdel Kader, of the Washington Islamic Centre; Bishop Shinsho Hanayama, of the Buddhist Churches of America; Dr. Isaac Franck, of the Jewish Community Council of Washington; and Dr. Duncan Howlett of All Souls' Church, Washington. Finley Peter Dunne, the Executive Director of the Temple of Understanding, was moderator. At lunch the eighty participants heard addresses by Mrs. Hollister, Dr. Amiya Chakravarty, who had been a secretary to Tagore and was Professor of Philosophy at the State University of New York, and Rt. Rev. Paul Moore, Jr., who was the Suffragan Bishop of the Episcopal Diocese of Washington.

[64]*The Temple of Understanding Newsletter,* spring, 1968, p. 2.

[65]The papers given at the conference are collected in *The World Religions Speak.* Edited by Finley P.

Dunne, Jr., published for the World Academy of Art and
Science by Dr. W. Junk, N.V. Publishers, The Hague, 1970.

[66]*Newsletter,* spring 1970, p. 2.

[67]*Newsletter,* summer 1971, p. 1.

[68]*Newsletter,* spring 1976, p. 1.

[69]*Ibid.*

[70]*Ibid.,* p. 2.

[71]*Ibid.,* p. 3.

[72]*Ibid.,* p. 5.

[73]*Ibid.*

[74]*Ibid.,* pp. 5-6.

[75]*Ibid.,* p. 7.

[76]*Ibid.*

[77]References are from *Towards A Global Congress of
World Religions.* Sponsored by the Unification Theological Seminary. Ed. Warren Lewis, Rose of Sharon Press,
1978, p. 28.

[78]*Ibid.*

[79]p. 29.

[80]pp. 29-30.

[81]p. vii.

[82]See relevant sections of *Investigation of Korean-
American Relations.* U.S. Government Printing Office,
Washington, D.C., 1978. The Unificationist reply is in
*Our Response,* New York, the Holy Spirit Association for
The Unification of World Christianity, 1979.

[83]Finley, P. Dunne in *The World Religions Speak,*
*op. cit.,* p. XII.

[84]George Appleton. *World Faiths,* No. 101, spring
1977, p. 3.

[85]Thomas Merton in *The World Religions Speak, op.
cit.,* p. 81.

## CHAPTER FOUR

[1]See *Pioneers for Peace Through Religion, Based on Records of The Church Peace Union* by Charles S. Macfarland. Introduction by Arthur J. Brown. Fleming H. Revell Co., New York, 1946, p. 26.

[2]Chapter 10, p. 163 ff.

[3]*Ibid.*, p. 164.

[4]*Ibid.*, p. 167.

[5]See *World Religions and World Peace.* Ed. Homer A. Jack, Beacon Press, Boston, 1968, p. 204.

[6]Quoted by Homer Jack, *op. cit.*, p. 204. From *The Japan National Conference for International Peace Through Religion.* Tokyo, 1931.

[7]Charles S. Macfarland, *op. cit.*, p. 196.

[8]*Ibid.*, p. 241.

[9] This account is based on *The Preface and Introduction to Religion and Peace.* Papers from the National Inter-Religious Conference on Peace, edited by Homer A. Jack and published by the Bobbs-Merrill Co., Indianapolis, 1966.

[10]p. IX.

[11]p. XIV.

[12]p. 39.

[13]*Ibid.*

[14]pp. 39-43.

[15]p. 89.

[16]p. 92.

[17]A note on prepositions: this is the most commonly used name. Although the legal name is World Conference of Religion for Peace. (Newsletter, *Religion for Peace,* Nov. 74, p. 3.) In November, 1974, the name of the Newsletter was changed from *Beyond Kyoto* to

*Religion for Peace.*

   [18]p. 6.

   [19]The report of the conference is *World Religions
and World Peace*. Edited by Homer A. Jack. Beacon
Press 1968. The account of the preparations is given
in the Introduction by Dana McLean Greeley. This quotation is from page XII.

   [20]p. 22.

   [21]p. 43.

   [22]Quoted, p. 76.

   [23]pp. 163-5.

   [24]p. 170.

   [25]p. 192.

   [26]This account is based on *Religion for Peace.
Proceedings of the Kyoto Conference on Religion and
Peace*. Ed. Homer A. Jack. Published by Gandhi Peace
Foundation, New Delhi and Bharatiya Bhavan, Bombay 7.
The introduction tells the story of the preparations
and the conference itself.

   [27]At Louvain, in 1974, where the same procedure
was adopted, there was considerable criticism of this,
because those present felt they were an uninvolved
audience watching others pray rather than themselves
participating. Judging from the texts of the prayers,
it seems that at least some of those who led them at
Kyoto  tried to involve those present. The Christian
prayers, for example, allowed for a congregational response. Another difficulty at Louvain was the presence
of film crews and photographers, so that the atmosphere
was restless.

   [28]p. 10.

   [29]pp. 118-9.

   [30]p. 99.

   [31]p. 107.

   [32]pp. 108-9.

[33]p. 109.

[34]p. 144.

[35]pp. IX-XII.

[36]p. 190.

[37]p. 21.

[38]p. 23.

[39]p. 149.

[40]p. 149.

[41]p. 150.

[42]*Disarmament, Development, Human Rights. The Findings of the World Conference on Religion and Peace.* Kyoto, Japan. Oct. 16-21, 1970. Introduction by Homer A. Jack. Published by the World Conference of Religions for Peace, New York, 1970, p. 47.

[43]The address is 777 U.N. Plaza, New York, N.Y. 10017, USA.

[44]WCRP, 1970-74. Four Year Report of the Secretary-General (cyclostyled), p. 3. The French spelling Louvain is traditional international usage, although it is a Flemish city, and at the conference, the Flemish name Leuven was used. Louvain is used in documents about the conference and is used here.

[45]*Religion for Peace.* Nov. 1974, p. 3. A Finance Committee was also elected. The nine elected to the Executive Board were: Mr. Abdul Ansari, a Muslim from India; Miss Jane Evans, a Jew from the USA; Rev. Shocho Hagami, a Buddhist of Japan; Professor Mohammed F. Jamali, a Muslim of Tunisia; Archbishop Marcos G. McGrath, a Christian of Panama; Dr. Howard Schomer, a Christian of the USA; Dr. Gopal Singh, A Sikh of India; Mr. August Vanistendael, a Christian of Belgium; and Mrs. Janet Wesanga, a Christian of Uganda.

[46]*Religion for Peace,* July 1976, p. 3.

[47]The regional addresses are: The Japanese WCRP, Fumon Hall, 2-6 Wada, Suginami-Ku, Tokyo, 166 Japan; The Gandhi Peace Foundation, 221 Deen Daya, Upadhyaya

Marg, New Delhi 1, India; The U.S. Inter-Religions Com-
mittee on Peace, 100 Maryland Avenue, NE, Washington,
D.C. 10002, USA; European Committee %Dr. Maria A.
Lücker, 25, Bismarckstr, 53 Bonn, German Federal Republic;
U.K./Ireland, %Pax Christi, Blackfriars Hall, Southampton
Rd, London NW5, England. At the end of 1975, a group was
formed in Canada: %Jack Shea, 3-104, Woodbridge Crescent,
Ottawa, Ontario.

[48]WCRP, 1970-74. Four year Report of the Secretary-
General (cyclostyled), p. 1. The account of activities
is largely based on this and copies of the Newsletter.

[49]*Religion for Peace*, Jan. 1975, p. 1.

[50]*Beyond Kyoto*, Nov. 1971, p. 2.

[51]*Religion and The Quality of Life.* Archbishop
Fernandes, p. 1 of the cyclostyled text of his speech. UNCTAD
III was the Third United Nations Conference on Trade and Development

[52]*Ibid.*, p. 4.

[53]*Ibid.*

[54]Opening Address of Ven. Thich Nhat Hahn. Cyclostyled, p. 1.

[55]*Ibid.*, pp. 1-2.

[56]*Religion for Peace*, Nov. 1974, p. 4.

[57]The Louvain Declaration. Cyclostyled text, p. 1.

[58]*Ibid.*, p. 2.

[59]*Ibid.*, p. 3.

[60]*Ibid.*, p. 5.

[61]*Religion for Peace*, February 1977, p. 1.

[62]*Conference Declaration.* Cyclostyled. p. 2.

[63]*Religion for Peace*, February 1977, pp. 1-2.

[64]*Religion for Peace*, July 1977, pp. 1 and 4.

[65]*Religion for Peace*, October 1977, pp. 1 and 2.

[66]*Religion for Peace,*   July 1977, p. 2.

[67]*Religion for Peace,*   July 1975, p. 2.

[68]*The Quest of World Religions for World Peace.*
Arya Samaj.  Centenary address.  Dr. Homer A. Jack,
cyclostyled, p. 5.

[69]*Ibid.,* p. 6.

[70]*Ibid.,* p. 6.

[71]I am indebted for much of this information to
a WCRP Report by Dr. Homer Jack, No. M5.


## CHAPTER FIVE

[1]Declaration on the Relationship of the Church to
Non-Christian Religions in *The Documents of Vatican II.*
Ed. W. M. Abbott, S. J.; Geoffrey Chapman, 1966, p. 660.

[2]*Ibid.,* p. 661.

[3]*Ibid.,* p. 662.

[4]*Ibid.,* pp. 662-3.

[5]Discourse to the Sacred College.  23.6.1964.  AAS.
Vol. 56, p. 584.

[6]*Bulletin* of the Secretariat for Non-Christians.
4.3.1967, p. 29.

[7]*Ibid.,* p. 33.

[8]*Ibid.,* p. 33.

[9]*Ibid.,* p. 35.

[10]*Ibid.,* p. 37.

[11]*Ibid.,* p. 38.

[12]*Ibid.,* p. 39.

[13]*Ibid.,* pp. 39-40.

[14]*Ibid.,* p. 31.

[15]*The International Review of Mission.* 1970, p. 173ff. See also S. J. Samartha, *Dialogue as a Continuing Christian Concern, Ecumenical Review,* XXIII, p. 128. Samartha refers to the following meetings, amongst others: Christian-Hindu, Kottayam, India, Oct. 14-16, 1962; Christian-Muslim, Birmingham, Jan. 27-8, 1968; Christian-Buddhist-Confucian, Seoul, Korea, Oct. 8-19, 1967.

[16]S. J. Samartha, *The World Council of Churches and Men of Other Faiths and Ideologies. Ecumenical Review XXII,* p. 192.

[17]Quoted by S. J. Samartha, *op. cit.,* from the Minutes of the Central Committee, Geneva, 1969, p. 29.

[18]Ecumenical Review XXIII, p. 134.

[19]S. J. Samartha, *Dialogue: Significant Issues in the Continuing Debate.* Ecumenical Review, XXIV, p. 328, 1972.

[20]*Study Encounter.* Vol. X 3, 1974, World Council of Churches, Geneva.

[21]Samuel Rayan S. J., *The Ultimate Blasphemy, International Review of Missions,* LXV No. 257, Jan. 1976, p. 131. See also S. J. Samartha in *World Faiths,* No. 100, 1976, p. 33ff, and Rabbi Arnold Jacob Wolf in *Common Ground,* summer 1976. The Rabbi was one of the non-Christian observers invited to the Assembly.

[22]Samuel Rayan, *op. cit.,* p. 132.

[23]*Ibid.,* p. 133.

[24]*Breaking Barriers.* Nairobi, 1975. Edited by David M. Paton, S.P.C.K., London, 1976, pp. 73-74.

[25]*Ibid.,* p. 75.

[26]*Ibid.,* p. 75.

[27]*Ibid.,* p. 76.

[28]*Ibid.,* p. 76.

[29]*Ibid.,* para. 20, p. 77.

[30]*Ibid.,* para. 22, p. 77.

³¹*Ibid.*, para. 23, pp. 77-8.

³²Quoted by David M. Paton, *op. cit.*, pp. 71-2.

³³*Ibid.*, pp. 72-73.

³⁴*Dialogue in Community.* Text of the statement of the Chiang Mai Consultation (cyclostyled). Para. 19, p. 10. See also S. J. Samartha, *Dialogue in Community, A Pause for Reflection* and *Dialogue in Community, A Step Forward.* (Both cyclostyled from World Council of Churches).

³⁵*Dialogue in Community*, para. 19, p. 10.

³⁶S. J. Samartha, *Dialogue in Community, A Step Forward*, p. 5.

³⁷*Dialogue in Community*, para. 9, p. 6.

³⁸S. J. Samartha, *Dialogue in Community, A Step Forward*, p. 1.

³⁹Referred to in Gwen Cashmore's report of Chiang Mai in *World Faiths*, No. 103, 1977, p. 27.

## CHAPTER SIX

¹*William Wynn Simpson* by James Parkes. *Common Ground*, XXVIII 3, autumn 1974, 5.

²W. W. Simpson in *Where Two Faiths Meet.* CCJ, 1955, p. 4.

³*Ibid.*, p. 15.

⁴*Loc. cit.*

⁵*Loc. cit.*

⁶*Ibid.*, pp. 15-16.

⁷*Ibid.*, p. 16.

⁸*In Spirit and in Truth, Aspects of Judaism and Christianity.* Edited for the Society of Jews and Christians by G. A. Yates. Hodder & Stoughton, London, 1934, p. XII.

[9]*Retro-Circum-Prospect.* W. W. Simpson. *Common Ground* XXVIII, 3, autumn 1974, p. 5.

[10]*Where Two Faiths Meet.* *op. cit.,* p. 16.

[11]For a time in the fifties Roman Catholic support was withdrawn because the Vatican thought the methods— not the objects—employed by the Council tended towards "indifferentism". See *Common Ground* IX, 2, March 1955.

[12]*Ibid.,* p. 18.

[13]*Freedom, Justice and Responsibility.* Conference Report, CCJ, 1946.

[14]Quoted in *Christian Teaching and Anti-Semitism.* CCJ Leaflet, n.d., after 1968.

[15]*Twenty Years After,* CCJ, 1966, p. 11.

[16]*Christian-Jewish Conclave Condemns Hijacking.* *Jerusalem Post,* 9-7-76.

[17]Quoted by Geoffrey Wigoder. *Fighting Intolerance.* *Jerusalem Post,* July 1976. See also *ICCJ Jerusalem Encounter* in *Christian News from Israel,* XXVI 1, 1976, pp. 2-6; and *Jerusalem 1976* by W. W. Simpson in *World Faiths,* No. 100, 1976, p. 13ff. The five Working Groups were on:

1) Israel - people, land and state - from the historical, theological and ideological aspects of the Jewish-Christian dialogue.

2) The significance of the State of Israel for present-day Christian-Jewish relations, with special emphasis placed on Christian-Jewish relations in the Diaspora, the Christian presence in a Jewish state, and the role played by the city of Jerusalem in Christian-Jewish relations in Israel and in the Diaspora.

3) Israel's present-day realities and problems, legitimate aspirations and responsibilities and relationship to Christians and Jews throughout the world.

4) The significance of the heritage of both Jews and Christians in their approach to problems of the world today, especially in relation to Islam, the Third World, secularized ideologies such as Marxism, modern culture, the Death-of-God movement, and the many issues created by the rise of the new Israel.

5) Christian ecumenism and Christian-Jewish rela-

tions, with special attention paid to the need for
"dialogue" and the dangers of "missionizing" or "proselytizing".

[18]Dr. Ezra Spicehandler. *Is Dialogue possible in
Jerusalem? World Faiths,* spring 1977, No. 101, p. 13.

[19]Dr. Coos Schoneveld. *Towards a New Jewish-
Christian Understanding in Israel. Judaism,* 86, vol.
22, No. 2.

[20]Fr. Dubois in *Inter-Faith Dialogue in Israel.
Retrospect and Prospect.* An inter-faith symposium held
in May, 1973. Published by *Immanuel,* as a special sup-
plement in 1973, p. 23.

[21]*Ibid.,* p. 13.

[22]Spicehandler, *op. cit.,* p. 13.

[23]Professor R. J. Zwi Werblowsky. *Inter-Faith
Dialogue in Israel, op. cit.,* page 33.

[24]*Ibid.,* p. 34.

[25]Fr. Elias Chacour. *Ibid.,* p. 25.

[26]*Ten Years Ecumenical Fraternity. Retrospect and
Prospect.* Talk by Schoneveld. Cyclostyled, 1976, p. 1.

[27]Spicehandler, *op. cit.,* pp. 13-14.

[28]Dr. Goldstein in *Judaism, op. cit.,* p. 204.

[29]Werblowsky, *op. cit.,* p. 33.

[30]Schoneveld. *Dialogue with Jews* in *Immanuel* No.
6, spring 1976, p. 68. See also *Judaism, op. cit.,* p.
206. In 1977 a difficult situation developed, after a
letter was printed on January 7th in the London *Times*
protesting the eviction of Arabs from their homes in
Old Jerusalem. It was signed by four Anglican clergy,
of whom one, Fr. Murray Rogers, was a member of the
Rainbow Group. A past Chairman of the group demanded
Fr. Rogers' expulsion from the group, saying that membership involved "an ideological commitment to the State of
Israel". After much discussion, he was finally expelled
for the "tone and style" of his actions. Fr. Rogers re-
counts his version of events in his Jyotiniketan Letter
No. 24 of December 1977. What happened is a reminder

that inter-faith dialogue in Israel cannot escape being influenced by the political situation there.

[31]*Ten Years Ecumenical Fraternity. op. cit.,* p. 1.

[32]Debbi Dunn. *People Can Get Along Better than Governments. The Kansas City Jewish Chronicle,* 12-7-74.

[33]*Neve Shalom.* Cyclostyled leaflet.

[34]*Christian News from Israel.* XXIII, spring 1973, p. 243.

[35]Dr. Uriel Tal. *The New Pattern in Jewish Christian dialogue. Immanuel,* No. 1, summer 1972, p. 54.

[36]Professor Shemaryahu Talmon. *Inter-faith Dialogue in Israel. op. cit.,* p. 10.

[37]*Ibid.,* p. 11.

[38]*Immanuel,* 1, summer 1972, p. 58.

[39]*Immanuel,* 5, p. 97.

[40]*Op. cit.,* p. 15.

[41]See Coos Schoneveld. *Dialogue with Jews, op. cit.,* p. 66.

[42]Dr. Hartman, *Immanuel,* 5, p. 98.

[43]*Op. cit.,* pp. 18-19.

[44]Rabbi Henry Siegman in *The Church and the Jewish People.* Newsletter, WCC, Geneva, No. 2, 1976, p. 13.

[45]*Jewish Christian Dialogue.* Published by IJCIC and WCC, 1975, pp. 17-8. The First National Colloquium on Greek Orthodox——Jewish Relations was held in the USA in 1972, the Jewish-Christian Orthodox Encounter in Lucerne in March, 1977, the First Episcopal-Jewish Colloquium in the USA in 1975. A Lutheran-Jewish consultation was held in Berlin in February 1979.

[46]*Ibid.,* p. 7.

[47]*Loc. cit.*

[48]*Ibid.,* p. 8.

[49]*Ibid.*, p. 9.

[50]*Loc. cit.*

[51]Fr. Bruno Hussar, OP. *Some Reflections on the Declaration by The Second Vatican Council on The Attitude of the Church Towards the Non-Christian Religions* in *Christian News from Israel* (CNI) XVII, 1, 1966, p. 10. See also Professor Krister Stendahl *Judaism and Christianity II - After a Colloquium and a War.* CNI, XIX, 1-2, 1968, pp. 21-30.

[52]CNI, XVI, Dec. 1965, pp. 3-6.

[53]Fr. J. M. Dubois. *The Catholic Church and the State of Israel after 25 Years. Petahim* No. 3 (25) July 1973, p. 9. See also CNI XXIII 4, 1973, p. 221.

[54]The text is printed in CNI XXIII 4, spring 1973, p. 252.

[55]*Ibid.*, pp. 252-3.

[56]*Ibid.*, p. 253.

[57]*Loc. cit.*

[58]*Ibid.*, p. 253.

[59]*Ibid.*, p. 254.

[60]CNI XXV 2, 1975, p. 92.

[61]*Ibid.*, p. 92.

[62]Quoted in *Rome and Geneva in Jerusalem.* CNI XXV 4, 1976, p. 183.

[63]Quoted by W. W. Simpson in *Jerusalem, 1976. World Faiths*, No. 100, 1976, p. 14.

[64]CNI XXV 2, 1975, p. 92.

[65]Professor Talmon in *Christian-Jewish Dialogue, a 'common search for spirituality'.* Article in the Jerusalem Post, 19.3.1976.

[66]Professor R. J. Zwi Werblowsky. *Jewish-Christian Relations.* CNI XXIV 2-3, 1973, p. 117. There are also those Christians who see Messianic significance in the

return of the Jews.

[67]Professor Talmon. *Op. cit.*

[68]*Christian-Jewish Dialogue, a 'common search for spirituality', op. cit.*

[69]*The Church and the Jewish People.* WCC Newsletter 2, 1976, p. 9.


CHAPTER SEVEN

[1]The relevant documents have been collected in *Christians Meeting Muslims.* WCC, Geneva, 1977, where the original references are given. This quotation is from p. 92. A valuable attempt to open Christians and Muslims to each other's devotional idiom is *Alive to God,* compiled by Kenneth Cragg, and published by The Oxford University Press in 1970.

[2]*Christians Meeting Muslims,* p. 112.

[3]*Ibid.,* p. 113.

[4]*Ibid.,* p. 114.

[5]*Ibid.,* p. 123.

[6]*Ibid.,* p. 125.

[7]See the *International Review of Missions.* LXV. 260, October 1976.

[8]*The Bulletin* of the Secretariat for non-Christians, 1976, XI/I, 31, p. 10.

[9]*Ibid.,* p. 21.

[10]*Ibid.,* p. 13.

[11]*Ibid.,* p. 13.

[12]See for example *A New Threshold* by D. Brown. British Council of Churches, 1976.

[13]Press release of the Conference of European Churches, No. 78, 3 efg., and also a report (cyclostyled) by R. Trudgian.

¹⁴This information is based on the following written sources:

   1) *J.C.M. Newsletter* 1 (July 1972); 2 (Feb. 1973);
3 (July 1973); 4 (Jan. 1974); 5 (June 1974).

   2) *Practical Ecumenism:* Jews, Christians and Muslims in Europe. Lionel Blue, *Journal ₒf Ecumenical
Studies,* Vol. 10, No. 1, 1973.

   3) Articles reprinted from *European Judaism,* winter
1974-75: *The New Paradigm of Europe,* Lionel Blue; *Islam
and The Muslims in Europe Today,* Kurshid Ahmad; *The
Christian Presence in Europe and The Encounter with Islam and Judaism,* W. Maechler.

   4) *The Faith of Our Fathers - The Fate of Our
Children.* Proceedings of the European Conference held
in London, 1972.

¹⁵*Christians Meeting Muslims. Op. cit.,* Foreword.

¹⁶*Ibid.*

¹⁷Mr. A. K. Brohi in an address to an International Seminar on Muslim Communities in Non-Muslim States,
held in London in July 1978, reported in the Times,
25.7.1978, p. 6.

# CHAPTER EIGHT

¹Vivekananda. Selections from Swami Vivekananda,
Calcutta, 1957, pp. 17-18.

²See above, Chapter Three, pp. 19-20.

³W. Miller. *The Madras Christian College.* Edin-
burgh, 1905, p. 8.

⁴Kaj Baago. *Pioneers of Indigenous Christianity.*
Christian Literature Society, Madras, 1969, p. 75.
Baago associates T. E. Slater with Farquhar's views

⁵Gandhi. *Satyagraha in South Africa.* S. Ganesan,
Madras, 1928, p. 165, quoted in *Mahatma Gandhi and
Hindu-Christian Dialogue.* Nirmal Minz. C.L.S. Madras,
1970.

[6]Gandhi. *All Religions are True*, p. 228.   Quoted Minz. *op. cit.*, p. 51.

[7]*Ibid.*, p. 26, quoted Minz. *op. cit.*, p. 52.

[8]Gandhi. *The Story of My Experiment with Truth.* Ahmedabad, 1927, p. 343.   Minz, p. 55.

[9]Gandhi. *The Way to Communal Harmony*, p. 406. Minz, p. 56.

[10]Gandhi. *The Message of Jesus Christ.*   Ahmedabad, 1940, p. 28ff.

[11]*The Aims and Basis of the All-Kerala Inter-Religious Student Fellowship,* printed as an Appendix in *The Witness of S. K. George,* by T. K. Thomas, C.L.S. Madras, 1970, pp. 149-150.

[12]*Ibid.*

[13]S. K. George. *Gandhi's Challenge to Christianity.* Ahmedabad, 1960, p. 47.   The book was written during the year he spent in 1938 at Manchester College, Oxford, at the invitation of the General Assembly of Unitarians.

[14]*Ibid.*, pp. 38-40.

[15]This is recounted by S. K. George in the Fellowship of Friends of Truth Quarterly, vol. V, No. 1 and reprinted in *The Witness of S. K. George, op. cit.*   I am also grateful for material supplied by the secretary, Ruth Richardson.   See also *Quakers Encounters,* vol. 3; *Whispers of Truth* by John Ormerod Greenwood, Sessions of York, 1978, pp. 232-33.

[16]The original statement says: "The Fellowship of the Friends of Truth is alive to the urgent need in the world today of bringing together people of different faiths in common endeavour to realize the good life for all through the way of truth and love.   It attempts to do this on the basis: (1) of reverence for all religions, implying thereby a frank acceptance of the fact of variety in men's growing apprehension of truth; (2) of silent worship; (3) of united brotherly action on non-violent lines."   Only one alteration has been made to this original statement.   The word "meditation" has been added after "silent worship".

[17]See above, p. 65.

[18]P. Chenchiah in *The Pilgrim,* reprinted in *The Theology of Chenchiah.* Ed. D. A. Thangasamy, C.I.S.R.S. Bangalore, 1966, p. 181.

[19]*Ibid.,* p. 183.

[20]*Ibid.,* pp. 192-93.

[21]H. Kraemer. *The Christian Message in a Non-Christian World.* Lutterworth, London, 1938, p. 302.

[22]Abhishiktananda. *Hindu-Christian Meeting Point.* Institute of Indian Culture, Bombay and C.I.S.R.S., Bangalore, 1969, p. 4.

[23]I discuss these developments in my book, *The Undiscovered Christ.* C.L.S. Madras, 1973. See also *Inter-Religious Dialogue,* ed. H. J. Singh, CISRS, 1967.

[24]*Dialogue on India.* Fr. A. Nambiaparambil. Varanssi. Quoted in *Religion for Peace,* July 1976. I have not been able to obtain a copy of the original report.

[25]This information is based on a private letter from Fr. Albert Nambiaparambil. I saw some of the easy co-operation between faiths on the WCF tour to India in 1978 at the Vaswani School in Poona, at Auroville and at the Tamilnad Theological College in Madurai.

[26]*Buddhist-Christian Encounter.* Papers from a consultation held at Rangoon in 1961, published by the Christian Institute of Buddhist Studies, Colombo.

[27]The Story of Devasaranaramaya is told in *If They Had Met,* published by the Community in 1968. See also *The Inner Eye of Love,* by William Johnston, Collins, 1978.

[28]Information about the Congress of Religions, Ceylon, is to be found in *The World Religions Speak,* ed. Finley P. Dunne, pp. 189-196. Information about the Inter-Religious Organization in Singapore is contained in booklets published by that body, and in reports that I have received from the secretary, Mr. Mehervan Singh.

## CONCLUSION

[1]*The Louvain Declaration.* Cyclostyled text, p. 1.

[2]G. Appleton. *Faiths in Fellowship. World Faiths,* No. 101, spring 1977, pp. 4-5.

[3]Quoted in *Breaking Barriers.* Ed. David M. Paton, p. 236.

[4]*Ibid.,* p. 73. See also *Religion and Society,* XXIII, No. 3, September 1976, pp. 1-3.

## APPENDIX A

This account is based on *World Fellowship. Addresses and Messages by leading spokesmen of all Faiths, Races and Countries.* Edited by Charles Frederick Weller (General Executive, World Fellowship of Faiths). Liveright Publishing Co., New York, 1935.

[1]p. 536.

[2]p. 10.

[3]See also p. 155.

[4]p. 502. See alsl Chapter IV.

[5]p. 534.

[6]Sung to the tune of "My Country 'Tis of Thee" or "God Save The Queen". At the opening ceremony and at subsequent sessions, prayers, drawn from the scriptures of the eleven faiths represented, were read.

# BIBLIOGRAPHY OF BOOKS AND
# ARTICLES MENTIONED IN THE TEXT

ABBREVIATIONS

| | |
|---|---|
| CCJ | Council of Christians and Jews. |
| CNI | *Christian News from Israel.* |
| ER | *Ecumenical Review.* |
| IRM | *International Review of Missions.* |
| J.C.M. | Jews, Christians and Muslims. |
| WCC | World Council of Churches. |
| WCF | World Congress of Faiths. |
| WCRP | World Conference on Religion and Peace. |
| WF | *World Faiths.* |

Books are published in London unless otherwise stated

\* \* \*

*Actes du Premier Congrés International d'Histoire des Religions.* Ernest Leroux, Paris, 1901.

Ahmad, Khurshid. *Islam and The Muslims in Europe Today. European Judaism.* Winter 1974-75.

Appleton, George. *Faiths in Fellowship, WF* 101, spring 1977.

Abhishiktananda. *Hindu-Christian Meeting Point.* Institute of Indian Culture, Bombay and Christian Institute for the Study of Religion, Bangalore, 1969.

Baago, K. *Pioneers of Indigenous Christianity.* Christian Literature Society, Madras, 1969.

Barrows, John Henry. *The World's Parliament of Religions.* An illustrated and popular story of the World's First Parliament of Religions, held in Chicago in connection with the Columbian Exposition of 1893. 2 vols. The Parliament Publishing Company, Chicago, 1893.

*Beyond Kyoto.* Newsletter of WCRP.

Bleeker, C. J. *The History of Religions, 1950-1975.* University of Lancaster, n.d.

_____. The Future Task of the History of Religions
     Numen VII, 1960.

Blue, Lionel. Practical Ecumenism: Jews, Christians and
     Moslems in Europe. Journal of Ecumenical Studies.
     Vol. 10, No. 1, 1973.

_____. The New Paradigm in Europe  European Judais
     Winter 1974-75.

Boeke, R. Interreligio Netherlands. WF 105, summer 197
     p. 7 ff.

Braybrooke, Marcus. Faiths in Fellowship. WCF. London
     1976.

_____. Inter-Faith Worship. Galliard, 1974.

_____. Together to the Truth. Christian Litera-
     ture Society, Madras, 1971.

_____. The Undiscovered Christ. Christian Litera-
     ture Society, Madras, 1973.

Breaking Barriers. Ed. David M. Paton, SPCK, 1976.

Brown, David. A New Threshold. British Council of
     Churches, 1976.

Buddhist-Christian Encounter. A Consultation at Rangoon
     in 1961. Christian Institute of Buddhist Studies,
     490 Havelock Road, Colombo 6, Ceylon, 1964 edtn.
     (cyclostyled).

Carman, J. B. Continuing Tasks in Inter-Religious Dia-
     logue, ER XXIII.

Carpenter, Edward. A Pluralist Society. The St. Paul's
     Lecture, London, 1975.

Cashmore, Gwen. Report on Chiang Mai. WF 103, 1977.

Cousins, B. Introducing Children to World Religions.
     CCJ, 1965.

Christians Meeting Muslims. WCC Papers on 10 Years of
     Christian-Muslim Dialogue, WCC, 1977.

Cragg, Kenneth (ed). *Alive to God*. Oxford University Press, 1970.

*Dialogue in Community*. Statement of the Chiang Mai Consultation. Cyclostyled WCC, 1977.

*Disarmament, Development, Human Rights*. WCRP, New York, 1970.

Dubois, Fr. J. M. *The Catholic Church and the State of Israel After 25 Years*. *Petahim*, No. 3, July 1973; CNI, XXIII, 4, 1973.

Dunn, Debbi. *People Can Get Along Better Than Governments*. *The Kansas City Jewish Chronicle*, 12-7-74.

*The Faith of Our Fathers——The Fate of Our Children*. Proceedings of the European Conference of J.C.M., J.C.M., 1972.

*Faiths and Fellowship*. The Proceedings of the World Congress of Faiths, 1936. Ed. A. Douglas Millard, published for WCF by J. M. Watkins, London, 1936.

Fernandes, Archbishop. *Religion and The Quality of Life*. Cyclostyled text of his speech at the Louvain Conference, 1974.

Foxe, Barbara. *The Long Journey Home*. A Biography of Margaret Noble (Nivedita). Rider and Co., London, 1975.

*Freedom, Justice and Responsibility*. Conference Report, CCJ, 1946.

Goldstein, Dr. Israel. *Inter-faith Relations in Israel*. *Judaism*, 86, vol. 22, No. 2.

Gandhi, M. K. *My Experiment with Truth*. Navajivan Publishing House, Ahmedabad, 1927.

_____. *Satyagraha in South Africa*. S. Ganesan, Madras, 1928.

_____. *The Message of Jesus Christ*. Ahmedabad, 1940.

_____. *India of My Dream*. Comp. by R. K. Frabhu. Hind Kitab, Ltd, Bombay, 1947.

George, S. K. *Gandhi's Challenge to Christianity.*
    Ahmedabad, 1960.

Hare, William Loftus, ed. *Religions of the Empire.* Duck
    worth, 1925.

Havens, Teresina. Article on Religious Education in *WF*,
    73, p. 9.

Hayes, Will. *Every Nation Kneeling.* Order of the Great
    Companions, 1954.

Hick, John. *Christian Theology and Inter-Religious Dia-*
    *logue.* *WF*, 103, autumn 1977, pp. 2-3.

_____. *Death and Eternal Life.* Collins, 1976.

Hinnells, John R. ed. *Comparative Religion in Education.*
    Oriel Press, Newcastle-upon-Tyne, 1970.

Humbertclaude, Fr. Article in *The Bulletin of The Secre-*
    *tariat for non-Christians*, 4-3-67.

Hussar, Fr. Bruno, OP. *Some Reflections on the Declara-*
    *tion by The Second Vatican Council on the Attitude*
    *of the Church Towards the Non-Christian Religions.*
    *CNI*, XVII, 1, 1966, p. 10.

Henderson, K. D. D. *Obituary of H. N. Spalding.* *The*
    *Oxford Magazine*, LXXIX, 9, 1-21-54.

_____. *The Work of the Spalding Trust and the Union*
    *for the Study of the Great Religions.* In *World*
    *Faiths*, 79, spring 1970.

*In Spirit and In Truth. Aspects of Judaism and Christian-*
    *ity.* Ed. G. A. Yates, Hodder and Stoughton, London,
    1934.

*Inter-Faith Dialogue in Israel. Retrospect and Prospect.*
    An Inter-Faith Symposium, May 1973. *Immanuel* Sup-
    plement, 1973.

*Is Religion Necessary?* Inter-Religious Organization,
    Singapore, 1974.

*If They Had Met.* The first ten years of Devassranaramaya
    Published by Devassranaramaya, Ibbagamuva, N.W.P.
    Ceylon, 1968.

Jack, Homer A. ed. *World Religions and World Peace.*
        Beacon Press, Boston, 1968.

_____ ed. *Religion and Peace.* Bobbs-Merrill Co.,
        Indianapolis, 1966.

_____ ed. *Religion for Peace.* Proceedings of the
        Kyoto Conference on Religion and Peace. Gandhi
        Peace Foundation, New Delhi, and Bharatiya Bhavan,
        Bombay 7, 1973.

_____ . *WCRP, 1970-74.* Cyclostyled report.

_____ . *The Quest of World Religions for World Peace.*
        Arya Samaj Centenary Address. Cyclostyled.

*JCM Newsletter. passim.*

*Jesus Christ Frees and Unites.* WCC, 1974.

*Jewish-Christian Dialogue.* WCC, 1975.

Kraemer, H. *The Christian Message in a Non-Christian
        World.* Lutterworth, London, 1938.

*The Louvain Declaration.* 1974, cyclostyled WCRP.

Macfarland, Charles S. *Pioneers for Peace Through Reli-
        gion.* Fleming H. Revell Co., New York, 1946.

Maechler, W. *The Christian Presence in Europe and the
        Encounter with Islam and Judaism. European Judaism,*
        winter 1974-75.

Menuhin, Yehudi. Conference Message. *WF* 101, spring
        1977, p. 2.

Minz, Nirmal. *Mahatma Gandhi and Hindu-Christian Dialogue.*
        Christian Literature Society, Madras, 1970.

*Nes Ammim.* Pamphlet, n.d.

*Neve Shalom.* Cyclostyled Leaflet, n.d.

Palmstierna, Erik. *The World's Crisis and Faith.* John
        Lane, Bodley Head, 1941.

Parkes, James. *William Wynn Simpson. Common Ground,*
        XXVIII, 3, autumn 1974, p. 5.

Peacock, A.  *Fellowship Through Religion.*  WCF, 1956.

Prickett, John.  *World Religions.  Humanists and Religio*
    *Education.*  WF 94, 1974.

*Proceedings of the Ninth International Congress for the*
    *History of Religions.*  Maruzen, Tokyo, 1960.

Radhakrishnan, S.  *Eastern Religions and Western Thought*
    Oxford, 1939.

_____.  *Religion and Society.*  Kamala Lectures,
    Allen and Unwin, 1947.

_____.  *Religion in a Changing World.*  Allen and Un-
    win, 1967.

_____.  *Fragments of a Confession* in *The Philosophy*
    *of Sarvepalli Radhakrishnan.*  Ed. A. Schilpp, Tudor
    Publishing Co., New York, 1952.

Rayan, Samuel S. J.  *The Ultimate Blasphemy.*  IRM, LXV,
    Jan. 1976.

*Religion for Peace.*  Newsletter of WCRP.  *passim.*

Samartha, S. J.  *Dialogue in Community. A Pause for Re-*
    *flection.*  Cyclostyled, WCC, Geneva, 1977.

_____.  *Dialogue in Community: A Step Forward.*
    Cyclostyled, WCC, Geneva, 1977.

_____.  *Dialogue As A Continuing Christian Concern.*
    *ER,* XXIII, p. 128.

_____.  *Dialogue: Significant Issues in the Contin-*
    *uing Debate. ER,* XXIV, p. 327.

_____.  *Reflections on a Multilateral Dialogue.  ER*
    XXVI, p. 367.  Also article in Study Encounter, 197(

_____, ed.  *Living Faiths and the Ecumenical Move-*
    *ment.*  WCC, Geneva, 1971.

_____.  *More Than An Encounter of Commitments.  IRM*
    vol. 59, 1970, p. 393.

_____.  *The World Council of Churches and Men of*
    *Other Faiths and Ideologies.  ER,* XXII, p. 190.

_____. *Courage for Dialogue*. *WF,* 100, 1976, p. 33.

Schimmel, Annemarie. *Summary of the Discussion*. *Numen,*
    VII, 1960.

Schoneveld, Coos. *Dialogue with Jews*. *Immanuel,* 6,
    spring 1976, p. 68.

_____. *Towards a New Jewish-Christian Understanding
    in Israel*. *Judaism,* 86, vol. 22, 2.

_____. *Ten Years Ecumenical Fraternity*. Cyclostyled,
    1976.

*School Assemblies for Worship*. Report of WCF Education
    Advisory Committee. *WF,* 86, 1972, p. 1ff.

Seaver, George. *Francis Younghusband*. John Murray, 1952.

Sharpe, E. J. *Comparative Religion: A History*. Duckworth,
    1975.

Siegman, Rabbi Henry. *The Church and the Jewish People*.
    WCC, Newsletter, Geneva, No. 2, 1976.

Simpson, W. W. *Jerusalem 1976*. *WF,* 100, 1976, p. 13 ff.

_____. *Retro-Circum-Prospect*. *Common Ground,* XXVIII,
    3, autumn 1974.

_____. *Where Two Faiths Meet*. CCJ, 1955.

*Six Rays of Hope*. Leaflet of the Temple of Understanding,
    undated.

Sorensen, Reginald. *I Believe in Man*. The Lindsey Press,
    1970. Conference Sermon, *WF,* 77, autumn, 1969, p.
    19.

Spicehandler, Ezra. *Is Dialogue Possible in Jerusalem?*
    *WF,* 101, spring 1977, p. 13.

Statement on Religious Education of WCF Education Advisory
    Committee. *WF,* 81, 1970, p. 20.

Stendahl, Krister. *Judaism and Christianity*. *After a
    Colloquium and a War*. CNI, XIX, 1-2, 1968.

Tal, Uriel. *The New Pattern in Jewish-Christian Dialogues*.
    *Immanuel,* No. 1, summer 1972.

Talmon, S.  *Christian-Jewish Dialogue: A Common Search*
    *for Spirituality.*  *Jerusalem Post,* 3-19-76.

Temple of Understanding Newsletter.  *passim.*

Thangasamy, D. A., ed.  *The Theology of Chenchiah.*  Chris-
    tian Institute for the Study of Religion, Bangalore
    1966.

Thich Naht Hahn.  Opening Address at Louvain Conference,
    1974, cyclostyled.

Thomas, T. K., ed.  *The Witness of S. K. George.*  Chris-
    tian Literature Society, Madras, 1970.

*Twenty Years After.*  Conference Report, CCJ, 1966.

*Toward a Global Congress of World Religions.*  Edited by
    Warren Lewis.  Sponsored and published by Unifica-
    tion Theological Seminary, Barrytown, New York,
    1978, Rose of Sharon Press.

*Union for the Study of Great Religions.*  Leaflet, 1954.

Vivekananda.  *Selections from Swami Vivekananda.*  Calcutt
    1957.

Ward, Marcus.  *Our Theological Task.*  Christian Literatur
    Society, Madras, 1946.

Werblowsky, R. J.  Zwi.  *The Hibbert Journal.*  LVIII, p.
    34.  *Jewish-Christian Relations.*  *CNI,* XXIV, 2-3,
    1973.

*What Future for the Agreed Syllabus?*  A Report to the Re-
    ligious Education Council, 1976.

*Where are we after Nairobi?* WCC, 1977.

*Where do we go from Nairobi?*  WCC, 1977.

Wolf, Rabbi Arnold Jacob.  *Impressions of Nairobi.*
    *Common Ground,* 1976.

*World Fellowship.  Addresses and Messages by Leading*
    *Spokesmen of all Faiths, Races and Countries.*  Ed.
    Charles Frederick Weller, Liveright Publishing Co.,
    New York, 1935.

*The World Religions Speak.*  Ed. Finley P. Dunne, Jr.

Published for the World Academy of Art and Science by
Dr. W. Junk.   N. V. Publishers, The Hague, 1970.

Younghusband, Francis.   *Vital Religion*.   John Murray,
1940.